WARSHIPS OF THE GREAT LAKES

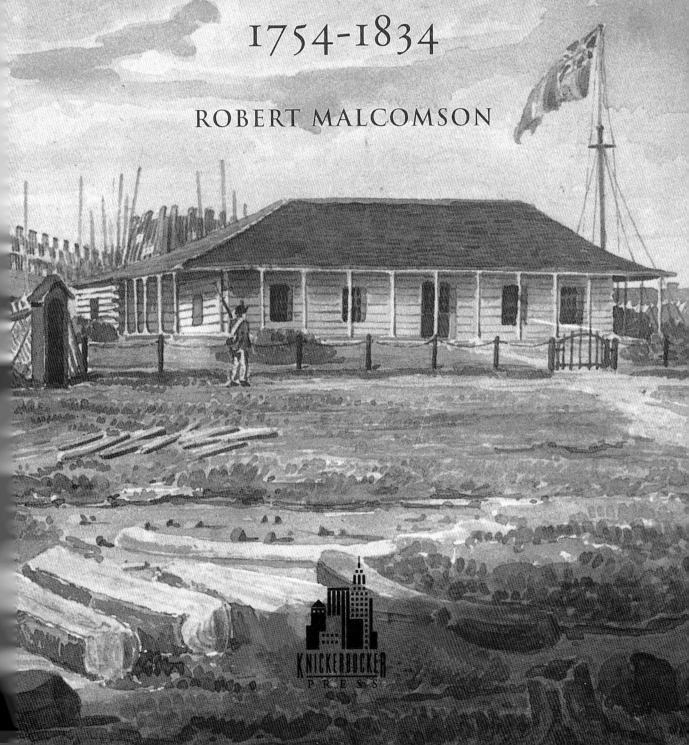

WARSHIPS OF THE
GREAT LAKES
1754-1834

ROBERT MALCOMSON

KNICKERBOCKER
PRESS

For Jennie Theresa Malcomson

This edition published in 2004 by
KNICKERBOCKER PRESS
a division of BOOK SALES, INC.
114 Northfield Avenue
Edison, New Jersey 08837
Under License From The Caxton Publishing Group.
Copyright © Robert Malcomson 2001

First published in Great Britain in 2001 by Chatham Publishing,
an imprint of Gerald Duckworth & Co Ltd,
61 Frith Street, London WID 3JL

The editorial office of Chatham Publishing is at
99 High Street, Rochester, Kent ME1 1LX

British Library Cataloguing in Publication Data
A catalogue record for this book is available from the
British Library

ISBN 0-7858-1798-0

Typeset and designed by Roger Daniels

Printed and bound in Dubai

Frontispiece: The naval dockyard at Point Frederick, Kingston in 1815. This watercolour
by Emeric Essex Vidal shows the Royal Navy Commander's Office to the right, with the
incomplete hulls of the three-deckers *Canada* and *Wolfe* rising behind it. (Royal Military
College, Kingston)

Contents

Introduction

WHILE THE GREAT FLEETS battled for international dominion on the ocean seas, the age of fighting sail also evolved in the interior of North America. For eighty years freshwater was the home to warships that ranged in size from the simplest gunboat to a First Rate that could have held its own in Nelson's line of battle. This book presents the history of the navies developed by the French, British and Americans on the Great Lakes and Lake Champlain, its primary objective being to provide the reader with a comprehensive description of the warships, their design and construction and their utilisation during war and peace.

Although armed sailing ships appeared on the lakes late in the 1600s and their remains spawn intensive archaeological investigation today, the specific period of study here ranges from 1754 until 1834. It was in 1754 that the British Admiralty issued instructions to commence building a naval presence on the lakes. In 1834 it formally closed the last of the establishments where the warships under sail had operated.

It is best to begin with a quick overview of the waterways upon which the ships sailed, which were, primarily, the vast bodies of freshwater known as the Great Lakes. The five lakes (and Georgian Bay) drain the North Central Basin in North America, an area approximately 291,000 square miles in size. Lake Superior is located farthest west and is the largest, with a surface area of 31,700 square miles and a maximum depth of 1333 feet. It meets Lake Michigan near the head of Lake Huron (23,000 square miles in surface area) which takes their waters down to Lake Erie.

Having a prominent place in this historical study, Lake Erie is the fourth largest of the Great Lakes with a surface area of 9910 square miles, a length of 241 miles, a maximum width of 57 miles and a maximum depth of 210 feet. Its waters empty northward, along the thirty miles of the Niagara River, tumbling over the 183-foot high falls at Niagara half way to Lake Ontario. This lake, the smallest of the five, measures 193 miles long and up to 53 miles wide (with a maximum depth of 802 feet) for a surface area of 7340 square miles. Lake Ontario's waters drain into the St Lawrence River for an 800-mile trip to the Gulf of St Lawrence and the sea.

Before the 1900s there were two water routes to the Great Lakes. The first ran up the St Lawrence River to Montreal, where a series of rapids and shoals alternated with stretches of smooth water for nearly 100 miles. Shallow-draught transports could reach Montreal from the Atlantic, but from there all traffic went by small boat or by foot and wagon on portages to the location of Prescott, Ontario today. Beyond that point boats and small sailing craft could navigate the last sixty miles up the river to Lake Ontario.

The second route originated at New York City, heading north for 140 miles on the Hudson River to Albany and then overland to where Schenectady sits on the bank of the Mohawk River. In high-water season, the Mohawk was navigable for ninety miles to present day Rome, where a portage was necessary to reach the creek that ran down to Oneida Lake and on to the Oswego, or Onondaga, River and down to Lake Ontario, 300 miles from New York.

In between the St Lawrence and the Hudson, however, there is another waterway system which became an integral part in the story of the freshwater warships. It began with an overland connection between the Hudson River above Albany and the southern tip of Lake George and flowed down that narrow thirty-mile body of water to its outlet into Lake Champlain. With a surface area that measures about one-seventeenth the size of Lake Ontario, Champlain is not considered one of the Great Lakes, but along its 125 miles of water, never wider than 12 miles, occurred some of the most significant events during the eighty-year span of this history. From Whitehall at its southernmost tip near the Poultney River to Ticonderoga, Plattsburgh and the head of the Richelieu River (seventy miles above the St Lawrence at Sorel), the Champlain Valley was a key to the invasion of Canada and, in return, a route for penetrating deeply into the American states.

Commerce prompted the initial building of sailing vessels on the lakes, but war altered their development, escalating their size and strength. The limitations of this study, however, do not allow for much detail about the political elements of the story. There is room for only the briefest treatments of the wars, the critical moments in battles, and contributions made by the most influential individuals, since the description of the more than 150 warships, excluding gunboats, demands considerable space.

Although some of their names appear in the general and particular histories of the late 1700s and early 1800s, the vessels have often been confused or inaccurately described or forgotten completely. To uncover the truth about the warships, I have investigated primary sources, relying on archival sources and the letters of key military and naval officers during the wars and the periods of peace. I also used a number of fine books and articles devoted to specific topics, especially those dealing with archaeological work, and to more general texts on naval development in order to place the freshwater warships in the context of their times.

There are gaps in the attainable resources, however; very little information exists about the vessels involved in the Seven Years War, for instance, and none of Henry Eckford's draughts from the War of 1812 have been found. Similarly, there are no detailed contracts, nor progress books, barely a sailing quality report, and only for a brief time during the American Revolution and after the summer of 1814 were consistent records of surveys and summaries compiled. The spelling of various names has led to confusion as in the case of the British sloop which was alternately identified as the *Messasague*, *Messasaga* and *Missassago*; here, the name has been standardised (as have other spellings) to the modern *Mississauga*. In the case of the repeated use of favourite names (there were five vessels named the *Mohawk*, for instance), the vessels have been identified in the tables and index in alphabetical order by their launch date (*ie Mohawk* (A) 1756; *Mohawk* (B) 1759; etc).

Despite these problems, the reader should gain an insight into the development of the sailing warships on the lakes. The vessels were similar in design to their saltwater cousins, although the narrow and shallow confines of the lakes required that they be built with generally shallow draughts. Long periods of peace meant that innovations in design and construction were slow in coming to the lakes, although the corvette-style sloop and the use of riders as bracing for hulls, as well as other progressive building techniques, eventually became key aspects in the contest waged by the nations to achieve supremacy on the water. In the end, the freshwater warships certainly equalled their oceanic contemporaries in might and sailing qualities. Hopefully, their place in the historiography of the sailing navies will be established by this book.

I am pleased to thank a number of individuals and institutions for assistance during the course of this work. Early forms of the manuscript were read by Brian Dunnigan, Gary Gibson, Jonathan Moore and Peter Rindlisbacher, all of whom provided me with useful information and worthwhile advice. Other individuals who contributed to, and influenced, my undertaking include: Don Boisvenue, Robin Brass, John Burtniak, Kevin Crisman, Ron Dale, Donald E Graves, Bob Garcia and Ross MacKenzie. The staffs and facilities at the following institutions were essential to the success of this project: the James A Gibson Library at Brock University, St Catharines, the Niagara-on-the-Lake Public Library, the Archives of Ontario, the Toronto Reference Library, the National Archives of Canada in Ottawa, the Royal Military College at Kingston, Ontario, Parks Canada, the United States National Archives in Washington, DC, the William L Clements Library at the University of Michigan, the Smithsonian Institute and the United States Naval Historical Center. Robert Gardiner suggested this work in 1998 and I appreciate very much his encouragement and the attention to detail that his co-workers at Chatham Publishing have afforded it.

As always, I am especially indebted to my wife Janet who encourages my writing and always enjoys the places it leads us, and to our ever-supportive daughters. It was in my parents' home that I first found HMS *St Lawrence*, so it is only fitting that I dedicate this book to my mother.

ROBERT MALCOMSON
2 April 2001

'To cause proper vessels to be built'

1675 TO 1763

SAILING SHIPS first appeared on the Great Lakes in the 1670s as the French consolidated their colony along the St Lawrence River and extended their holdings to the west. Prior to that time, transportation on the waters had been limited to the bark canoes of the indigenous peoples, but the European impact upon trade and control of the territories created a necessity for larger carriers. In 1670 Jean Talon, the intendant of New France, called for a vessel to be built on Lake Ontario 'in the form of a galley with both sails and oars, to look into all parts of the lake.'[1] As a transport, it would carry supplies to posts near the western end of the lake and return with furs, for a fee to the trading company that would offset the government's expenses for operating the vessel. Shipbuilding began in 1673 when the French erected Fort Frontenac at the mouth of the Cataraqui River (Kingston, Ontario) and established a dockyard where craft of 10 and 20 tons were launched. The explorer René Robert Cavelier de La Salle sailed in such a vessel to the Niagara River in 1678 and, while some of his men remained there to construct Fort Conti at the river's mouth, he trekked above Niagara Falls to begin work on a vessel in the upper river near Cayuga Creek on the mainland north of Grand Island. This was the legendary *Griffon* which, in 1679, became the first sailing ship to navigate the upper lakes. It disappeared later that year while returning from Lake Michigan with a hold full of peltries, earning another distinction as the first wreck in those waters; the vessel that carried La Salle to Niagara had been lost on Lake Ontario near Fort Conti during the previous winter.

The early French vessels were lightly armed in case the native nations became hostile, which is what happened in September 1687 when a party of Iroquois attacked a vessel setting sail from Fort Frontenac. Caught in a lull, the French crew members defended themselves with musketoons and four swivel guns and, since the craft had no bulwarks, lay on the deck to avoid being shot, until a breeze rose and they made their escape. When the Iroquois raids became too dangerous in 1689, the French evacuated Fort Frontenac, scuttling three of their vessels, one of which was raised and refitted several years later when the French returned. They maintained their base at the fort for the next sixty years, keeping one or two vessels afloat to move men, provisions and furs.

The British appeared on Lake Ontario in 1727, setting up a fur trading post (Fort George) on the western bank of the mouth of the Oswego, or Onondaga River. Their arrival aroused concern in New France that British vessels would soon ply the lake, but nearly three decades passed before there was a real challenge to French mastery of the waterway. It came in 1754 in response to warfare breaking out between the French and British in the Ohio River valley and which became known locally as the French and Indian War. By the time Britain and France were formally engaged in the Seven Years War (1756-1763), the first opposing squadrons on Lake Ontario were preparing for battle.

As part of a strategy to cripple the French supply line to their string of forts between the lakes and the Ohio River, the British planned to capture Fort Niagara in 1755, which had been built on the site of Fort Conti. Vessels were needed on Lake Ontario to support land operations so the Admiralty ordered Commodore Augustus Keppel, commanding a squadron at Virginia, 'to cause proper Vessels to be built and fitted upon the Boarders of the Lake in the most frugal manner.'[2] Keppel was instructed to utilise rigging, stores and guns from his command to supply the vessels and to send a party of officers and seamen to crew them; he was to submit his bills to the Navy Board which provided him with the draught for a vessel of 60 tons.

Through Keppel the Royal Navy supplied equipment for the warships, but detached only two lieutenants and, perhaps, a few hands to supervise the work; late in the spring of 1755 Lt Housman Broadley and a second officer identified only as Laforey arrived at Oswego.[3] They were in company with a 2400-man army commanded by Major General William Shirley who

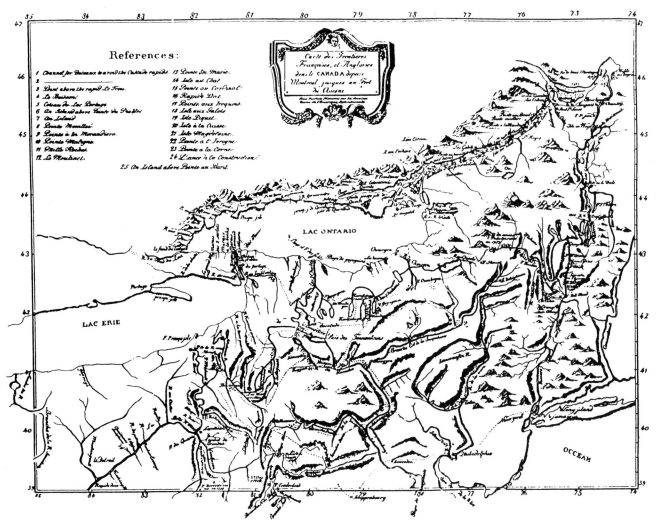

References:

1. Channel for Bateaux to avoid the Cascade rapids
2.
3. Head above the rapid Le Trou
4. Le Baubant
5. Coteau du Lac Portage
6. An Island above Pointe du Diable
7. An Island
8. Pointe Maurlou
9. Pointe à la Morandiere
10. Pointe Maligne
11. Petite Rocher
12. Le Moulinet
13. Pointe Ste Marie
14. Isle au Chat
15. Pointe au Corbeau
16. Rapid Plat
17. Pointe aux Iroquois
18. Isle aux Galois
19. Isle Picquet
20. Isle à la Cuisse
21. Isle Magdeleine
22. Pointe à l'Ivrogne
23. Pointe à la Corne
24. L'ance à la Construction
25. An Island above Pointe au Baril

Carte des Frontieres Françoises, et Angloises dans le CANADA depuis Montreal jusques au Fort du Quesne

LAC ONTARIO

LAC ERIE

OCCEAN

This map of the region around the lower Great Lakes was drawn in 1758 by Pierre Pouchot, commandant at both Fort Niagara and Fort Lévis when they fell to the British. (From Pouchot's *Memoirs* and in E B O'Callaghan, *Documents Relative to the Colonial History of the State of New York,* 15 volumes, Albany, 1856-7)

was the governor of Massachusetts and commander-in-chief of British forces in North America; the colonial governments were actively involved in supporting operations against the French and Shirley obtained shipwrights and crews from colonial seaports for the vessels on Lake Ontario. While the army erected additional fortifications at Oswego, Broadley supervised the work in the newly cleared dockyard on the bay near Fort George. Progress was good and a 70-ton schooner, the *Oswego*, was launched in July, followed the next month by a sloop, the *Ontario*, of similar size and two 20-ton schooners, identified in some sources as the *Valiant* and *George*. The first two vessels were each fitted to carry six 4pdrs and ten swivel guns with a crew of 45, while the schooners carried only swivel guns. Broadley made a brief cruise or two, after which he re-rigged the *Oswego* as a sloop to improve its sail-

ing qualities, and then set out on a voyage of exploration in October. Without charts, he felt his way to the west, noting prevailing winds and currents, before bad weather drove him back to Oswego. By that time, the attack on Fort Niagara had been postponed due to the lateness of the season, and the vessels were laid up at Oswego where about 1000 troops spent a miserable winter.

Contemporary artwork indicates that Broadley's sloops had bulwarks to protect the crew on the main deck, which was flush with the fore-castle. Swivel guns might have been mounted on the raised quarterdeck, below which was adequate space for accommodating the senior officers. The vessels had sharply raked masts, long booms and short gaffs, probably square topsails, and lengthy bowsprits like sea-going merchant vessels with a 'Bermudoes' or Bermudian rig. F H Chapman featured the draught of a vessel of this type in his

Architectura Navalis Mercatoria (1768) that carried ten 4pdrs and twelve swivels. This was a popular rig for commercial vessels and well known to the Royal Navy; the Virginia sloop *Mediator*, for example, was bought into the service in 1745 and proved very useful. It measured 61ft on deck, 44ft between perpendiculars by 21ft 2in extreme breadth by 9ft 9in in the hold, for a burthen of 104 tons. It seems that Broadley's sloops were smaller versions of this type of craft and that his little schooners, lacking square topsails, were typical of the popular rig used by merchants along the eastern seaboard and in the West Indies trade.[4]

During his brief voyages on Lake Ontario in 1755, Housman Broadley did not encounter French vessels then afloat, the schooners *Huralt*, of 12 guns, and *Louise*, 6, and the sloop *Victor*, 6. At Fort Frontenac during the winter of 1755-6 Louis-Pierre Poulin de Courval Cressé, a master shipbuilder from Quebec, built the schooner *Marquise de Vaudreuil*, which was large enough to mount eight 8pdrs, eight 6pdrs and eight 2pdr swivel guns. Captain René Hippolyte La Force, a veteran Canadien mariner, arrived in the spring to take command of the new vessel and the

squadron.[5] Another experienced seaman, Pierre Boucher de La Broquerie, captained the *Huralt* and was the artist/cartographer who portrayed the French and British lake vessels in insets on his *Carte du Lac Ontario*. While the *Vaudreuil* was larger than Broadley's original vessels, the other three appeared similar in size to the British sloops; La Broquerie depicted each of the two larger French vessels with a single square main topsail, although from a practical sailing point of view, the craft probably carried such sails on their foremasts as later British vessels did. While French documents generally referred to their lake vessels as 'barks' without specifying their rigs, La Broquerie's illustration identifies them as schooners and a sloop; British reports noted that all four French vessels were schooner rigged.

The governors of the colonies decided late in 1755 to increase their naval presence on Lake Ontario.[6] When Broadley, recently promoted to master and commander, returned to Oswego with Laforey and a few men the next spring, the colonial governments took full responsibility for financing the new vessels without support from the Royal Navy. Several merchant captains were

Sloops built by the British on Lake Ontario during the Seven Years War appear to have been modelled after the Bermudian sloop, popular in the West Indies trade and utilised during this period by the Royal Navy for inshore operations. This aquatint, showing one such vessel from three angles, was not published until 1807, but the type had not changed substantially in the previous half-century. (National Maritime Museum, neg A4020)

Although misleading in its depiction of the terrain and settlement at the mouth of the Oswego River, this view indicates the approximate location of the dockyard established by the British in 1755. (From the *London Magazine*, 1760)

hired to command the sloops and schooners on the lake while shipwrights and seamen from New York, Pennsylvania and New England signed on to build and man the vessels. Conditions at Oswego were dangerous owing to persistent raids from native groups allied with the French who also attacked supply convoys coming from New York, delaying their progress and retarding work in the dockyard. Despite the difficult situation, the British launched three new vessels in July and August: the sloop *Mohawk*, 12, the brigantine *London*, 18, and the snow *Halifax*, 18. The sloop's dimensions, 45ft (keel) by 18ft (beam) by 7ft (hold), may represent the proportions of the *Ontario* and *Oswego*, whereas the brigantine, at 60ft by 21ft by 7ft, may have closely resembled the *Marquise de Vaudreuil* in size. Measuring 80ft 6in on deck, 66ft 10¼in by 22ft by 8ft 7in, the snow *Halifax* was clearly meant to face down the French flagship. The length and breadth of the vessels were similar to the dimensions of typical ocean-going vessels of each type during this period of time, although the depth of their holds was less.[7] The shallower holds indicate that Broadley's new vessels were built with shallow draughts so they could pass over the bar obstructing the narrow channel winding out of Oswego Bay.

While the army fortified Oswego and prepared for a campaign against the French posts on the lake, Broadley made a couple of cruises in the vessels launched the previous year. On 27 June he encountered the French squadron twenty miles southwest of Fort Frontenac and, deciding that he was outgunned, turned tail and fled toward Oswego with the French in pursuit. Only one of the small schooners was with Broadley on that occasion and failed to keep up with the *Oswego* and *Ontario*. Broadley ordered its master to veer away and try to elude the French, but this effort failed when Captain La Force detached two of his vessels to capture it, which they did. La Force soon gave up his chase of the British sloops, which returned safely to Oswego where Broadley remained through July waiting for the guns and men to complete his new vessels.

Only a portion of the munitions and seamen intended for the British squadron arrived by the end of the month so Broadley shifted his crews and guns to the best advantage and set sail on 30 July. His squadron consisted of his flagship, the brigantine *London*, armed with fourteen 6pdrs and 4pdrs, the sloop *Mohawk*, four 4pdrs and two 3pdrs, and the *Ontario*, six 4pdrs and four 4pdrs. The snow *Halifax* had been launched but there were neither men nor guns to outfit it and it remained at anchor in Oswego Bay with the *Oswego* and the other vessel; a new schooner was laid down in the dockyard to replace the one that

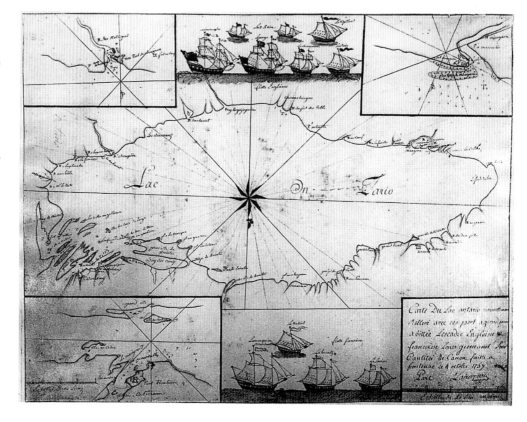

Pierre Boucher La Broquerie drew this map of Lake Ontario with the northern shore of the lake at the bottom. The Niagara River is in the upper right-hand corner, the Oswego, or Onondaga, River and Oswego are in the upper left-hand corner and Fort Frontenac is in the bottom left-hand corner by Grande Island (Wolfe Island) and the head of the St Lawrence River. Among the insets La Broquerie detailed are the vessels in the British and French squadrons. (Toronto Reference Library, T14112)

had been captured. Broadley's cruise was as unsuccessful as his previous voyages because bad weather sprung spars in the *London* and *Ontario*, the magazines of the new vessels were discovered to be made of such green and wet timber that they ruined the powder supplies and, in attempting to negotiate the tricky channel to the bay, the *London* ran hard aground.

By 11 August Captain Broadley was ready to sail again, but on that day the British discovered that a 3000-man army of French soldiers and their native allies was about to besiege Oswego. Under the command of Louis-Joseph Marquis de Montcalm, the French had crossed the lake from Frontenac to Niaouaré Bay (the vicinity of Henderson Harbour) and had proceeded by land and by batteaux and canoe to Oswego.[8] The French squadron had not accompanied them and, fortunately for the French, the British had failed to detect their flotilla of boats and canoes advancing along the shoreline. Broadley sent the *Ontario* and *Mohawk* to reconnoitre the French column on 11 August, but they returned quickly after being hulled by shot from a battery a short distance east of Oswego. Finding the British ill-prepared to

defend themselves, the French quickly pressed their attack, capturing an outpost on the eastern side of the river and crossing over on the morning of 14 August. Harbour-bound by adverse winds, Broadley withdrew his men to the *London*

TABLE 1		
Sloop *Mohawk* – legend of particulars		
Launched: July 1756, Oswego		
Hull Dimensions		
Keel	45ft	
Beam	18ft	
Hold	7ft	
Spar Dimensions		
Main mast		
To the hounds	58ft	head 7ft
Bowsprit	43ft	
Main boom	59ft	
Square sail yard	26ft	
Jibboom	26ft	
Ordnance		
Pierced for	12	
Armed with	4-4pdrs	
2-3pdrs		

Source: Broadley to Admiralty, 14 January and 26 September 1756, cited in Grant, 'The Capture of Oswego in 1756'.
Broadley was informed by the congress of American governors that the sloop was to have these dimensions.

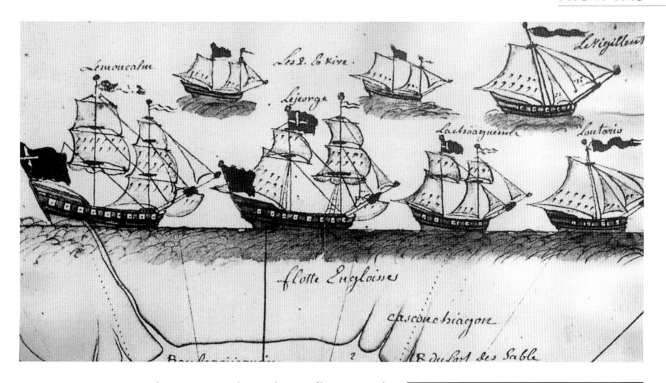

This detail of La Broquerie's map shows the British squadron: top, left to right, Captain Broadley's two schooners and one of his 1755 sloops; bottom, left to right, the snow *Halifax*, brigantine *London*, *Mohawk* (depicted as a schooner) and the second 1755 sloop.(Toronto Reference Library, T14112)

after preparing to destroy the rest of his command. The military commander's announcement that he would negotiate a settlement with the French caught Broadley by surprise and prevented him from setting the vessels aflame, which under the terms of surrender fell into French hands. Over the next five days the French packed all the stores they wanted from the British post into their prizes and La Force's vessels which had arrived from Fort Frontenac and burned the rest. The new schooner in the dockyard was destroyed while the three sloops, one brigantine, one snow and a schooner sailed under the French flag; Broadley and his men were sent to Montreal as prisoners.

Montcalm's victory at Oswego more than doubled the naval force at Fort Frontenac but campaign priorities on other fronts drew men and resources away from Lake Ontario and the potential of the vessels at the French base was never utilised effectively. In August 1758 Lieutenant Colonel John Bradstreet led a force of 3000 men in batteaux across Lake Ontario to attack Fort Frontenac. Fewer than 100 French soldiers and their families were in the garrison and it quickly fell to the British. Captains La Force and La Broquerie attempted to flee with two of the vessels, but when they were headed off by armed batteaux they ran their vessels ashore and escaped on foot

TABLE 2			
Brigantine *London* – legend of particulars			
Launched: July 1756, Oswego			
Hull Dimensions			
Keel	60ft		
Beam	21ft		
Hold	7ft		
Spar Dimensions			
Main mast			
To the hounds	53ft	head	7ft
Main topmast			
To the hounds	23ft	head	3ft
Boom	54ft		
Topsail yard	26ft		
Crossjack yard	30ft		
Fore mast			
To the hounds	42ft	head	8ft
Fore topmast			
To the hounds	28½ft	head	3½ft
Topgallant mast	15ft	head	3½ft
Fore yard	42ft		
Topsail yard	32ft		
Topgallant yard	21ft		
Bowsprit	38ft		
Jibboom	28ft		
Spritsail yard	30ft		
Ordnance			
Pierced for	18-6pdrs		
Armed with	14-6pdrs and 4pdrs		

Source: Broadley to Admiralty, 14 January and 26 September 1756, cited in Grant, 'The Capture of Oswego in 1756'.
Broadley was informed by the congress of American governors that the brigantine was to have these dimensions. The *London* sprung its gaff during its first voyage, although the gaff was not listed among its spars.

into the woods. Bradstreet now turned the tables on the French, seizing all the stores and munitions his force could carry and blowing up Fort Frontenac. He also burned and sank all the warships in the bay except for the brigantine and schooner he used to carry the booty back to Oswego. Lacking orders to establish a squadron there, Bradstreet burned the two vessels and withdrew to New York, leaving Lake Ontario without a naval vessel afloat.[9]

The British and French had also fought in the vicinity of Lake George from 1755.[10] At Fort William Henry at the southern end of the lake the British set up a large camp and built whaleboats, batteaux, three scows and four sloops. The latter ranged from 20 to 30 tons, were armed with swivel guns or a handful of small-calibre cannon and two of them were identified as the *George* and *Earl of Loudoun*. They were intended to support a campaign against the French Fort Carillon on Lake Champlain, but in 1757 a French army attacked and destroyed Fort William Henry, all the shipping and most of the boats. In 1758 while Bradstreet conducted his Lake Ontario expedition, a British army of 15,000 under General James Abercromby assaulted Fort Carillon and was badly beaten by a much smaller force commanded by General Montcalm. Abercromby withdrew to a camp near the ruins of Fort William Henry and began to prepare for a new campaign in the following year.

Realising that shipping was essential, the British brought shipwrights and seamen from the ports on the Atlantic seaboard under the command of Captain Joshua Loring, RN, to do the work. A native of Massachusetts, Loring had been given a lieutenant's commission in the navy in 1745 and served for four years until going on half pay and purchasing an estate near Roxbury, Massachusetts with money he had earned as a privateer. At the outbreak of war, he was promoted to the rank of master and commander and put in charge of transports at Boston, from which post he was ordered to New York to act as the commissary superintending the building and operation of boats and vessels in North America with the new rank of post captain.[11]

At Fort William Henry early in August 1758, Loring's shipbuilders launched a sloop, the *Earl*

TABLE 3

Snow *Halifax* – legend of particulars

Launched: August 1756, Oswego

Hull Dimensions

Deck	80ft 6in
Breadth extreme	22ft
Keel for tonnage	66ft 10¼in
Hold	8ft 7in
Depth in waist	3ft 6in
Upper deck plank to quarterdeck plank	5ft 9in
Forecastle ditto	4ft 11in
Height between deck and gangways	5ft 2in
Burthen in tons	172

Spar Dimensions

	Length	Diameter
Main mast	54ft	15in
Yard	44ft	10½in
Topmast	31ft 4in	9¼in
Yard	31ft 9in	8½in
Topgallant	16ft	5¼in
Yard	18ft 6in	5in
Fore mast	49ft	14in
Yard	38ft 6in	10in
Topmast	29ft	9in
Yard	27ft 6in	7¾in
Topgallant mast	14ft 6in	5in
Yard	16ft	4½in
Bowsprit	33ft	11½in
Yard	27ft 6in	7¾in
Flying jibboom	25ft	5in

Ordnance

Pierced for:	18-6pdrs
Armed with:	0

Source: Broadley to Admiralty, 14 January and 26 September 1756, cited in Grant, 'The Capture of Oswego in 1756'.
Broadley was informed by the congress of American governors that the snow was to have these dimensions.

---

of *Halifax*, of about 100 tons in burthen, measuring 51ft on the keel and pierced for fourteen 4pdrs and a dozen swivels. The *Halifax* patrolled Lake George while work continued in the dockyard where two row galleys and a radeau were soon launched. The latter vessel was a strange looking craft proposed by John Dies, a ship outfitter and land speculator from New York who appears to have served during the war as an army contractor. While discussing warships for the lakes in 1755, Dies had suggested that a shipbuilder's 'Flatt … by which they C[a]reen the Vessels might be modified to have stoutly-built sides with ports for guns and oars that would serve as a Breast work to cover the Men.'[12] The radeau on Lake George was such a craft; named the *Land Tortoise*, it had three ports on one side offset from

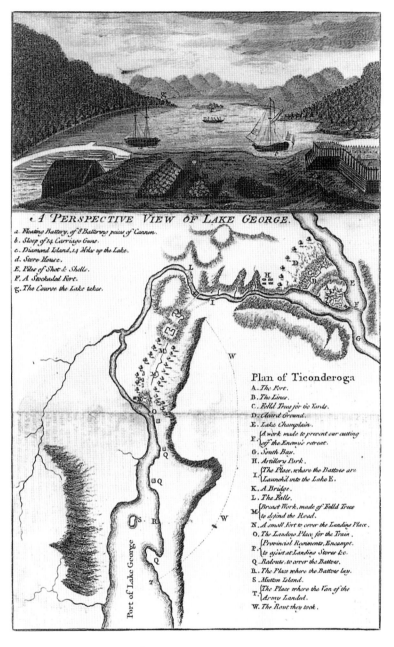

A PERSPECTIVE VIEW OF LAKE GEORGE.

a. Floating Battery, of 8 Battery peices of Cannon.
b. Sloop of 14 Carriage Guns.
c. Diamond Island, 14 Miles up the Lake.
d. Store House.
E. Piles of Shot & Shells.
F. A Stockaded Fort.
g. The Course the Lake takes.

Plan of Ticonderoga

A. The Fort.
B. The Lines.
C. Felld Trees for 60 Yards.
D. Cleard Ground.
E. Lake Champlain.
F. A work made to prevent our cutting off the Enemy's retreat.
G. South Bay.
H. Artillery Park.
I. The Place, where the Battoes are Launchd into the Lake E.
K. A Bridge.
L. The Falls.
M. Brest Work, made of Felld Trees to defend the Road.
N. A small Fort to cover the Landing Place.
O. The Landing Place for the Train.
P. Provincial Regiments, Encampt. to assist at Landing Stores &c.
Q. Redouts, to cover the Battoes.
R. The Place where the Battoes lay.
S. Mutton Island.
T. The Place where the Van of the Army Landed.
W. The Rout they took.

Port of Lake George

Adjoined to this map of the outlet connecting the northern reaches of Lake George to Lake Champlain at Fort Ticonderoga is a view of the British fortifications on the southern shore of Lake George. Moored offshore are the radeau *Invincible* (left) and the sloop *Earl of Halifax*. (From *The Universal Magazine*, London 1759)

and put into service, but the *Land Tortoise* was not retrievable. Underwater archaeologists discovered the hull in 1990 in near-pristine condition at a depth of 107 feet and examined it in detail, revealing that it was built of oak and pine and measured 52ft long by 18ft wide and probably drew about 5ft of water.

Late in 1758 Major General Jeffrey Amherst became the commander-in-chief of the forces in North America and took personal command of an 11,000-man army at Lake George.[13] Captain Loring was once again in charge of naval operations and raised the *Halifax* and numerous smaller craft from their underwater storage as well as supervising the building of the radeau *Invincible*, 8, and a large scow named the *Snow Shoe*. In July Loring's squadron escorted the flotilla of batteaux, whaleboats and rafts that carried Amherst's army to the outlet at the northern end of Lake George that flowed into Lake Champlain. The larger vessels were left at that point while the army proceeded to attack and capture the French Fort Carillon which was improved and renamed Fort Ticonderoga. Amherst's force moved north to seize a second French position at Crown Point, but there the general stopped his campaign to allow time for completion of new fortifications and for Loring to construct warships.

The French had four vessels under sail on Lake Champlain in 1759, all of them appearing to have been constructed at the French settlement of St Jean, located twenty-four miles down the Richelieu River at the head of the rapids that barred easy access to the St Lawrence River. The sloops were the *Musquelongy, Brochette* and *Esturgeon*, each armed with eight guns, and the 10-gun schooner *La Vigilante*, all under the command of Joseph Payant St Onge who had been the master of French vessels on Lake Champlain from as early as 1742. Most of the French army on the lake had retreated from Fort Carillon and Crown Point to Isle aux Noix, situated eight miles down the Richelieu River. St Onge kept his naval force on the lake to keep an eye on the British and impede their movement north.

To contend with St Onge's squadron, Joshua Loring built two warships at Ticonderoga, the brig *Duke of Cumberland*, 20, and the sloop *Boscawen*, 16, while the radeau *Ligonier*, 7, was

four ports opposite to allow space for its battery of 12pdrs to recoil. Its flat bottom, sides that flared out and bulwarks that tilted inward led locals to nickname it 'Ord's Ark' after Thomas Ord, the New England artillery captain who built it.

The Lake George vessels were intended to escort the army when it moved north against the French, but the season grew too late for further operations and the British withdrew to Albany. To protect them from French marauders, all the vessels were sunk near the British fortifications. The next year the *Halifax* and galleys were raised

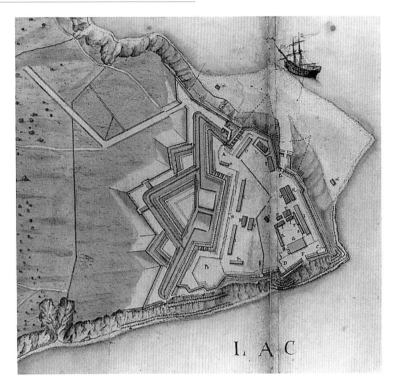

L A C

Pierre Pouchot recorded the layout of Fort Niagara, before becoming its commandant during the British siege in July 1759, and inserted a moored vessel that is thought to have been the *Marquise de Vaudreuil*. (British Library, Add MSS 15332-H)

constructed at Crown Point. The brig was 155 tons in burthen, mounting twenty 6pdrs and 4pdrs and twenty swivels and crewed by 70 seamen and 60 soldiers. The sloop was 80ft on deck by 24ft abeam and had a burthen of 115 tons, its crew made up of 60 seamen and 50 soldiers and its armament including sixteen 6pdrs and 4pdrs, plus twenty-two swivel guns. Like its cousins on Lake George, the *Ligonier* was 84ft by 20ft, flat-bottomed and convex-sided and built stoutly enough to mount six 24pdrs and a mortar. Delays caused by short supply of fittings and breakdowns in a nearby sawmill made Loring's task difficult and frustrated Amherst's ambitions to advance north. Archaeological examinations of one of several wrecks (believed to be the *Boscawen*) found near Ticonderoga revealed that construction was hurried: bark was not removed from the underside of deck beams, and shavings and waste wood were not cleared from the bilge, leaving the limber holes clogged and useless. The builders used white oak for most of the vessel, fastening its components securely with iron bolts, spikes and treenails.[14]

Manning the squadron posed problems for Loring and Amherst and due to the absence of experienced naval officers or even merchant cap-

tains, military officers took commissions afloat while their rank and file went before the mast. The most prominent of the army officers was Lieutenant Alexander Grant from Montgomery's Highlanders, the 77th Regiment of Foot, a 25-year-old who had served for a brief period in the navy before joining the army in 1757. Grant took command of the *Boscawen*, thus beginning a career on the lakes that would last for five and a half decades.[15]

Amherst finally started his movement north from Crown Point on 11 October. The next day, as he scouted ahead of the army flotilla, Loring spotted St Onge in the *Vigilante* and gave chase, but the *Cumberland* and *Boscawen* both ran aground trying to follow the experienced French captain through a narrow channel. After getting his vessels afloat, Loring encountered the three French sloops and pursued them to Cumberland Bay (Plattsburgh, New York), trapping them there as night fell. The next sunrise revealed that the French crews had abandoned their vessels after cutting up their rigging and trying to scuttle them. In time, all three were taken into the British squadron (with one of them apparently being renamed the *Amherst*), but by then Amherst had heard that General Wolfe's army had captured Quebec, and expecting that the French force collecting on the Richelieu would be too strong for his army, he ended his campaign and withdrew to Crown Point and Ticonderoga for the winter.

French control on Lake Ontario suffered a setback in 1759 also. Within weeks of the destruction of Fort Frontenac in August 1758, the French opened a new dockyard on the north shore of the St Lawrence River near Point Baril, about fifty miles downstream from the lake and nine miles up from the mission settlement at La Présentation (Ogdensburg, New York).[16] As well, they began constructing a fortress (Fort Lévis) on a island just below La Présentation to act as a rear guard for Montreal. The master shipbuilder Louis-Pierre Poulin de Courval Cressé arrived at the dockyard, named Ance á la Construction, in November 1758 to lay the keels for the schooner *Iroquoise* and the brig *Outaouaise*, which were launched the following April. Details about their construction are missing, although they are said to have measured about eighty feet in length and

TABLE 4
French vessels, 1754-1760

Vessel	Launch	Place	Rig	Remarks
Lake Ontario				
Hurault, 12	1753?	Fort Frontenac	schooner	Aug 1758 destroyed at Ft Frontenac by British
Victor, 6	1753?	Fort Frontenac	sloop	Aug 1758 destroyed at Ft Frontenac by British
Louise, 6	1753?	Fort Frontenac	schooner	Aug 1758 destroyed at Ft Frontenac by British
Marquise de Vaudreuil, 16	1755	Fort Frontenac	schooner	Aug 1758 destroyed at Oswego (?) by British
unidentified	1759?	Fort Niagara?	schooner	Aug 1759 British prize *Farquhar* *
unidentified	1759?	Fort Niagara?	sloop	Aug 1759 British prize *Mississauga* *
Iroquoise, 10	1759	Point Baril	schooner	Aug 1760 British prize *Anson* *
Outaouaise, 10	1759	Point Baril	brig	Aug 1760 British prize *Williamson* *
unidentified	1760	Point Baril	schooner	Aug 1760 British prize *Johnson* *
Lake Champlain				
Vigilante, 10	1757	St Jean	schooner	Aug 1760 British prize; laid up and decayed
Musquelongy, 8	1759	St Jean	sloop	Oct 1759 British prize *
Brochette, 8	1759	St Jean	sloop	Oct 1759 British prize; not listed after 1761
Esturgeon, 8	1759	St Jean	sloop	Oct 1759 British prize; not listed after 1761
Waggon	1759?	St Jean	sloop	Aug 1760 British prize; laid up and decayed
Grand Diable	1759	St Jean	radeau	Aug 1760 British prize; Oct 1761 wrecked

* see Table 5.

Amherst's gunboats capture the French brig *Outaouaise* on 17 August 1760 in the St Lawrence River above Fort Lévis. (Thomas Davies, National Gallery of Canada, 6271)

were armed with ten guns and various swivels. Captains La Force and La Broquerie arrived from Quebec to take command of them.

A British army under Brigadier General John Prideaux set up camp at Oswego in the spring of 1759 intent on capturing Fort Niagara.[17] In July Prideaux's force proceeded in a flotilla of batteaux along the Lake Ontario shore toward the fort where it would have been an easy target for the French warships. The *Outaouaise*, however, had been badly damaged in a storm earlier in the month and had gone to Ance á la Construction for repairs, leaving La Force in the *Iroquoise* alone on the lake. It arrived at Fort Niagara on 6 July, the same day the British army did, but somehow La Force failed to detect the British flotilla. In the following weeks, he bombarded their camp several times, but was unable to provide any significant service to the land force and after a siege lasting nearly three weeks, the small garrison at Fort Niagara surrendered on 25 July. The British now occupied Fort Niagara and prepared to build vessels in the shipyard nearby, consolidated their force at Oswego and made plans for an attack on the St Lawrence River valley the next spring.

Shortly after the capture of Fort Niagara, Amherst ordered the construction of two heavily armed vessels on Lake Ontario to contend with the *Iroquoise* and *Outaouaise* when he commenced operations in that quarter in 1760. Although the former dockyard at Oswego was restored and used in 1760, the British chose the former French yard just within the mouth of the Niagara River as the site for building their new vessels, because of the excellent harbour that lay under the fort and the proximity to a plentiful supply of oak. There they had found a French sloop and schooner (they may have been two of the 1756 vessels refloated by the French at Fort Frontenac), which they re-named the *Mississauga* and *Farquhar*, respectively. A master shipbuilder from Pennsylvania named Peter Jacquet, hired by Loring, arrived at Fort Niagara in the summer of 1759 with a small crew of shipwrights and began work on the warships Amherst had ordered. The first of these vessels, a snow named the *Mohawk*, 16 (the second British warship to bear that name) was launched early in the autumn of 1759 and made one return trip to Oswego, under the command of Lieutenant Thomas Thornton. Thornton then made several cruises in the *Mississauga* and *Farquhar*, but ran into a snow-storm early in December that covered the schooner and sloop in ice. He managed to save the crews by grounding his vessels thirty miles east of Oswego, but both were so badly

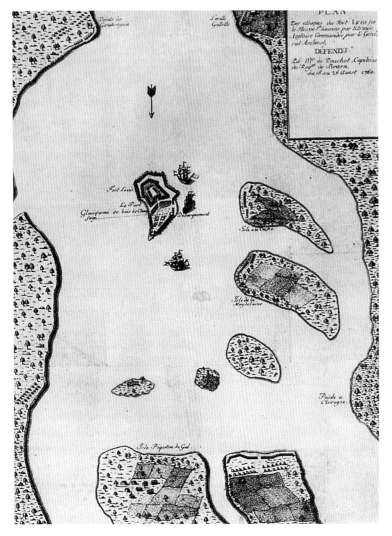

Pierre Pouchot, the commandant of Fort Lévis, depicted the attack on his garrison by the British on 23 August 1760. One of the British vessels has fallen below the fort, (the arrow indicates the direction of the current), while the second passes the island. The *Onondaga* continues to engage at close range. (William L Clements Library)

age of equipment and stores. Amherst arrived at Oswego expecting to see his warships ready for action, but was frustrated to observe the *Iroquoise* and *Outaouaise* cruising in the offing, ready to intercept the expedition he planned to make down the St Lawrence. When Loring finally appeared on 14 July, Amherst hurried reinforcements to him, urging him to cruise near the entrance of the St Lawrence and catch the French before they could get into the river. Although the two forces came within sight of each other briefly, a thick fog separated them, allowing La Force and La Broquerie to sail down to Fort Lévis.

Before commencing his descent of the St Lawrence, General Amherst hosted a grand ceremony at Oswego on 1 August, designed to solidify the alliance he had made with local native nations. The chiefs had informed him that they would like to see the *Apollo* renamed the *Onondaga*, so, as Amherst wrote:

> I had a large flag made with an Onondaga Indian painted on it. This was hoisted just as I christened the Snow by breaking a bottle on the head. … All this pleased the Indians extremely and I … gave them some Punch and they were greatly delighted with the whole, promised to be fast friends and said they were ready to go with me.[19]

damaged that he eventually stripped them of useful fittings and burned the remains.[18]

In spring 1760 Amherst sent an army to Oswego while other British forces prepared to close in on Montreal from the directions of Quebec and Lake Champlain. Captain Loring reached Oswego in June with a naval detachment made up of merchant seamen under contract and volunteers from colonial regiments; except for Loring's involvement, all naval matters on the lakes were now under the complete control of the army. Supervised by a builder named Gliden and army contractor John Dies, the dockyard at Oswego was busy with the building of five row galleys each capable of carrying a single 12pdr gun. Loring proceeded to Niagara to await the imminent launch of the second snow, the *Apollo*, 18, but its final fitting out was delayed by a short-

The army set out on 10 August and, despite some rough weather during the passage along the shore, entered the St Lawrence safely, reaching Point Baril six days later. Loring had preceded him in the *Onondaga* (formerly the *Apollo*) with Thornton as his first officer and a crew of 100 seamen and 25 soldiers. The snow carried four 9pdrs and fourteen 6pdrs while the *Mohawk*, commanded by Lieutenant David Phipps, had a crew of 90 seamen and 30 soldiers and a battery of sixteen 6pdrs. Amherst sent native guides to act as pilots, but this proved to be unhelpful and the warships sailed into a shallow, dead end channel, and had to be laboriously kedged upstream in full view of the army passing down in the vast flotilla of batteaux, whaleboats and row galleys. The uncharted waters had also embarrassed the French. While heading to Fort Lévis after eluding Loring, La

TABLE 5

British vessels launched and acquired, 1754-1762

Vessel	Launch	Place	Rig	Remarks
Lake Ontario				
Oswego, 6	1755	Oswego	sloop	Aug 1756 French prize; Aug 1758 destroyed at Ft Frontenac by British
Ontario (A), 6	1755	Oswego	sloop	Aug 1756 French prize; Aug 1758 destroyed at Ft Frontenac by British
Valiant (?)	1755	Oswego	schooner	Aug 1756 French prize; Aug 1758 destroyed at Ft Frontenac by British
George (B)(?)	1755	Oswego	schooner	Aug 1756 French prize; Aug 1758 destroyed at Ft Frontenac by British
London, 18	1756	Oswego	brigantine	Aug 1756 French prize; Aug 1758 destroyed at Oswego (?) by British
Mohawk (A), 12	1756	Oswego	sloop	Aug 1756 French prize; Aug 1758 destroyed at Ft Frontenac by British
Halifax, 18	1756	Oswego	snow	Aug 1756 French prize; Aug 1758 destroyed at Ft Frontenac by British
Mississauga (A) ‡	1759	Fort Niagara	sloop	one of British 1755/6 sloops (?); Dec 1759 wrecked 30 miles east of Oswego
Farquhar ‡	1759	Fort Niagara	schooner	one of British 1755 schooners (?); Dec 1759 wrecked 30 miles east of Oswego
Mohawk (B), 16	1759	Fort Niagara	snow	1764 wrecked
Apollo/Onondaga (A),18	1760	Fort Niagara	snow	Aug 1760 abandoned after battle at Fort Lévis
Williamson ‡	1759	Point Baril	brig	ex-*Outaouaise*; autumn 1760 wrecked near Oswego
Anson ‡	1759	Point Baril	schooner	ex-*Iroquoise*; Nov 1761 wrecked 20 miles down St Lawrence
Johnson‡	1760	Point Baril	snow	unidentified French schooner; 1764 wrecked
Mississauga (B),10	1760	Fort Niagara	sloop	1765 wrecked
Mercury, 4	1760	Oswego	schooner	after 1765, not listed
Lake George				
George (A)	1755	Fort Wm Henry	sloop	1757 destroyed by French
Earl of Loudoun	1755	Fort Wm Henry	sloop	1757 destroyed by French
two unidentified	1755	Fort Wm Henry	sloop	1757 destroyed by French
Earl of Halifax, 14	1758	Fort Wm Henry	sloop	laid up after 1760, decayed
Land Tortoise, 7	1758	Fort Wm Henry	radeau	1758 scuttled, not retrieved
Invincible, 8	1759	Fort Wm Henry	radeau	laid up after 1760, decayed
Snowshoe	1759	Fort Wm Henry	scow	laid up after 1760, decayed
Lake Champlain				
Ligonier, 7	1759	Ticonderoga	radeau	laid up after 1761, decayed
Duke of Cumberland, 20	1759	Ticonderoga	brig	laid up after 1761, decayed
Boscawen, 16	1759	Ticonderoga	sloop	laid up after 1761, decayed
Musquelongy ‡	1759	St Jean	sloop	1767 Blackburn contract; 1771 decayed and replaced
Lake Erie				
Huron (A), 4	1761	Navy Island	schooner	after 1763 not listed; probably renamed *Victory* *
Michigan, 6	1762	Navy Island	sloop	Aug 1763 wrecked at Presque Isle

‡ prize vessel.

* see Table 9.

Force severely damaged the *Iroquoise* by sailing onto a shoal. When they reached Fort Lévis, the French concluded that they lacked the manpower to repair the schooner immediately and scuttled it in the lee of the island beside the hull of a third vessel that de Cressé had launched at Ance á la Construction but had not been able to outfit.

When Amherst's army encamped at Point Baril, the *Outaouaise* lay anchored in the river just above La Présentation as an advance guard for Fort Lévis. Fearing La Broquerie would attack his flotilla, Amherst sent Colonel George Williamson to seize the brig at dawn on 17 August. Five row galleys, each armed with a heavy gun, closed in on the *Outaouaise* as it got underway and after a two-hour engagement the British boarded it victoriously. The brig, which had a crew of 27 seamen and 73 soldiers (of whom 15 were casualties), was armed with one 18pdr, seven 12pdrs and two 8pdrs. To honour the colonel's successful assault, Amherst renamed the brig the *Williamson* and appointed Lieutenant Patrick Sinclair of the 42nd Regiment of Foot as its commander.[20]

Over the next several days, Amherst deployed his forces and erected batteries on the mainland and islands near Fort Lévis.[21] His plan was to land on the island under cover of a bombardment from the shore after his three warships (the *Onondaga* and *Mohawk* had made their appearance) had moved into position to fire on the fort at close range. On 23 August the vessels advanced and anchored near the island and engaged the French whose effective return fire forced the *Mohawk* and *Williamson* off their moorings and down stream out of range. The *Onondaga* held its place but suffered badly and when Loring attempted to follow the others, the current caught the snow and ran it hard aground closer to the island, where French batteries tore it to pieces. Amherst postponed his landing, but was slow to send reinforcements to the stricken warship where nearly one-third of the crew was killed or wounded; Loring himself received a severe leg wound. Some of the military observers, Amherst included, questioned Loring's handling of the *Onondaga*, especially when frantic crew members hauled down its flag. At one point in the action, Lieutenant Thornton went to parley with the French to gain time for the beleaguered crew, Loring explained later, but Amherst objected to such conduct and summarily dismissed Thornton from the service several days after the battle.

The British bombardment of Fort Lévis proved to be too much for the French to withstand and on 25 August they surrendered. Amherst named the fort William Augustus and, before proceeding to Montreal with his main force six days later, issued instructions for the restoration of the fort and the deployment of warships. In the weeks that followed, the British managed to raise and repair the *Iroquoise*, which was renamed the *Anson*, and the new French hull that had also been scuttled. This vessel, named the *Johnson*, was rigged as a snow, using gear from the *Onondaga* which was irretrievably aground. While the work was underway, a new sloop, the *Mississauga,* 10 (as with the *Mohawk*, the British re-used a popular name, a trend that would persist over the decades), apparently launched at Niagara in July, arrived with stores from Oswego. With the sailing season about to end, the British hurried to use all the vessels to carry supplies from Oswego (where a small schooner, the *Mercury*, 4, was launched in the autumn) to Fort William Augustus and Niagara. During this period Lieutenant Charles Robertson, 77th Foot, acted as the senior officer afloat in the place of Loring who had gone to Albany to recover from his wound.

While Amherst pursued his campaign on Lake Ontario, Colonel William Haviland led an army to attack the French base at Isle aux Noix, on the Richelieu River, during the latter half of August. Lieutenant Alexander Grant commanded the British squadron, which included the *Duke of Cumberland*, *Boscawen*, *Ligonier* and the three sloops captured the year before. After ten days of skirmishing and bombardments, during which three more French vessels, the *Vigilante*, the *Waggon* sloop and the radeau *Grand Diable* fell into British hands, the French withdrew from their fort. Haviland pressed on to Montreal, arriving there about the same time as Amherst and Brigadier General James Murray, marching from Quebec. Surrounded by British forces, the French surrendered their final post in Canada on 8 September 1760.[22]

The fall of New France presented the British with the problem of how to control the vast territory that spread from Quebec to the Mississippi River. Due to their proximity to New York, the posts on the Lake Ontario and Lake Champlain frontiers were relatively easy to sustain with reduced garrisons. The shipping in existence in 1760 was adequate to transport men and provisions so no new vessels were laid down on either lake. Only one or two of the warships on Lake Champlain, where Lieutenant Grant remained in command, saw service while all the craft at Oswego were employed as long as they lasted – the *Williamson* ran aground near Niagara late in 1760 and disappeared from the record, while the *Anson* (ex-*Iroquoise*) struck a shoal and sank in the St Lawrence twenty miles downstream from the lake in November 1761.[23]

Control of the territory south and west of Lake Erie, where French traders travelling up the Mississippi River continued to conduct business with the aboriginal nations, was a more complex problem. To establish their domain and secure the lucrative fur trade, the British instituted regulations in September 1761 restricting all interaction with the various nations to certified agents located at specific posts.[24] This policy required the manning of garrisons at places like Detroit and Mackinac, which in turn required the building of vessels to service those stations. General Amherst foresaw this need and put the wheels in motion in March 1761 to create a shipyard above Niagara Falls that could produce vessels capable of sailing up to Lake Superior. Joshua Loring was still the commissioner of the forces on the lakes, but he remained at Boston through most of 1761 recovering from his wound. Acting under Loring's instructions, Lieutenant Charles Robertson headed up the expedition to erect a new dockyard, assisted by John Dies who was to superintend the building. They selected a spot on Navy Island (originally called Dies Island) two miles above Niagara Falls and cleared land on its eastern shore facing Grand Island. Despite the many difficulties encountered by the men inhabiting this wilderness dockyard, the 80-ton schooner *Huron*, to carry four 4pdrs and six swivels, was launched late in 1761 and the 100-ton sloop *Michigan*, to carry six 6pdrs and eight swivels, went into the water the next summer.[25]

Captain Loring returned to the lakes in the

This map, showing the northern half of the Niagara River around 1762, is attributed to George Demler. Fort Niagara is at the mouth of the Niagara overlooking Lake Ontario (to the right). Other points salient to this chapter are the lower landing of the portage (2), the fortress at Little Niagara (3), and the falls of Niagara (4). Navy Island and the Chippewa Creek are above the falls (and off the map to the left). (British Library, King's Top, CXXI, 73)

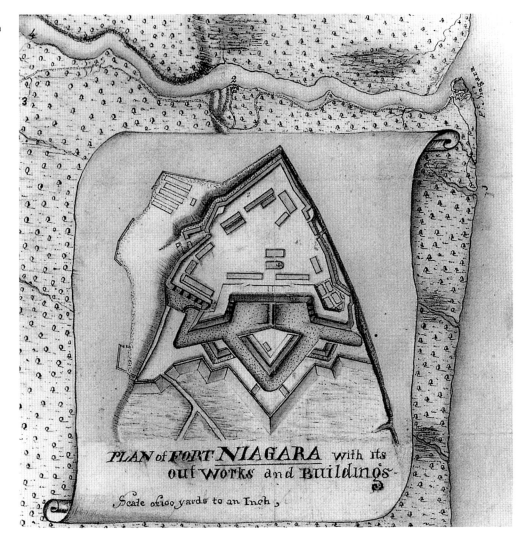

summer of 1762 and was present to see the *Huron* set out on its initial trip to Detroit, after having been laboriously hauled over the strong currents at the confluence of Lake Erie and the Niagara. The schooner was the first sailing vessel to navigate the upper lakes since La Salle's *Griffon* enjoyed its brief season eighty-five years before and it secured the link between the new British post at Detroit and vital resources to the east. Because of the importance of this post, Amherst appointed Major Henry Gladwin, 80th Foot, at Detroit to command the upper lakes region, with Loring and the vessels under his jurisdiction.[26] A regular circuit was to have been established in 1763 carrying provisions and reinforcements from Niagara to Detroit, while timber was cut for a third vessel and an attempt was made to navigate the St Clair River into Lake Huron. The plan suf-

fered a significant setback, however, when growing hostility among aboriginal nations on the frontier erupted into a violent and bloody uprising led by the Ottawa chief, Pontiac. Some of the men of Loring's party were attacked near Buffalo Creek and when Loring arrived at Detroit in July with intentions to build a vessel there, the presence of threatening native warriors prevented him from even building a proper wharf for the *Huron* and *Michigan*. To make matters worse, the *Michigan* went aground at Presque Isle in August and was wrecked; its cargo was saved, as were fittings and timbers that could be used to build a replacement vessel at Navy Island. The 1763 sailing season ended with the British maintaining a tenuous presence on the upper lakes while their vessels on Lakes Ontario and Champlain secured the vital link with New York and Quebec.

CHAPTER 2

'Upon a settled footing'

1764 TO 1783

THE SEVEN YEARS WAR provoked the first naval contest on Lakes Ontario and Champlain. Where only a handful of French transports had existed prior to the conflict, well-armed sloops, brigs and snows were launched for deployment during the military campaigns. The next period on the lakes witnessed a reduction in the warships so that only limited number remained in service transporting goods for the government and private entrepreneurs. When war broke out again in the 1770s, a sharp escalation in the size and force of the inland navies once more took place, producing larger squadrons with heavier firepower.

Pontiac's uprising threatened British control of the newly won territories south and west of Lakes Ontario and Erie, and in the summer of 1764 two military forces headed to the region to put down the insurrection. Colonel John Bradstreet led the expedition that re-established security at the posts along the Niagara River before heading to relieve the besieged garrison at Detroit in August. Hostilities in the area settled down when Bradstreet used diplomacy to make peace with the warring nations, rather than acting as aggressively as the British force approaching from Fort Pitt. Although Bradstreet was criticised for his passive approach by Major General Thomas Gage, who replaced Amherst as commander-in-chief in North America during the autumn of 1763, the peace agreements allowed the British to pursue their goal of controlling the upper lakes without having to fight for their survival at every turn.

The Royal Proclamation of late 1763 had reserved for the native nations the land west of the Appalachian Mountains (with the Mississippi River as the western boundary of British holdings) and forbade business transactions in that region, except through British officials. The widely separated British posts west of Lake Ontario depended on supply by water and, as a result, the dockyard on Navy Island was a busy place during 1764 with the launch of two schooners, the *Boston* and *Gladwin*, carrying eight guns apiece, and a sloop, the *Royal Charlotte*, 10. Documents of the period are scarce and contradictory, but indicate the launch of an un-named sloop in 1763, which was lost the following year, and another schooner named the *Victory*; the latter was most likely the *Huron* (launched in 1761) renamed to celebrate the end of the Seven Years War since the *Huron* disappeared from the record after 1763 without explanation. The vessels supported Bradstreet's expedition to Detroit as well as transporting sufficient supplies to that place, and the *Gladwin* was hauled over the shallows and rapids in the St Clair River and sailed into Lake Huron to the trading forts at Mackinac Island and beyond. During the winter some of the vessels returned to Navy Island where they were moored in a creek on Grand Island opposite the dockyard.[1]

A multitude of problems plagued the British as they struggled to govern their expanded holdings in North America: American colonists complained about taxes and the limits on their western expansion; encroaching settlers from the colonies clashed repeatedly with the natives; French traders persisted in travelling up the Mississippi to deal with the aboriginal nations; and the costs of enforcing laws and conducting commerce rose. Uncertainty prevailed about how best to deal with the various problems, including the maintenance of the armed vessels on the lakes and the expensive garrisons. Joshua Loring continued as HM commissary, superintending the building and operation of the vessels on the inland seas until late 1765 when he finally gained approval to attend the Admiralty office in England. Gage had delayed Loring's departure as he believed his expertise would be needed when orders finally arrived to put the marine department 'upon a Settled Footing on each of the lakes respectively; many Regulations to be made and some new Craft to be built.'[2]

Gage appointed Lieutenant Alexander Grant to replace Loring, but nothing appears to have been done to firmly establish the Great Lakes naval department. Following the burst of activity on Navy Island, shipbuilding there ended and no new public vessels were launched above Niagara Falls for the rest of the decade, although the *Victory* caught fire accidentally in 1766 and was destroyed at its winter anchorage on Grand Island, the same fate suffered by the *Boston* two years later. On Lake Ontario during this period there was only one vessel, the schooner *Brunswick*, launched at Oswego in 1765, despite the weakened state of the *Mercury* and the loss by shipwreck of the snows *Johnson* and *Mohawk* in 1764 and the sloop *Mississauga* the next year. More than one official proposed the employment of government vessels as transports for the goods of private merchants, the fees for which would sustain the service, but Gage rejected the idea, claiming that it would interfere with provisioning the garrisons. As well, Gage was concerned about rumours that the officers were receiving secret payments to carry private goods; 'the Masters of the Vessels may be perverted to bad Uses,' he claimed. 'Some are suspected now of playing tricks.'[3]

Dominating nearly every British debate over policies in North America following the Seven Years War was the need to reduce costs, which led eventually to a significant diminution in the forces on land and water. In 1767 the Lords Commissioners of the Treasury entered into a contract with John Blackburn, a London-based merchant and army contractor, to administer the manning, victualling and repairing of four government vessels on the lakes, the *Musquelongy* on Lake Champlain, the *Brunswick* on Lake Ontario, the *Charlotte* on Lake Erie and the *Gladwin* on Lake Huron; the remaining vessels on the lakes were allowed to rot at their moorings. Blackburn's contract provided for the employment of 12 officers and 40 seamen, so after the crews were discharged from the public payroll, some of them were rehired by Henry White, Blackburn's agent in New York, including Alexander Grant who acted as superintendent on the lakes. About the same time, most of the small frontier posts were closed while reduced garrisons remained at Mackinac, Detroit, Niagara, Oswego and Oswegatchie (Ogdensburg, New York).[4]

Blackburn completed his take-over of the vessels on the lakes in 1768, causing little apparent change in the normal routine of moving men and provisions to and from the trading posts. Gage's

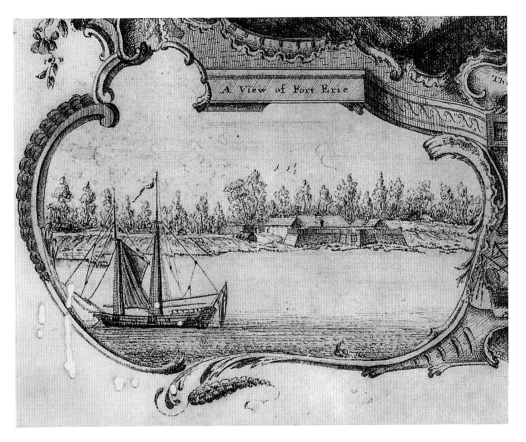

Henry DeBerniere portrayed a schooner lying off Fort Erie, at the head of the Niagara River, in 1773. It is either the public vessel *General Gage* or *Earl of Dunmore* or Alexander Grant's *Hope*. (National Army Museum, London, neg 19676)

objection to the transport of private goods was over-ruled and for a fee, and as space allowed, the vessels carried the personal property of people settling near the main outposts, as well as the merchandise and produce belonging to the merchants who had set up shop at Detroit and the other trading centres. The need for more carriers, and the promise of the profits they could accrue, prompted the building of the first private vessel, the sloop *Enterprise*, at Detroit in 1769 by Phyn, Ellice and Company of Schnectady, New York. An active dockyard developed thereafter at Detroit where a New York shipbuilder named Richard Cornwall set up shop in 1767. While still employed as Blackburn's superintendent, Alexander Grant saw the money to be made in shipping and paid for the building of the *Beaver* at Detroit in 1771. By 1774, at which time he took up permanent residence near Detroit, Grant owned two sloops, the *Angelica* and *Chippewa*, and two schooners, the *Hope* and *Faith*, on the upper lakes and the sloop *Charity* on Lake Ontario.[5]

Early in the 1770s the government vessels wore out and were replaced in the yards at Detroit, Fort Niagara and Oswegatchie, which had superseded Oswego as the main transhipment point for Lake Ontario; Navy Hall, a new depot on the west bank of the Niagara River across from Fort Niagara was built during this time. Labourers cut timber at these places so that it would have time to season properly and thereby inhibit the decay that consumed most of the freshwater vessels in seven or eight years; on Lake Erie stands of cedar were discovered at the Bass Islands and reserved for government use because of the wood's supposed durability. When new government vessels were ordered in 1771, Cornwall built two of them under the direction of Alexander Grant, who contracted the work for Blackburn's agent. The first of the vessels, the *General Gage*, measured 72ft on the deck, 62ft by 22ft 10in by 8ft 1in for a burthen of 154 tons. Originally rigged as a schooner, it was altered to a brig later in its career and carried twelve 4pdrs. The second vessel was a smaller schooner, the *Earl of Dunmore*, measuring 60ft on deck, 50ft by 20ft by 7ft 10in for a burthen of 106 tons and a battery of ten 4pdrs.[6] At St Jean on the Richelieu River, the 50-ton sloop *Betsy* was built in 1771 to replace the rotten *Musquelongy* using some equipment salvaged from the old *Duke of Cumberland* and *Boscawen*. The same year the first government vessel built at Oswegatchie, the 150-ton snow *Haldimand*, was launched. It measured 76ft on deck, 67ft by 24ft 8in by 8ft 8in and was pierced for sixteen 4pdrs.

The new crop of vessels closely resembled the warships of the Seven Years War, but served exclusively as transports, their armament being little more than 'show', as revealed in 1773 by the master of the *Gage* who complained about his vessel's 'defenceless state having on board only eight useless Muskets without Pistol, Sword or pike and only about two pounds of Powder, for the carriage guns.'[7] Locals had replaced the eastern seaboard mariners and military volunteers who had crewed the earlier warships. Some of the masters had left the army for permanent employment afloat and taken up residence on shore, while other men joined the lake service after giving up hope of promotion in the Royal Navy during the years of peace.[8]

The situation on the lakes changed dramati-

TABLE 6

Particulars of the British squadron on Lake Ontario, 1779-1783

Vessel	Rig	Tonnage	Keel	Deck	Breadth	Hold	Metal
Haldimand	snow	150	67ft	76ft	24ft 8ft	8ft 8in	16-4pdrs
Seneca	snow	130	72ft	84ft	24ft 6ft	9ft	10-4pdrs, 8-6pdrs
Caldwell	sloop	37	—	52ft	15ft	7ft	2-4pdrs
Mohawk	sloop	47	37ft 9in	51ft	15ft 2ft	8ft	4-12pdrs
Ontario	snow	231	68ft	77ft	25ft 6ft	9ft 3in	16-6pdrs, 6-4pdrs
Limnade	ship	226	—	80ft	24ft 4ft	9ft	16-6pdrs, 6-4pdrs

Source: NAC, RG 8, I, 722a, pp32-33, 46-7; Haldimand Papers, 21805, p107.

TABLE 7

Particulars of the British squadron on Lakes Erie, Huron and Michigan, 1779-1782

Vessel	Rig	Tonnage	Keel	Deck	Breadth	Hold	Metal
Gage	brig	154	62ft	72ft	22ft 10in	8ft 1in	12-4pdrs
Dunmore	schooner	106	50ft	60ft	20ft	7ft 10in	10-4pdrs
Hope	schooner	81	47ft	54ft 4in	18ft	6ft 8in	4-4pdrs; 6 swivels
Angelica	sloop	66	—	52ft	17ft 6in	8ft 3in	6 swivels
Felicity	sloop	55	—	57ft 6in	16ft	6ft	4 swivels
Faith	schooner	61	—	56ft	15ft 6in	6ft 4in	4 swivels
Welcome	sloop	30	47ft	—	—	—	—
Wyandot	sloop	47	37ft	44ft	15ft 6in	6ft	4 swivels
Adventure	sloop	34	—	44ft 6in	13ft	5ft 4in	2 swivels

Source: NAC, RG 8, I, 722a, pp34-5 and 44-5; *Collections and Researches made by the Pioneer and Historical Society of the State of Michigan* (Lansing 1888), 10, p620.

cally late in 1775 when the rebellion broke out in the Thirteen Colonies and threatened to expand northward. The Quebec Act of 1774 had undone many of the strictures of the unpopular 1763 Royal Proclamation by extending Quebec's borders to include the native territory southwest of the lakes and easing trade restrictions in that area; three civil governors were sent to govern the areas around Detroit, Vincennes (Indiana) and Kaskaskia (Illinois). American colonists considered the Quebec Act one of Britain's 'Intolerable Acts', and protested that their rights to settle in the area were under attack, gradually getting more militant as the government failed to respond adequately to their entreaties.

Promoted to the rank of lieutenant general in 1770, Thomas Gage was still the commander-in-chief of British forces in North America, while responsibility for commanding the province of Quebec was in the hands of Major General Sir Guy Carleton who realised that the transport service on the lakes needed to be put on a war footing. As a result, in August 1776 Carleton took control of the vessels that had been operated by John Blackburn. He forbade any private craft to be under sail and, to ensure that the needs of the outposts were met, he hired three of Alexander Grant's vessels on Lake Erie (the *Hope*, *Angelica* and *Faith*) and his new 37-ton sloop *Caldwell* on Lake Ontario to supplement the public vessels. Grant's sloop *Charity* on Lake Ontario also appears to have been used by the government for a brief time, before it wore out, as was his sloop *Chippewa* (wrecked on Lake Erie in 1775). Carleton also retained three other private vessels at Detroit, the *Felicity*, *Adventure* and *Wyandot* for employment on the upper lakes. In 1777 Carleton formally appointed Alexander Grant the commissioner of the squadrons on Lake Ontario and above, and gave commissions to the officers then serving in the vessels, making Richard Cornwall the master builder for all the lakes. Mindful

TABLE 8

Particulars of the British Squadron on Lake Champlain, 1777-1779

Vessel	Rig	Tonnage	Keel	Deck	Breadth	Hold	Waist height	Draught fore/aft	Metal
Royal George	ship	384	77ft 9½in	96ft 6in	30ft 6in	10ft	4ft 9in	8ft 6in/9ft	20-12pdrs, 6-6pdrs; 10 swivels
Inflexible	ship	204	65ft 7½in	80ft 1½in	23ft 10in	9ft	5ft 6in	8ft 4in/9ft 6in	16-9pdrs, 6-3pdrs; 10swivels
Maria	schooner	129	52ft 2in	66ft	21ft 6in	8ft 2½in	4ft 2in	7ft 4in/7ft 4in	14-6pdrs; 6 swivels
Carleton	schooner	96	46ft 4in	59ft 2in	20ft	6ft 6½in	4ft 2in	6ft 2in/7ft 4in	12-6pdrs; 6 swivels
Thunderer	ketch	422	71ft 9in	91ft 9in	33ft 4in	6ft 8in	3ft 6in	4ft 6in/4ft 6in	14-18pdrs; 4-8in howitzers
Washington	brig	127	59ft 3in	72ft 4in	19ft 7in	6ft 2in	4ft 5in	6ft 4in/7ft 4in	16-6pdrs, 4-3pdrs; 12swivels
Lee	sloop	47	33ft	43ft 9in	16ft 3½in	4ft 8in	3ft 2in	5ft 4in/5ft 4in	8-6pdrs; 4 swivels
Convert	hoy	109	50ft 8in	62ft 10in	20ft 3in	3ft 7½in	1ft 6in	3ft 0in/3ft 6in	7-9pdrs; 6 swivels
Jersey	hoy	52	43ft 9in	52ft 6½in	14ft 9in	4ft 8½in	3ft 6in	2ft 6in/2ft 6in	5-9pdrs; 6 swivels
Trumbull	galley	119	62ft 2in	74ft 10in	18ft 3in	5ft	3ft 8in	5ft 10in/6ft 8in	2-18pdrs, 2-6pdrs, 4-4pdrs; 18swivels
Liberty	schooner	37	31ft 8in	41ft 11in	14ft 9in	5ft 1in	2ft 10in	4ft 10in/5ft 10in	6-3pdrs; 6 swivels
Spitfire (B)	sloop	4	30ft 2in	—	9ft 8in	3ft 8in	—	3ft	4-2pdrs; 2 swivels
Spy	sloop	4	30ft	—	9ft 7in	3ft 9in	—	3ft	2-3pdrs; 4 swivels
Lookout	sloop	4	30ft 1in	—	9ft 9in	3ft 7in	—	3ft	1-4pdr; 2 swivels
Dispatch	sloop	4	30ft 3in	—	9ft 9in	3ft 9in	—	3ft	2-3pdrs; 2 swivels
Dilligence	sloop	4	30ft	—	9ft 8in	3ft 8in	—	3ft	2-3pdrs; 2 swivels
Nautilus	sloop	4	30ft	—	9ft 7in	3ft 7in	—	3ft	1-4pdr; 6 swivels
Camel	hoy	80	65ft	—	23ft	7ft 1in	—	4ft 11in	—
Commissary	hoy	50	56ft 2in	—	17ft 2in	7ft	—	3ft 8in	—
Ration	hoy	40	42ft 9in	—	13ft 6in	6ft 9in	—	3ft	—
Receipt	hoy	45	53ft 6in	—	17ft 8in	6ft 9in	—	3ft 4in	—
Delivery	hoy	45	53ft 4in	—	16ft 10in	6ft 9in	—	3ft 2in	—

Source: NAC, RG 8, I, 722a, pp20-21, 30-31.
Discrepancies sometimes appear between data in returns such as the ones used to compile this table and draughts of some vessels. Jonathan Coleman's draught of the *Washington*, for instance, shows the keel dimension as 60ft 6in which conflicts with the returns of this period. In the text, draught dimensions are used when available.

TABLE 9
British vessels launched and acquired, 1763-1783

Vessel	Launch	Place	Rig	Remarks
Lake Ontario				
Brunswick	1765	Oswego	schooner	1767 Blackburn contract; 1770 reported thoroughly rotten
Haldimand, 16	1771	Oswegatchie	snow	1785 last mentioned
Caldwell	1775	Niagara	sloop	1793 last mentioned
Charity †	1770	Niagara	sloop	1778 derelict at Carleton Island, burned
Seneca, 18	1777	Oswegatchie	snow	1789 last mentioned
Mohawk (C), 4	1778	Niagara	cutter	1785 last mentioned
Ontario (B), 22	1780	Carleton Island	brig	November 1780 wrecked east of Ft Niagara
Limnade, 22	1781	Carleton Island	ship	1786 last mentioned
Lake Erie				
unidentified	1763	Navy Island	sloop	1764 wrecked
Victory	1761	(?) Navy Island	sloop	nee *Huron* (?); 1766 accidentally burned at Grand Island
Boston, 8	1764	Navy Island	schooner	1768 accidentally burned at Grand Island
Gladwin, 8	1764	Navy Island	schooner	1767 Blackburn contract in service until 1772
Royal Charlotte, 10	1764	Navy Island	sloop	1767 Blackburn contract in service until 1772
Chippewa (A)†	1769	Detroit	sloop	November 1775 wrecked on Lake Erie
General Gage, 12	1772	Detroit	schooner/brig	1785 last mentioned
Earl of Dunmore, 10	1772	Detroit	schooner	1803 on shore at Amherstburg, decayed
Angelica †	1771	Detroit	sloop	Oct 1783 wrecked on Lake Erie
Hope, 4 †	1771	Detroit	schooner	Oct 1783 wrecked on Lake Erie
Felicity †	1774	Detroit	sloop	1796 powder hulk at Amherstburg
Faith †	1774	Detroit	schooner	Oct 1783 wrecked on Lake Erie
Archangel†	1774	Detroit	sloop	after 1775 no longer listed
Adventure †	1776	Detroit	sloop	1785 last mentioned
Welcome†	1777	Detroit	sloop	1781 last mentioned
Wyandot†	1779	Detroit	sloop	1789 wrecked on Lake Huron
Rebecca	1783	Detroit	snow	1785 last mentioned
Lake Champlain				
Betsey, 2	1771	St Jean	sloop	1775 taken by Rebels *
Royal Savage, 14	1775	St Jean	schooner	1775 taken by Rebels *
Loyal Convert, 7‡	1775	Ticonderoga	gondola-lugger	ex-*Hancock* or *Schuyler*; 1784 last mentioned
Inflexible, 22	1776	St Jean	ship	1785 last mentioned
Maria (A), 14	1776	St Jean	schooner	1793 last mentioned
Carleton, 12	1776	St Jean	schooner	1785 last mentioned
Thunderer, 18	1776	St Jean	radeau-ketch	1777 wrecked
Royal George (A), 26	1777	St Jean	ship	1785 last mentioned
Washington, 14‡	1776	Skenesborough	brig	1785 last mentioned
Lee, 8‡	1776	Skenesborough	sloop	1784 last mentioned
Jersey, 5‡	1776	Skenesborough	hoy	1784 last mentioned
Trumbull, 8‡	1776	Skenesborough	lugger	1785 last mentioned
Liberty, 6‡	1770?	Skenesborough	lugger	nee-*Catherine*; 1785 hauled up on shore, useless
six gunboats	1778	Isle aux Noix	sloop	
five transports	1778	Isle aux Noix	hoy	

† private vessel hired or purchased for government service. ‡ prize vessel. * see Table 10.

that the interruption of private shipping would be a hardship for the merchants involved, Carleton advised his captains to make every effort to accommodate commercial interests. As it was, the vessels were so burdened by private cargo that some of the masters petitioned Carleton in 1778 for an 'allowance of the freights', because they were 'having extraordinary trouble in carrying Merchandise, and [were] almost always crowded with Passengers, of Merchants, traders, Clerks, and others not employed in His Majesty's Services, but on their own immediate and most lucrative business.'[9]

Carleton's changes to operations on the upper lakes prepared the service to face war conditions, but no significant naval activity took place in that region. Instead, Lake Champlain became the most contentious freshwater theatre in the hostilities between Britain and the colonies.[10] The British had maintained garrisons at Ticonderoga, Crown Point and St Jean (referred to in British and American accounts as Saint Johns or St Johns) which was located on the Richelieu River twenty-four miles north of Lake Champlain and forty miles southeast of Montreal. In 1775 two of the handful of decked sailing vessels on Lake Champlain were the 50-ton government sloop *Betsey*, armed with two brass 6pdrs, and the 41ft schooner *Catherine*, owned by Philip Skene at Skenesborough (Whitehall, New York), a village at the southernmost end of the lake. In the spring of 1775 rebels seized the *Catherine*, renamed it the *Liberty*, and used it to transport a force that captured the weakly manned British forts at Ticonderoga and Crown Point in May. Benedict Arnold, a militia captain and experienced mariner from Connecticut, played a key role in these attacks, which netted the rebels nearly 200 pieces of ordnance. He followed up his early success by taking command of the *Liberty* and sailing for St Jean with a crew of 50 soldiers where he surprised the British guard and overpowered the 7-man crew of the *Betsey*. Naming their sloop the *Enterprise*, the rebels sailed back to Crown Point.

In June the Continental Congress appointed Philip Schuyler the major general in charge of an expedition into Canada. Schuyler made his headquarters at Lake George where he organised his army while batteaux and a pair of large gunboats

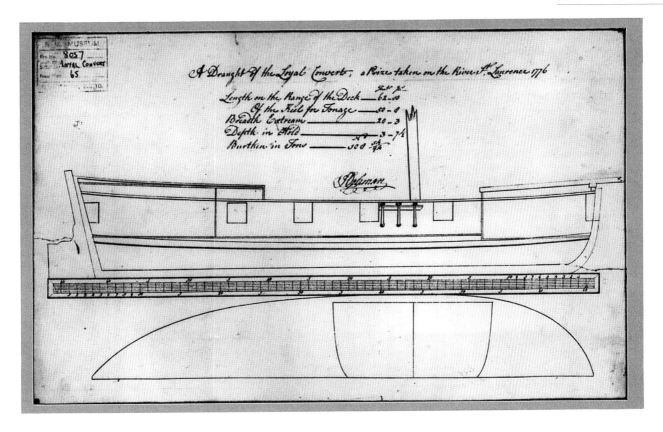

When they captured one of Benedict Arnold's gondolas (the *Hancock* or *Schuyler*) on the St Lawrence River early in 1776, the British renamed it the *Loyal Convert*. Jonathan Coleman, the master builder at St Jean, prepared this 'as built' draught of the gondola, which the British rigged as a hoy, for submission to the Navy Board. (National Maritime Museum, neg 8057)

– referred to variously as gondolas, gundalos or gundalows – were built on Lake Champlain to transport the force. At the end of August 1200 men embarked at Ticonderoga in a flotilla of batteaux supported by the *Enterprise* and *Liberty* and two sixty-foot gondolas, the *Hancock* and *Schuyler*, and headed for St Jean. Major General Carleton had sent reinforcements to the garrison as well as shipwrights and artificers who launched a schooner, the *Royal Savage*, 14, during the summer and set up the frames for a row galley. After two months of resistance, the British post fell to the persistent Americans on 1 November; the *Royal Savage* was sent to Ticonderoga with the components of the row galley on board. The Americans dragged their gondolas down the twelve miles of shoals and rapids between St Jean and Chambly, seizing that place before proceeding to Montreal and capturing it on 13 November. The long winter campaign against Quebec ensued and ended during the spring of 1776 with the withdrawal of a greatly depleted American army to Sorel, at the mouth of the Richelieu River, and then south to Ticonderoga.

Although the Americans failed to conquer Quebec, their invasion prevented the British from co-ordinating an immediate counter-attack on the rebel states by means of the Lake Champlain Valley. Major General Carleton's army re-occupied the Richelieu River late in June 1776 where work began to assemble a naval force at St Jean. Commodore Charles Douglas, who commanded the squadron that brought relief to Quebec the month before, supervised the establishment of the force, sending about 400 officers and men from his warships and 250 from transports in the St Lawrence to Chambly, at the foot of the rapids on the Richelieu.[11] It had been intended to haul the 100-ton armed schooner *Maria* overland to St Jean, but the road proved to be too soft and the schooner was disassembled nearly to the waterline so that it was light enough to be either moved on land or dragged up the river. Similar treatment was given to the transport schooner *Carleton*, while navy carpenters took down a 180-ton vessel on the stocks at Quebec so that its components could be sent up to St Jean. To that place, the British also moved a captured American gondola, either the *Hancock* or *Schuyler* (renaming it the *Loyal Convert*), sixteen Canadian-built gun-

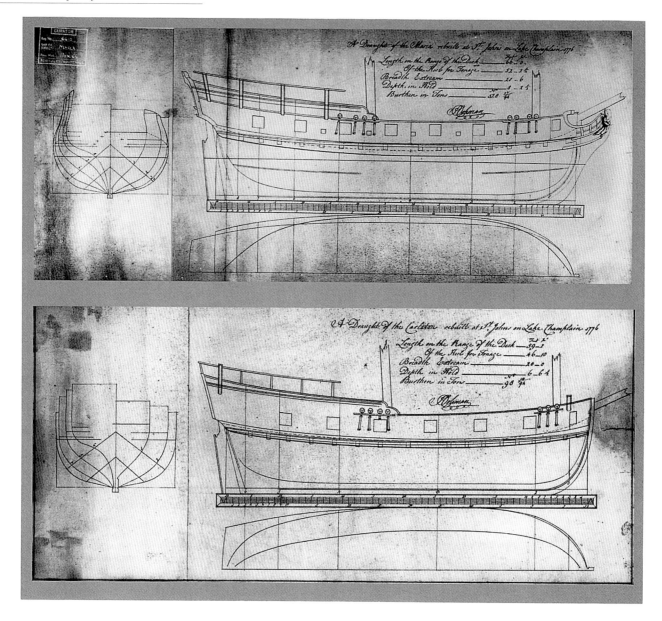

Commodore Charles Douglas ordered two schooners under his command (the *Maria*, top, and *Carleton*) sailed up the Richelieu River to Chambly where they were partially disassembled and hauled up to St Jean. Royal Navy carpenters hurried to reconstruct them and outfit them to meet the rebels. (National Maritime Museum: *Maria* neg DR6440; *Carleton* neg DR6369)

boats and a dozen other gunboats sent from England in parts.

The yard at St Jean was the scene of hectic activity with the ship from the Quebec yard, named the *Inflexible*, rising from keel to launch in twenty-eight days. It measured 80ft 1½in on deck, 65ft 7½in by 23ft 10in by 9ft for a burthen of 204 tons and was armed with sixteen 9pdrs, six 3pdrs and ten swivels. Drawing 8ft 6in of water forward and 9ft aft, the *Inflexible* was a deep vessel in comparison to the shallow conditions on the Richelieu and Lake Champlain; builders during the period of the War of 1812 were careful to keep the draught of water under 8ft, which

suggests that water levels might have been higher during the rebellion.

The rebuilt merchantmen drew less water. Measuring 66ft on deck, 52ft 2¼in by 21ft 6in by 8ft 2½ for a burthen of 129 tons, the *Maria* had little or no drag from bow to stern, drawing 7ft 4in at both ends. The smaller *Carleton* (59ft 2in on deck, 46ft 4in by 20ft by 6ft 6½in for a burthen of 96 tons) had more than a foot of drag and drew 7ft 4in aft. Like most, if not all, of the vessels then on the lakes, the three vessels put together at St Jean had raised quarterdecks which allowed for lighted accommodations aft on the main deck and, as contemporary artwork sug-

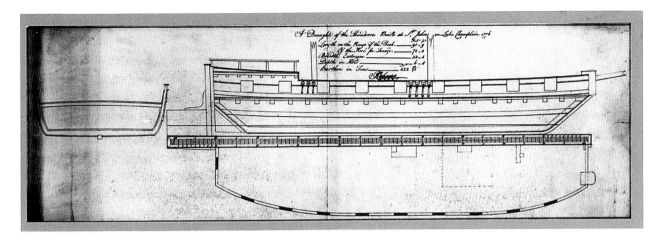

Having relied on radeaux during the Seven Years War, the British built another one for use against the American rebels. The *Thunderer* was larger and more powerful than its predecessors, with a raised quarterdeck and rigged as a ketch. Flat-bottomed and box-like, the radeau must have a difficult vessel to sail. It sank near Windmill Point in 1777 while carrying sick and wounded from the fighting at Saratoga back to St Jean. (National Maritime Museum, neg DR6406)

TABLE 10

Rebel Vessels on Lakes Champlain and George, 1775-1777

Vessel	Launch	Place	Rig	Remarks
Liberty, 8 †‡	1770?	Skenesborough	schooner	ex-*Catherine*; 1777 taken by British at Skenesborough »
Enterprise, 10‡	1771	St Jean	sloop	ex-*Betsey*; 1777 destroyed by British at Skenesborough
Royal Savage, 12	1775	St Jean	schooner	1776 destroyed by British at Valcour Bay
Hancock	1775	Ticonderoga?	gondola-lugger	1776 destroyed or captured by British »
Schuyler	1775	Ticonderoga?	gondola-lugger	1776 destroyed or captured by British »
unidentified	1775?	Lake George	schooner	1777 destroyed by British
Revenge, 6	1776	Ticonderoga	schooner	1777 destroyed by British at Skenesborough
Lee, 4	1776	Skenesborough	gondola-sloop	1776 taken by British after Valcour Bay »
Boston, 3	1776	Skenesborough	cutter	1776 destroyed by Americas after Valcour Bay
Connecticut, 3	1776	Skenesborough	cutter	1776 destroyed by Americas after Valcour Bay
Jersey, 3	1776	Skenesborough	cutter	1776 taken by British after Valcour Bay »
New Haven, 3	1776	Skenesborough	cutter	1776 destroyed by Americas after Valcour Bay
New York, 3	1776	Skenesborough	cutter	1777 destroyed by British at Skenesborough
Philadelphia, 3	1776	Skenesborough	cutter	1776 sunk at Valcour Bay
Providence, 3	1776	Skenesborough	cutter	1776 destroyed by Americas after Valcour Bay
Spitfire (A), 3	1776	Skenesborough	cutter	1776 destroyed by Americas after Valcour Bay
Congress, 9	1776	Skenesborough	lugger	1777 destroyed by British at Skenesborough
Trumbull, 9	1776	Skenesborough	lugger	1777 taken by British at Skenesborough *
Washington, 9	1776	Skenesborough	lugger	1776 taken by British after Valcour Bay *
Gates, 9	1776	Skenesborough	lugger	1777 destroyed by British at Skenesborough

† private vessel hired or purchased for government service. ‡ prize vessel. * see Table 9.

gests, ornate sterns; such arrangements would be considered extravagant and unnecessary by builders thirty-five years later.

In addition to the three reconstructions and numerous small craft, a radeau, the *Thunderer*, was built at St Jean. It resembled a scow with a flat bottom and sides that flared out, but it lacked the curious inward-slanting bulwarks and sparse quarters of the British radeaux built during the Seven Year War. The *Thunderer* was decked with a raised quarterdeck and stern accommodations and rigged as a ketch. It was larger that its predecessors, measuring 91ft 9in on deck, 71ft 9in by 23ft 4in by 6ft 8in for a burthen of 423 tons, and more heavily armed, bearing fourteen 18pdrs and four 8in howitzers.

Superintending the St Jean shipyard was a Royal Navy master builder named Jonathan Coleman who prepared 'as fitted' plans for all the vessels and sent them to the Navy Board. The Admiralty also ordered the preparation of draughts for a pair of 10-gun sloops to be built on Lake Champlain (they were not needed), the only time they had supplied the design for a vessel on the lakes, it appears, since sending the draught of a sloop to Commodore Keppel in 1754.[12] The preparation on Lake Champlain was also notable because it was the largest investment in men and munitions the Royal Navy had made on the lakes to date. This was due, in part, to the fact that the British could no longer call on the ports along the eastern seaboard for shipwrights and crews as they had done during the Seven Years War.

Unaware of the strength of the squadron being prepared at St Jean, American authorities chose

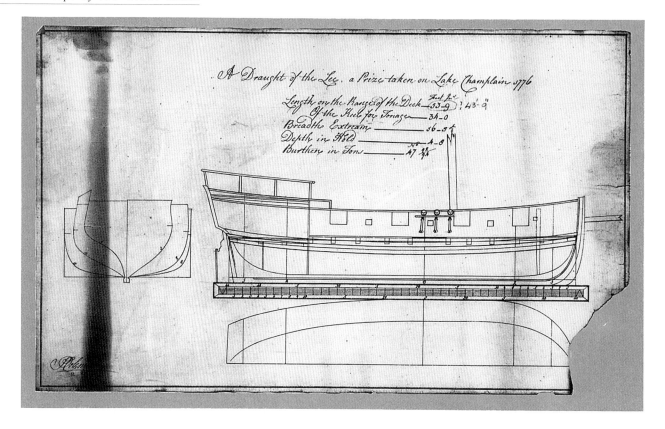

A Draught of the Lee a Prize taken on Lake Champlain 1776

Length on the Range of the Deck —— 53-9 { 43-9"
Of the Keel for Tonage —— 34-0
Breadth Extream —— 16-3½
Depth in Hold —— 4-0
Burthen in Tons —— 47 ½½

With its raised quarterdeck, bulwarks and finer lines, the gondola *Lee* was a more comfortable vessel than the eight gondolas built along Arnold's design. It fell into British hands and Jonathan Coleman recorded its design for the Navy Board. (National Maritime Museum, neg DR6407)

to increase their naval component by building smaller craft rather than heavily armed schooners or square rigged vessels. The *Revenge* schooner, 6, was built during the summer at Ticonderoga, while the rest of the work was done in the dockyard at Skenesborough, where two gondolas were launched by the end of June with two more under construction. Benedict Arnold, who took command of the Skenesborough yard when its production bogged down, is credited with the design of the Lake Champlain gondolas which was based on the barge-like river craft used to transport produce to colonial seaports.

Arnold's design called for a keel of 48ft, an extreme beam of 16ft and the depth amidships from floor to rail of 3ft 6in, but evidence shows that the Skenesborough gondolas were not identical. An extant gondola (the *Philadelphia*, raised from Lake Champlain and preserved in the Smithsonian Institute) reflects Arnold's design, measuring 53ft 2in overall by 15ft 2in by 4ft, while a gondola captured by the British (the *Jersey*) was found to be 52ft 6½in on deck, 43ft 9in by 14ft 9in by 4ft 8½in. The *Philadelphia*'s hull was sharp at both ends and flat-bottomed with no

deadrise. It carried a 12pdr on a slide on the forecastle, a pair of 9pdrs on regular carriage at its sides, offset from each other to allow space for recoil, and several swivel guns. The gondola was open to its internal planking between the forecastle and mast after which there was a low deck for the carriage guns with a raised quarterdeck beneath which stone ballast was carried to counter the weight of the long gun in the bow. The craft had little freeboard and, therefore, no protection for the crew; to cover the men, stanchions were inserted into the rails so that weather cloths could be rigged, but due to a lack of canvas, some gondolas sailed with pine boughs serving this purpose. A gondola carried a single mast, rigged with a square course and topsail and a jib, but the craft's poor sailing qualities made it dependent upon sweeps. By mid-September eight gondolas – the *New Haven, Providence, Boston, Spitfire, Philadelphia, Connecticut, Jersey* and *New York* – had been launched at Skenesborough. After being brought down the lake to Mount Independence on the Vermont shore opposite Ticonderoga where they were rigged and armed, the gondolas joined the squadron anchored under Arnold's command at

While at Chambly in May 1776 with the American force retreating from the winter campaign to Quebec, Benedict Arnold produced this design (here redrawn by Chapelle) for the gondolas he would later command at the battle of Valcour Bay. (Chapelle Collection, Smithsonian Institute)

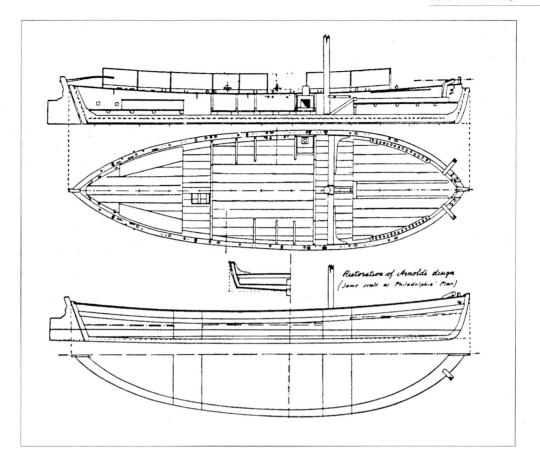

One of the prizes taken during Major General Schuyler's attack on St Jean in the autumn of 1775 was the British *Royal Savage*. Its name left intact, the 14-gun schooner is depicted here under the rebel flag. (Watercolour in Schuyler Papers, Rare Books and Manuscripts Division, New York Public Library.)

A VIEW OF THE NEW ENGLAND ARM'D VESSELS, IN VALCURE BAY ON LAKE CHAMPLAIN, 11 OCTOBER, 1776

1—Royal Savage—8 Six Pounders and 4 4 pounders—Burnt 11 Octr. 2—Revenge*—Eight Guns 4 & 3 pounders. 3—Enterprise*—10 4 poundrs. 4—Lc Octr. 5—Trumble*—One 18, One 12, two 9, & Six Six prs with Swivels &c. 6—Washington mounted same as Trumble taken 13 October. 7—Congress Ar 1, 12. & 2. 9 prs Burnt 15 Octr. 9—New York ♀ do Arm'd. 10—Jersey ♀ do—taken 12 Octr. 11—Connecticut ♀ Burnt 13 Octr. 12—Providence ♀—Sun Burnt 13 Octr. 14—Spitfire ♀ Burnt Dᵒ. 15—Boston ♀ Sunk 11 Octr.

N B the Liberty Schooner & a Row Galley at Tyconderoga with those Mark'd * were taken or Destroy'd in 1777, those Mark'd ♀ Carried same Nu the Above Vessels were Command'd by Benedict Arnold.

A VIEW OF HIS MAJESTY'S ARMED VESSELS ON LAKE CHAMPLAIN OCTOBER 11, 1776

1—Carleton—14 Six pounders (Lt. Dacres). 2—Inflexible—18 twelve pounders (Lt. Shank). 3—Maria—16 six pounders (Lt. Stark). 4—Convert- —6 twenty-four pounders; 18 twelve pounders (Lt. Scott). 6—A Long Boats. 7—Gun Boats. 8—Valcure Island—

N B there were three Longboats with 2 two pounders on Sliders, 17 Gun boats, having one Gun—from Six to 24 pounders. Commander Captn Thos on board the Maria in Both Actions.

Engraved after a contemporary watercolour by Lieutenant C Randle, RN, these twin views show the American (top) and the British squadrons at Valcour Island. The annotation identifies the ships and their force. (Naval Institute Press)

Valcour Island (three miles south of Plattsburgh).

Three row galleys the *Trumbull*, *Congress* and *Washington* eventually made their way to Arnold's squadron. Like the gondolas, they were not identical; the *Washington*, as measured by the British, was 72ft 4in on deck, 60ft 6in by 19ft 7in by 6ft 2in for a burthen of 123 tons and the *Trumbull* (or *Trumble* in some accounts) was 74ft 10in on deck, 62ft 2in by 18ft 3in by 5ft. Each of them was outfitted with two lateen-rigged masts and thirty-six sweeps. There was an 18pdr in the bow, two 12pdrs in the stern and three 6pdrs on each side. The galleys were more comfortable vessels than the gondolas, being decked and having cabins aft, and they sailed better since their bottoms had a slight deadrise, and a smooth contour

12, One 9 & 4 4 prs—Taken 1
: 15th Octr. 8—Philadelphia—
Squall. 13—New Haven ♀ –

of Metal as the Philadelphia—

Lt. Longcroft). 5—Thunder

Navy—Sir Guy Carleton wa

fore and aft. A fourth vessel, referred to as a galley in some sources and a cutter or sloop or gondola in others, was the *Lee*, 4. It was only 43ft 9in on deck, 34ft by 16ft 3½in by 4ft 8in for a burthen of 48 tons and had been built from frames confiscated at St Jean the previous year.[13]

The British finished outfitting their squadron at St Jean and, as a vanguard for an army of 7000 that would depart later, it sailed for Lake Champlain on 4 October, taking up an anchorage on 6 October near Grand Isle, ten miles north of Valcour Island. Commodore Douglas had appointed Captain Thomas Pringle of HMS *Lord Howe* to command the squadron now consisting of the schooner *Maria*, 14, carrying his pendant (with General Carleton in attendance on board), the *Inflexible*, 22, Lieutenant John Schank, the *Carleton*, 12, Lieutenant James Richard Dacres, the *Thunderer*, 18, Lieutenant George Scott and the *Loyal Convert*, 7, Lieutenant Edward Longcroft as well as upwards of twenty gunboats (with single long guns and some howitzers) and other craft, mounting in all more than ninety guns.

The Americans were surprised to discover the strength of the Pringle flotilla, having been ill-informed by their sources at St Jean. Though some officers believed that Arnold's squadron, now consisting of two schooners, the *Royal Savage*, 12, and *Liberty*, 8; a sloop, the *Enterprise*,

10; the galley *Lee*, 4; three other galleys and eight gondolas (for a total of about 80 guns), would be best deployed in a running withdrawal to Ticonderoga, Arnold decided to remain at Valcour Island. He anchored the vessels in a line between the island and the mainland and waited for the British to make their appearance.

Unaware of the precise American anchorage, Pringle led his squadron past Valcour Island on 11 October and, upon sighting the Americans lying in the mile-wide span between the island and the mainland, tacked to sail up into the bay. From his place in the *Congress*, Arnold sent the *Royal Savage* and his four galleys forward to meet Pringle, and the battle commenced around 10:00am. Lightly damaged, the *Royal Savage* ran aground on Valcour Island and was captured while Pringle, whose *Maria* was unable to enter the action, left it up to the *Inflexible*, *Carleton*, *Convert* and the gunboats to do most of the fighting. The *Carleton* was in the forefront and was just barely saved from destruction by the efforts of 19-year-old Midshipman Edward Pellew (the future Lord Exmouth) who succeeded to command on board when the senior officers fell wounded. Despite their advantages in weight of metal and manoeuvrability, the British only managed to sink one gondola, the *Philadelphia*, before Pringle signalled a withdrawal at sunset. He arranged his line

A contemporary print, published in London in December 1776, of the Battle of Valcour Island supposedly 'from a sketch taken by an officer on the spot'. (Beverley R Robinson Collection, Annapolis)

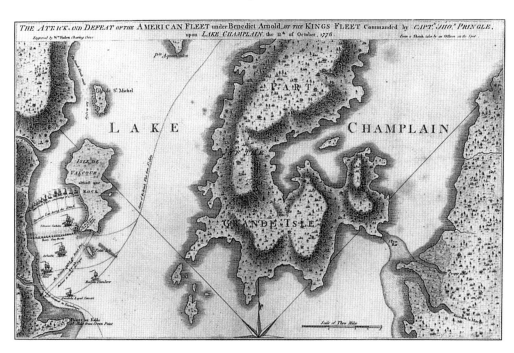

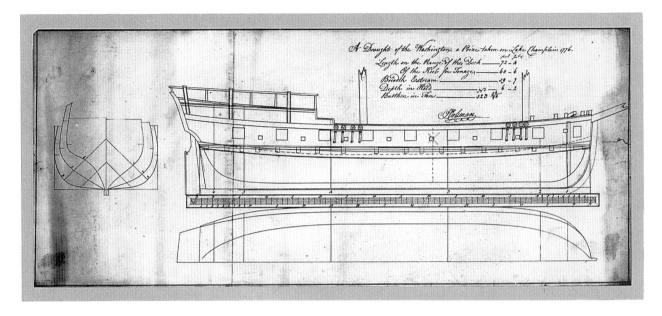

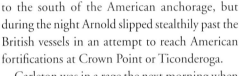

The row galley *Washington* also became a British prize and was recorded by Coleman. Impressed with its stability and sturdiness, the British re-rigged it as a brig. (National Maritime Museum, neg DR6409)

John Schank (*circa* 1740-1823) began his naval career as an able seaman in 1757 and was rated a midshipman three years later. Obtaining a lieutenant's commission in 1776, he was given the transport *Canceaux* as his first command. Renowned for his inventiveness, Schank rose in the service to become admiral of the blue in 1821. (Toronto Reference Library, T14872)

to the south of the American anchorage, but during the night Arnold slipped stealthily past the British vessels in an attempt to reach American fortifications at Crown Point or Ticonderoga.

Carleton was in a rage the next morning when he discovered the Americans had fled and ordered Pringle to pursue them. Over the next two days the British captured the *Lee*, *Washington* and *Jersey* while the Americans scuttled one gondola and burned four others and a galley after running them on shore at Schuyler Island. Only the *Enterprise*, *Revenge*, *Trumbull* and *New York* made it to safety at Ticonderoga. Although the American squadron had been virtually ruined, at the cost of more than eighty casualties compared to the British loss of about forty killed and wounded, the strength of the American presence on Lake Champlain and Benedict Arnold's stand at Valcour delayed Carleton's advance on the lake long enough for the general to conclude that the season was too far gone for further campaigning and he withdrew his force to Canada.

In 1777 General John Burgoyne commanded the 8000-man army collected at St Jean for the next campaign against the Americans. He began his advance in June, utilising the squadron, now commanded by Captain Skeffington Lutwidge, which had been strengthened by its American prizes (Jonathan Coleman submitted as-built draughts to the Navy Board) and the construction during the winter at St Jean of the *Royal*

George, 26. This ship was the largest vessel yet built on Lake Champlain (or any other lake), measuring 96ft 6in on deck, 77ft 9½in by 30ft 6in by 10ft, for a burthen of 384 tons. Designed by Coleman, the ship had very little deadrise and a commodious hold, an enclosed gundeck, raised forecastle and quarterdeck and comfortable accommodations in the stern with quarter galleries; it carried twenty 12pdrs and six 6pdrs. Burgoyne's force easily took control of Lake Champlain, capturing two more American vessels, the schooner *Liberty* and the galley *Trumbull*, at Skenesborough and burning several others. In July most of the British vessels on Lake Champlain were disarmed so that they could serve exclusively as transports for the army which was advancing to Lake George; eighteen gunboats

were hauled up the outlet between the two lakes to support the army's advance. The British also captured an un-named schooner built by the Americans on Lake George and added it to their gunboat flotilla, but the key naval actions in the freshwater theatre of war were finished. Months of bloody fighting on land frustrated Burgoyne's strategies and led to his ultimate defeat at Saratoga on 17 October.

Seeking to regulate the far flung elements of the naval service on the lakes, in 1778 Carleton looked to Lieutenant John Schank, formerly the commander of the converted merchantman *Canceaux* in Commodore Douglas's squadron, whose energetic efforts he had observed firsthand during the previous two years, and appointed him 'Commissioner of all His Majesty's Naval Yards or

The two British ships shown in this view of Lake Champlain from Fort Ticonderoga are the *Inflexible* and *Royal George*. Details on the vessel in the foreground reveal its ornate, lighted stern and lateen mizen sail. (National Archives of Canada, C040336)

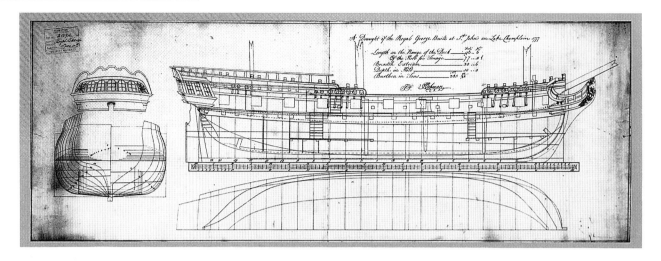

The British launched the 26-gun ship *Royal George* at St Jean in 1777. Jonathan Coleman based his draught on ocean-going vessels and, apart from a shallow, flat-bottomed hull, made few of the concessions that later builders would make when designing heavily armed warships for service on Lake Champlain. (National Maritime Museum, neg DR2994)

Docks upon the Lakes.' Carleton arranged with the Admiralty for Schank to be seconded from the Royal Navy and placed under his authority at Quebec since Carleton believed the service on the lakes should operate independently of the regular service. Hard-pressed by urgent matters on numerous fronts, the Admiralty acceded to Carleton's request and in so doing fostered the creation of a naval department at Quebec that would come to be known as the Provincial Marine and remain independent of the Royal Navy until the War of 1812. Commissioner Schank had barely taken office when Carleton, who resigned his post as governor-in-chief of Quebec after hearing criticisms for the lack of aggressiveness in his campaign of 1776, sailed for England upon the arrival of his replacement, Sir Frederick Haldimand, in June 1778. Having served in North America from the time of the Seven Years War, Haldimand was familiar with conditions in Canada and welcomed a restructuring of the naval force under Schank. Despite the considerable authority of his command, Schank continued as a lieutenant until Haldimand's influence encouraged the Admiralty to promote Schank to master and commander in 1780; he advanced to post rank in 1783.[14]

Haldimand pushed forward Carleton's plans for the naval department and issued a series of regulations, some based upon Royal Navy standards recommended by Schank, that affected everything on the lakes from pay to rations, from slops to the monthly reading of the Articles of War. To maintain tight control of all shipping on the lakes, Haldimand stipulated that 'No vessel [was] to be constructed, or the Establishment of any Kings Vessel altered without an Order from the Command in Chief, nor is any private person whatsoever to Build any Vessel or Boat or even Navigate a Caneau without a proper passport on any Lake.'[15] Haldimand divided the force into three separate divisions, each with its own senior officer: Lake Champlain – Lieutenant William Chambers, RN, from the squadron in the St Lawrence; Lake Ontario – Master and Commander James Andrews, who had been on the lakes for years; and, Lake Erie and the upper lakes – Alexander Grant. On each station, however, the naval commander was immediately responsible to the senior military officer present, with ultimate control of the force being held by the quartermaster general's office at Quebec, thereby continuing the arrangement begun during the Seven Years War of the army having jurisdiction over the naval department.

Personnel from warships and transports in the St Lawrence, some of whom had been with Pringle and Lutwidge on Lake Champlain, were sent to crew the vessels on each station; musters surviving from 1779 show 171 officers and men in the ships and dockyards on Lake Ontario, 118 men employed under Grant's command at Detroit and 182 at St Jean.[16] Apart from the Royal Navy seamen and the hands who had been employed by Blackburn, there were French Canadian 'provincials' in the naval service as well; the snow *Seneca*, 18, launched at Oswegatchie in 1777, was crewed exclusively by French Canadian sailors and captained by Jean-Baptiste

Bouchette, who had been commissioned the same year by Carleton. In part to encourage the employment of more French Canadians, in 1779 Commissioner Schank accepted the services of René-Hippolyte La Force who had commanded the French squadron on Lake Ontario during the Seven Years War. Another veteran of that conflict made his re-appearance in 1779 when Patrick Sinclair, the army officer who commanded one of the vessels during the battle at Fort Lévis in 1760 returned to Canada as lieutenant governor of the post on Mackinac Island.[17]

Among the changes in the department was the relocation of the shipyard at Oswegatchie to a point nearer Lake Ontario. Oswegatchie had been a British transhipment depot from the time of the Seven Years War, but its works had fallen into disrepair, and sailing up and down the river had always proven difficult. Governor-in-Chief Haldimand at first planned to move the base to Cataraqui, the site of the former French dockyard at Fort Frontenac, and he sent a large detachment there in 1778 to make preparations. Along the way, the British officers, who included Lieutenant Schank, stopped at Buck Island, located six miles from the opening to Lake Ontario and ten miles southeast of Cataraqui. Situated in the middle of the main channel of the St Lawrence, south of Grand Island (later Wolfe Island), the

island featured a lofty bluff perfect for fortifications, and two deep, well-sheltered harbours separated by a narrow, low lying neck of land. The officers suggested to Haldimand that Buck Island was a better place to set up the naval establishment and by the end of the summer 1778 they had renamed the island after Sir Guy Carleton, and the soldiers and artificers were laying out the footings for Fort Haldimand. The governor-in-chief had expected to use the post as a jumping off point for an expedition to rebuild a fort at Oswego, but this plan did not come to fruition. Instead, the creation of a strong garrison on Carleton Island proved to be one of several deterrents to an American plan in 1779 for building a naval force at Oswego and launching an attack down the St Lawrence as Amherst had done nearly two decades before.[18]

Although some limited contact between the British and the Americans took place near Carleton Island, and the posts at Niagara, Detroit and Mackinac were on constant guard against an attack from the Americans, no fighting of any importance occurred on the Great Lakes. As a result, very little shipbuilding took place in that area compared to the activity on Lake Champlain, which appears to have continued after the launch of the *Royal George* with the building of six sloop-rigged gunboats and five shallow-draught transports. The dockyard at

The draught of the *Ontario*, drawn by master builder Jonathan Coleman, shows that this ill-fated vessel was very similar in form to the *Royal George* built by Coleman on Lake Champlain. (National Maritime Museum, neg DR3643)

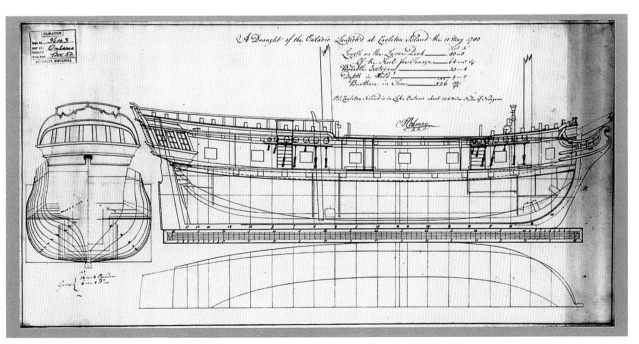

This view of the ship *Limnade* reveals its gentle sheer, raised quarterdeck and ornate stern. The ship is shown moored at Cataraqui in 1783. (Painting by James Peachey, Toronto Reference Library, T15311)

James Andrews was appointed commanding officer on Lake Ontario after Governor Haldimand's organisation of the Provincial Marine. He took command of the snow *Ontario* after its launch in 1780 and was lost when the ship sank on 31 October of that year. (Toronto Reference Library, T15488)

Niagara, presumably at Fort Niagara rather than Navy Hall, produced the *Mohawk* in December 1778. Originally intended to be a row galley like the two-masted, lateen-rigged craft on Lake Champlain, the *Mohawk* was set up as a sloop-rigged transport since the decaying state of the *Haldimand* had made that vessel all but unserviceable. The *Mohawk* measured 51ft on the deck, 37ft 9in by 15ft 2in by 8ft for a burthen of 47 tons and was armed with four 12pdrs. In the spring of 1779 Schank asked Haldimand to send gunboats up from Montreal as he lacked enough small armed craft to patrol the St Lawrence above Oswegatchie. A shortage of suitable timber prevented him from building gunboats immediately at Carleton or proceeding very far with the snow *Ontario*, which was meant to take the place of the *Haldimand*.

In the spring of 1779 work began in earnest on the *Ontario* and progressed slowly under the watchful eye of Jonathan Coleman, who had spent part of the past year at Niagara repairing the *Angelica* on the upper river and building the *Mohawk* at Fort Niagara. As a smaller version of the *Royal George* on Lake Champlain, the *Ontario* measured 77ft on deck, 68ft by 25ft 6in by 9ft 3in for a burthen of 231 tons.[19] It had a stern cabin with full quarter galleries and was pierced to carry six guns on its quarterdeck and fore-castle besides sixteen on its main deck. Apart from a platform below that deck in the bow, the hold ran the length of the hull, its shallow deadrise making the hold large enough to suit the *Ontario*'s prime function as a transport. Finally launched on 10 May 1780 and rigged as a snow, the *Ontario* had a brief career; after spending the summer transporting men and goods between Niagara and Carleton Island, it disappeared in a violent storm east of Niagara late on 31 October 1780, taking with it Master and Commander James Andrews, his crew of 40, a company of the 34th Foot and several army officers, including the former commandant at Fort Niagara.

Following Andrews's death, there was a squabble between J B Bouchette and R H La Force (then superintending the dockyard at Carleton Island) over who should assume command on Lake Ontario. The matter was resolved when the latter returned to Quebec and Bouchette took over for a short time. Master and Commander David Betton, a officer who had served mainly on Lake Erie since receiving a commission from Amherst in 1763, rose to command on Lake Ontario by 1781 and when the ship-rigged *Limnade*, virtually identical in dimensions to the *Ontario*, was launched that year at Carleton Island, he raised his pendant in it.

The dockyard at Detroit had produced no vessels during the American Revolution, since the *Gage* and *Dunmore* had been amply supplemented by hired sloops and schooners during that period. A 1778 return showed that the keel, stern and stem of a snow to be named the *Ottawa* were in place on the stocks at Detroit, but work on that project was stopped and, following the loss of the *Ontario* in 1780, resources were devoted to replacing that vessel before anything new was launched on Lake Erie. After appealing to Halidmand that the warships on the upper lakes were wearing out, Grant received approval to launch a new vessel in 1782; a return later that year noted 'A New Vessel on the Stocks of One hundred and Thirty Six Tons and pierced for 14 Guns but no men or Guns for her.'[20] Whether a wholly new vessel or an alteration of the frame that had been set up in 1778, the snow *Rebecca* was launched in 1783.

Following the British defeat at Yorktown in October 1781, final resolution of the Revolutionary War had only to be negotiated. Receipt at Quebec of the preliminary terms of peace in 1782 prompted the commencement of the customary post-war reductions in the British forces. Of the 468 officers and men then in the naval department 266 (and 35 of the 47 men in the dockyards) were discharged in 1783, their num-

bers including R H La Force and Jonathan Coleman.[21] Haldimand wanted only two vessels in service on Lake Ontario and two more on the upper lakes, but when merchants complained that their transportation needs would never be met by such a meagre force, he increased the number to three. As well, he supported the North West Company when it built a small vessel on Lake Superior. On Lake Champlain all the vessels were dismantled and sunk for preservation purposes except for the 1776 schooner *Maria*.

The 1783 Peace of Paris required the establishment of a boundary line between the United States and British North America. It would run down the middle of Lakes Huron, Erie and Ontario and part way down the St Lawrence River; Haldimand and his advisors believed that Carleton Island would become American territory. As a result, Haldimand stopped further development on Carleton Island and ordered a re-assessment of Cataraqui as the key transhipment point on the lake. By July of that year, the small garrisons at Oswego and Oswegatchie had moved to Cataraqui and work began on a fortified outpost and a town site on the west bank of the mouth of the Cataraqui River. The first parties of United Empire Loyalists, refugees of the American Revolution, set up camps at Cataraqui during the summer of 1783 and, within a year, they had constructed mills, a wharf, storehouses (including one dedicated to naval equipment) and residences.

Haldimand detained Schank in Canada to oversee the changes until 1784 after which there was no longer a commissioner for the marine department and the quartermaster general's office at Quebec took over all responsibilities for the department's operation. The senior officers, Grant on Lake Erie, Betton on Lake Ontario and Adam Bairnfair on Lake Champlain, were responsible to the military commandants at the posts and had to pass all their transactions through the local deputy assistant quartermaster general. The force shrank to fewer than 100 individuals before Governor-in-Chief Haldimand left Canada in 1784. The Provincial Marine became once again a transport service, as it had following the Seven Years War, although the fact that there were more vessels under sail reflected the growing population and commercial traffic around the lakes.

'Of little military service'

1784-1807

FOLLOWING THE AMERICAN REVOLUTION, a reduction took place in the number and size of the freshwater warships, just as it had in the 1760s. For more than two decades the armed government vessels performed their traditional role as transports with meagre crews and only basic upkeep. The spread of privately owned merchantmen further reduced their importance and while wars across the ocean led to changes in warship design,

innovations in construction and armament were slow in being adopted on the lakes.

The 1780s brought some fundamental political changes to the Great Lakes. United Empire Loyalists who were forced out of the rebellious American colonies or refused to live under the Stars and Stripes opened land on the rims of Lakes Ontario and Erie while American settlers spread across Pennsylvania and into Michigan territory. An economic depression followed the war, however, owing in part to the loss of rich military contracts, driving into bankruptcy some individual merchants and partnerships in settlements on the lakes. British traders who remained solvent appealed to the government at Quebec that there were not enough vessels available to forward their goods expeditiously. They wanted the regulation

Origins of this view of Detroit are uncertain, although it seems likely to date from the early 1780s. The size of the vessel and its rig suggest that it is the snow *Rebecca*. It lies off the empty dockyard where a smaller hulk is pulled up on the shore. (Service Historique de l'Armée de Terre)

TABLE 11

Return of the Marine Establishment in the Provinces of Lower and Upper Canada, 24 October 1793

Lakes	Vessels	PRESENT ESTABLISHMENT			NEEDED TO COMPLETE NEW ESTABLISHMENT		NEW ESTABLISHMENT	
		Tons	*Crew*	*Guns*	*Crew*	*Guns*	*Crew*	*Guns*
Lake Champlain	*Maria*	128	25	8	59	6	84	14
	Royal Edward	147	—	—	—	—	—	—
Lake Ontario	*Onondaga*	100	22	6	50	6	72	12
	Mississauga	100	22	6	50	6	72	12
	Caldwell	80	9	2	15	4	24	6
Lake Erie and Huron	*Ottawa*	100	22	6	50	6	72	12
	Dunmore	106	22	4	10	4	32	8
	Chippewa	100	22	6	50	6	72	12
	Felicity	55	11	2	5	2	16	4

Source: NAC, MG 11, CO 42/97, p170.

In anticipation of hostilities erupting with the United States, a new establishment for the Provincial Marine was designed and approved by Lord Dorchester. This return tabulated improvements needed to raise the current establishment to the new guidelines. A note beside the *Royal Edward* indicated: 'Not in Commission, to replace the *Maria* next Spring.' Added to the bottom of the return was: 'The Guns and Ammunition to complete the above vessels for war is lying at the several posts of St Johns, Kingston and Detroit. There is in store here [Quebec] rigging for two vessels of about 150 tons each and timber cut, squared, marked and numbered at St Johns for to build two vessels of the above burthen.'

of 1777 which strictly limited freshwater transport to be lifted so that they could build their own carriers and, as a result of their requests, a loosening of the shipping restrictions began before Governor-in-Chief Frederick Haldimand's departure from Quebec in 1784 and continued during the two-year term of his temporary replacements. The first large batteaux built by the merchants soon evolved into sloops and schooners and by the time Sir Guy Carleton, now Lord Dorchester, arrived at Quebec in 1786 to take up the duties of governor-in-chief, there was one vessel on Lake Ontario and as many as six private craft operating on Lake Erie.[1]

Dorchester established a commission in 1787 to examine the problems of the inland navigation. The inquiry revealed that the vessels of the Provincial Marine had been busily involved in transporting public and private goods, but that the system was fraught with problems. The individual masters in the marine department were in charge of loading their own vessels following a system of rotation; once the government's particular cargo of military or civil items was embarked; the balance of a vessel's capacity was taken up with an equal proportion of each proprietor's merchandise waiting for shipment. Crafty traders abused this procedure, however, by inflating the report of their stock so that when the proportion they were allowed was put on board it took up most, if not all, of the packs of peltries or barrels of flour they had in store. At the same time, the government coffers suffered because merchants were slow to pay their fees or defaulted outright: one report showed that only £9096 was collected out of the £23,505 in fees charged between 1777 and 1783.[2]

Dorchester's commission resulted in the enactment of the Inland Navigation Act, which opened the lakes to private carriers as they had been prior to the Revolutionary War. Among its many articles, the act established offices for superintendents at the key ports who would record the arrival, departure and cargo of each vessel and ensure that the masters of private outbound vessels filled any remaining space in their holds with other merchandise waiting for shipment. Commercial craft

were also limited to 90 tons in burthen, a stricture which was followed closely except in the instance of vessels such as the *Lady Dorchester*, 120 tons, and the *Governor Simcoe*, 137 tons, launched at Kingston in 1788 and 1793 respectively.[3] The change in policy promoted business and the rapid development of private shipping on the lakes, especially at Detroit.

The Inland Navigation Act eased the burden on the Provincial Marine vessels, all of which had been built during the Revolutionary War and were wearing out. On Lake Ontario the cutter *Mohawk*, launched in 1778, and the ship *Limnade* (1781) were no longer entered in the records at the end of the 1780s. The senior officer on the lake, David Betton, who by this time was being referred to as 'the commodore,' only had the old sloop *Caldwell* (1775) and the snow *Seneca* (1777) under his command, but the latter was badly decayed and probably ended up in 1793 as the 'large vessel ... condemned at Kingston'.[4]

Formerly the townsite of Cataraqui, Kingston grew rapidly during the 1780s. Although doubts lingered about whether Carleton Island was in British or American territory, the Provincial Marine offices and dockyard were moved to Kingston in 1789 and set up on the wide, low lying peninsula across the Cataraqui River from the town. The peninsula was originally labelled Point Montreal but soon became known as Navy Point or Point Frederick. A wharf and storehouses appeared and the government vessels took up anchorage in Haldimand Cove (later Navy Bay) which lay between the peninsula and Point Henry, the rise of ground to the east of the bay. Some officials still considered Carleton Island as a better location for naval headquarters and transhipment, but the dockyard was abandoned and gradually fell into decay; small British detachments manned the post until the Americans seized the island at the outbreak of the War of 1812.[5]

Plans for two new vessels on Lake Ontario appear to have developed during 1788 and the next summer, while the *Seneca* was being careened for repairs at Point Frederick, a pair of schooners rose on the stocks. The building site was not at Kingston, however, but fifteen miles down the St Lawrence at Raven Creek (near Gananoque); the proximity of suitable timber might have

Grand Isle (Wolfe Island) creates two channels at the head of the St Lawrence River. The location of the Provincial Marine dockyard in the late 1770s, identified on this map as the 'Harbour', was on Carleton Island in the middle of the southern channel. The dockyard was later moved to Point Frederick off the Kingston Channel. (National Archives of Canada, NMC 19618)

The ramparts and outbuildings of Fort Niagara were portrayed *circa* 1783 by James Peachey. Anchored at the dock is a two-masted vessel which is most likely the *Seneca*. On the opposite shore (bottom right) is located Navy Hall, the Provincial Marine depot that had developed during the latter half of the 1770s. (National Archives of Canada, C2035)

prompted the decision to build away from Kingston. At 100 tons in burthen, the schooners were considerably smaller than the *Seneca* and *Limnade* since there was less freight for the government vessels to transport and fewer hands in the Provincial Marine to build or sail the craft. The schooners, named the *Mississauga* and *Onondaga*, slid down the ways in 1790 apparently and were soon supplemented by two new 44-ton gunboats, the *Sophia* and *Catherine* (also known respectively as the *Bear* and *Buffalo*). As in the case of the schooners, no dependable record of the dimensions of the gunboats or their construction has survived. The gunboats were large enough, however, to make regular voyages up and down the lake laden with cargo during the 1790s.[6]

The situation on the upper lakes was very similar. Despite being launched in 1783, the snow *Rebecca* had been laid up and was no longer noted by 1790, whereas the old schooner *Earl of Dunmore* (from 1772) and the sloop *Felicity* (1774) still worked a full season, primarily on Lake Huron. The same initiative that led to the launch of new vessels on Lake Ontario also resulted in the building of a pair of unidentified gunboats

and two 100-ton schooners at Detroit around 1790, the *Ottawa* and the *Chippewa* (the latter was said in one primary source to have been known originally as the *Tebicas*). Details about their launch dates are lacking, but some evidence suggests that the schooners' first full sailing season was 1792 because the following February 'Commodore' Grant, as he had become widely known, wrote that 'the schooner *Ottawa* from the length and weight of the main boom and rather sharp build in the bows makes her pitch much in a head sea, to ease this defect, I intend rigging her this Spring snow fashion.'[7] From 1793, both vessels were referred to as snows.

Of the station at St Jean during this period, very little was written. In 1789 one observer mentioned 'seven stout ships of different strengths and Portage [on the Great Lakes]. To which may be added four more in the harbour of St Johns at the entrance and for the defence of Lake Champlain.'[8] Other sources show that only the *Maria* was still afloat, though barely, and under the charge from 1791 of Master and Commander John Steel, who had joined the Provincial Marine in 1785. The *Maria*, a dismantled merchantmen rebuilt at St Jean in

1776, was nearing the end of its career, however, and just as new vessels appeared on the other lakes, the 100-ton *Royal Edward* was launched into the Richelieu River at St Jean in 1794.

During the early 1790s the international boundary was confirmed and the British turned over their holdings on American soil south of the lakes and established new settlements and garrisons along the line. In response to the influx of people to the Great Lakes region, and to the threat posed by the expansion of the United States, the British government passed the Constitutional Act in 1791, splitting the reduced province of Quebec into two colonies, Lower and Upper Canada, the boundaries of which closely matched those of the modern provinces of Quebec and Ontario. The villages of Newark (also known as Niagara), Queenston, Chippewa and Fort Erie developed along the Niagara River while townsites were still under consideration along the Detroit. The post on Mackinac Island became an American holding, leaving the British to establish a new garrison on St Joseph Island on the northern shore of Lake Huron. In 1796 the Lake Erie dockyard was finally moved from Detroit to the military post of Malden (soon to be part of the village of Amherstburg) at the mouth of the Detroit River.

In June 1792 Colonel John Graves Simcoe arrived at Kingston to begin his term as lieutenant governor of the province of Upper Canada.[9] A well-reputed veteran of the Revolutionary War, Simcoe had ambitious ideas on how the new colony should be organised and administered. He first experienced the Provincial Marine when he took passage from Kingston to Niagara on board the *Onondaga* and what he saw left him unimpressed. By autumn he was writing that 'this department is without any kind of discipline and obedience ... the refuse of the Merchants' seamen [are] picked up at a bounty to remain for three years and who are the most profligate men I have ever heard of.'[10] Simcoe later wrote that the vessels were 'well calculated for the purpose of Transport [but] ... of little Military Service.'[11] His wife, Elizabeth, echoed his opinions, remarking on one occasion 'the men who navigate the Ships on this Lake have little nautical knowledge and never keep a log book.'[12]

Shortly after Governor Simcoe's arrival in Canada, fear arose that the United States would go to war with Britain as an offshoot of the hostilities that had commenced in Europe. Simcoe was quick to make recommendations for improving the province's defences to Lord Dorchester at Quebec and to the home government, including how the Provincial Marine could be put on a war footing. His suggestions included a plan to fully arm and man the existing vessels and build heavily armed gunboats and ten new ships, carrying

Elizabeth Simcoe, the wife of Lieutenant Governor John Graves Simcoe, painted this watercolour of the salute fired by the Provincial Marine schooners *Onondaga* and *Mississauga* at York in August 1793 to commemorate the victory of the Duke of York at the siege of Famars. Simcoe used this event to honour the duke by renaming the old French post of Toronto after him. (Toronto Reference Library, T10334)

TABLE 12

British vessels launched, 1784-1807

Vessel	Launch	Place	Rig	Remarks
Lake Ontario				
Onondaga (B), 12*	1790	Gananoque	schooner	1798 condemned
Mississauga (C), 12	1790	Gananoque	schooner	1801 laid up
Mohawk (D), 12	1795	Kingston	schooner	1803 laid up
Catherine/Buffalo	1792?	Kingston	schooner (?)	1797 condemned
Sophia/Bear	1792?	Kingston	schooner (?)	1797 condemned
Swift	1798	Kingston	schooner	1806 worn out
Speedy	1798	Kingston	schooner	1804 wrecked at Presque Isle
Toronto	1798	York	schooner	1811 on shore at York, unserviceable
Duke of Kent	1802	Kingston	snow	1811 laid up, barracks
Earl of Moira, 14	1805	Kingston	ship	1814 renamed *Charwell*; 1817 in ordinary; 1830s sold
Duke of Gloucester, 6	1807	Kingston	schooner	1813 taken by Americans, renamed *York*, magazine hulk
Lake Erie				
Ottawa, 12	1791?	Detroit	schooner/snow	1803 condemned
Chippewa(B), 12	1791?	Detroit	schooner/snow	1803 on shore, decayed
Francis	1795	Detroit	sloop	last mentioned, 1803
Maria (B)	1796	Detroit	schooner	out of service by 1803
Earl of Camden	1803	Amherstburg	snow	1811 unserviceable
General Hope, 12	1804	Amherstburg	schooner	1805 wrecked at St Josephs
General Hunter, 12	1807	Amherstburg	schooner/brig	1815 sold to private owners
Lake Champlain				
Royal Edward, 12	1794	St Jean	schooner	1812 unserviceable

* Ordnance strength for some vessels is not shown here due to lack of dependable information.

TABLE 13

American vessels launched, 1790s-1807

Vessel	Launch	Place	Rig	Remarks
Tracy	1790s	Detroit?	schooner	post 1800 sold to private owners
Niagara (A)	1790s	Detroit?	sloop	post 1800 sold to private owners
Adams, 6	1801	River Rouge	brig	1812 taken by British, renamed *Detroit*; recaptured by Americans, destroyed

ten or twelve 4pdrs, 6pdrs or 9pdrs. Because he believed that the naval headquarters at Kingston was ill-placed and that the town itself was indefensible, Simcoe wanted the marine department moved to the new village of York (Toronto) where he would soon relocate the colony's capital from Newark. He also advised that the Lake Erie dockyard be set up at Chatham on the Thames River, and considered establishing a naval depot in Matchedash Bay in the southeast corner of Georgian Bay. Simcoe disapproved of the inconsistencies he detected in the operations of the various naval stations and blamed them on the great distance between the headquarters of the quarter-

master general at Quebec and the remote outposts. There was a deputy assistant quartermaster general at each place, but Simcoe wanted an officer appointed in Upper Canada to act as Commissioner Schank had done, co-ordinating the elements of the naval force after close consultation with Simcoe who was also the province's military commander; in fact, in 1794 Simcoe requested that Schank be reassigned to the lakes.[13]

Simcoe's ideas about the navy on the lakes drew comments from his superiors and friends in England. Henry Dundas (the future Viscount Melville), treasurer of the Admiralty, agreed that 'a Naval Force, properly constructed for the Lakes, [is] a matter of great future import and consequence, as tending to form the most natural and efficient, as well as the cheapest, mode of Defence for the province of Upper Canada.' Dundas called for the framing of regulations to provide the discipline Simcoe had said was lacking and agreed that Captain John Schank 'is a Person peculiarly well qualified to superintend the Construction and Management of a Naval Force upon the Lakes.'[14] He added that he would speak to their Lordships at the Admiralty about the matter. Hugh Percy, the second Duke of Northumberland, a prominent military officer in England, offered to send Simcoe a model of a gunboat he had found useful during his tour of duty in New England and suggested that sliding keels might be employed in the warships so that they could carry heavy metal while maintaining shallow draughts suitable for inshore fighting. 'I will talk to my friend Shank (*sic*) on this subject,' wrote Northumberland, referring to Schank's experiments with centreboard-like sliding keels which had won the approval at the Admiralty.[15] Schank was on assignment in the West Indies at the time, however, and did not return to Canada. War clouds eventually vanished in North America and Lieutenant Governor Simcoe's saw few of his plans for the improvement of the Provincial Marine put into effect before he left Upper Canada on sick leave in 1796. The organisation of the marine remained as it had been, its role continuing to be that of a low level transport service consisting of a handful of small vessels manned by skeleton crews. The increase in private vessels and the better wages offered to sailors had made the acquisition of crews for the public vessels more difficult and the quartermaster general's department barely filled the paltry 22-man establishments of the largest vessels in the squadrons. Between 1794 and 1801 only 189 seamen were entered into the service, of whom 50 deserted, the others usually leaving when their three-year term was up. Repeatedly, the vessels lay inactive at their moorings for want of hands unless draughts of soldiers could be found to make up the crews. Private schooners were routinely hired to carry public goods.[16]

A dozen or so new officers were commissioned during the war scare of 1792 and 1793, but the men were suddenly discharged in 1796 without half pay, which they had been promised they would receive in such an event; several of them were able to rejoin the next year. David Betton died in December 1794 and was replaced by Jean-Baptiste Bouchette, who had left his Lake Ontario command after the Revolutionary War and returned to the service in 1791; his son Joseph Bouchette held a lieutenant's commission in the department during this period and completed hydrographic surveys at York and elsewhere. The senior Bouchette's term as commodore was marked by controversy, however, and came to an end in 1803 when he was pushed out of office and pensioned

off; John Steel took over from him as senior officer on Lake Ontario. Alexander Grant remained in command on the upper lakes, as he had been for nearly forty years, and was accustomed to exercising considerable power as the commodore; Simcoe had made him a member of the executive council of the province's government. On more than one occasion, however, government officials reprimanded Grant for running up accounts on work that had not been approved.[17]

On Lake Erie the old *Felicity* finally wore out, ending its days in 1796 as a temporary powder magazine at Amherstburg before being laid up. The *Earl of Dunmore* was rebuilt from its lower futtocks during the summer of 1794 and lasted past 1800. The newer vessels, *Ottawa* and *Chippewa*, lacked such durability and by 1795 both needed extensive repairs, the estimates for which provide glimpses of the schooners' construction and appearance. The *Ottawa* needed the planking of its main and quarterdecks replaced, including the planksheers (widest planks along edge of the deck), waterways, and quickwork (planking on the bulwarks between the ports); 210 feet of wale was to be replaced and the vessel had to be careened and re-caulked. Pine was slated for use on the deck in strakes measuring 2in moulded by 3¼in sided for planking and 7½in sided for

This view of York in 1803 by Edward Walsh shows a small vessel offshore which may be one of the converted gunboat/schooners (*Speedy* or *Swift*), or the schooner *Toronto*. (Edward Walsh, William L Clements Library)

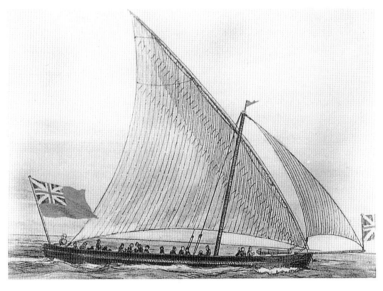

Simcoe wanted gunboats built for defence of the rivers and shorelines and proposed several different designs, including a lug-rigged boat pulling thirty-two oars, and a 'Spanish' gunboat with a large lateen rig and a heavy gun in the bow. (Toronto Reference Library, T16944, T16948)

British government were the sloop *Francis* and the schooner-gunboat *Maria*. Built by William Baker along the lines of the private sloop *Detroit* which Lieutenant Governor Simcoe had admired, the *Francis* was intended as a replacement for the *Felicity* and measured 49ft (on the keel) by 19ft by 7ft. The *Francis* was launched late in 1795 and during the winter Baker built the *Maria* to be 38ft 10in by 14ft by 4ft, dimensions probably typical of gunboats during the Simcoe regime. Originally intended to be given over to the officials of the British Indian Department (for which two other schooners the *Miamis* and *Shawnee Feather* had been built), the *Maria* ended up as a regular element of the Provincial Marine.[18]

A new *Mohawk* (the fourth vessel on the lakes to be so named) was launched at Point Frederick in May 1795. It was described as 'a government boat of 80 tons … the size of the *Mississauga*' and was pierced for twelve 6pdrs, although a special requisition had to be made to find guns that would suit the schooner's dimensions.[19] The *Mohawk* was originally intended to replace the *Onondaga* which had run heavily aground at York late in 1793 and remained high and dry for nearly three months before a persistent Lieutenant Bouchette and his crew managed to get it afloat again. In November 1797 the *Onondaga* barely survived a violent storm and limped into Kingston where it was surveyed during the following winter and condemned; the same board of survey declared the gunboats *Sophia* and *Catherine* unserviceable. Plans for building a replacement for the *Onondaga* were debated, but delayed when officials decided to raise the sides of two of five gunboats then on the stocks at Point Frederick as a temporary solution for the shipping shortage. Originally meant to be part of Simcoe's gunboat programme, the vessels were each built up by two feet, increasing their burthen to 44 tons, and were launched as the schooners *Speedy* and *Swift* late in the summer of 1798. A similar modification was later ordered by Alexander Grant for the *Maria* at Amherstburg. He had the deck of that gunboat-class vessel raised two feet to allow an additional layer of barrels in the hold and 'to prevent her being so wet on deck when sailing in anything of a sea.'[20]

the waterways. Oak plank 3in moulded by 7½in sided was used apparently for the quickwork, while 4in by 9½in oak plank went into the wale. The *Chippewa* required the same work on deck, as well as new lower masts, one cedar beam (20ft by 7½in by 7½in) and four cedar knees. An identical amount of paint was ordered for each snow: 196 pounds of white, 100 pounds of red, 60 pounds of yellow and 50 pounds of black. In consultation with the local military commander and the deputy commissary, William Baker, the master builder, estimated that the work, including the price of labour, on the *Ottawa* would cost £305-18-4 and £369-5-10 on the *Chippewa*.

The last two vessels built at Detroit for the

A third small vessel was launched on Lake

Edward Walsh depicted Detroit in 1804, from the Canadian shore, showing a two-masted vessel at the dockyard which may be the US Army armed transport *Adams*, launched in 1801. (William L Clements Library)

Ontario in 1798. This was the *Toronto*, commonly referred to as a yacht and rigged as a schooner. Peter Hunter, the current lieutenant governor, had complained that government business was often delayed by the lack of available transportation and he asked his superiors in England for permission to build a craft reserved for the specific use of civil officials. When approval arrived, he contracted a private shipbuilder named John Dennis to do the work. Dennis, a Pennsylvanian Quaker and Loyalist who had come to Upper Canada to build gunboats at Simcoe's invitation, owned property by the Humber River at York where he built the *Toronto* and launched it in September 1799, 'one of the handsomest vessels, of her size, that ever swam upon the Ontario. ... she bids fair to be one of its swiftest sailing vessels ... [and] well calculated for the reception of passengers.'[21]

Discussions regarding the vessel to replace the *Onondaga* continued through 1798, the plan being at first to build it on the model of the *Mohawk*. The preference turned, however, to constructing a 'vessel to be double decked and of about one Hundred and Fifty tons ... [and] better adapted for transporting the King's troops and effects.'[22] Approval for the scheme came from Quebec, and Silas Pearson, the master builder at Point Frederick, laid down the keel just before the year ended. Pearson became ill and the project lagged through the next year and into 1800. Although reports showed the vessel on the stocks, already identified as the *Duke of Kent*, and arrangements being made for its launch, the event was postponed, partly because local officials were expecting the Duke of Kent, senior military commander in North America, to visit the lakes and participate in the launch. The Duke did not travel to Kingston in time and in October 1801 the *Duke of Kent* was launched after having sat ready for nearly two years on the stocks. Finally commissioned the following spring, it was rigged as a snow and put into service with the *Swift*, *Speedy* and *Mohawk*. The *Mississauga* was laid up by that point, its sailing days done, a fate that claimed the *Mohawk* early in 1803, after barely eight navigation seasons.

On Lake Erie the *Ottawa*, *Francis* and *Maria* operated past the turn of the century after under-

Edward Walsh painted the view of Fort Niagara in 1804 from the Provincial Marine depot at Navy Hall on the west side of the Niagara River. Details of the stern of one of the Provincial Marine schooners is evident in the vessel in the foreground. (Edward Walsh, William L Clements Library)

going extensive repairs, while the *Chippewa* and *Dunmore* had been condemned and were moored along the shore at Amherstburg. Just as a larger vessel had been built on Lake Ontario to replace the schooners of 1790, John Normand, who had taken over from William Baker as the master builder at Amherstburg, laid down the keel of a 180-ton vessel with dimensions of 66ft by 22ft by 9ft in 1801. It was launched two years later as the *Earl of Camden* and given a snow rig. That same season, the *Ottawa* was surveyed, declared unserviceable and left to rot at Bois Blanc Island, directly opposite Amherstburg, while the *Chippewa* and *Dunmore*, which had been scavenged for iron and sound timbers, were pulled out of the river where they had been causing a silt bar to form.[23]

A new project was rising on the stocks at Point Frederick late in 1803 based upon a detailed draught prepared by Alexander Munn, a shipbuilder at Quebec. This was to be a two-masted, 90-ton vessel measuring 53ft (keel) by 18ft by 9ft 6in that differed from earlier Provincial Marine vessels in that it had a fairly sharp hull with a midships deadrise of about 12 degrees; by way of comparison, the draught of the *Ontario* launched at Carleton Island in 1780 showed a midships deadrise of about 5 degrees. The new vessel also lacked the raised quarterdeck and forecastle that the warships of the Revolutionary War period had, having instead a flush deck in the corvette style. Nevertheless, room was made for a set of four stern lights and a badge on each quarter because the vessel was designed to carry passengers; there were four staterooms fitted with ventilation ports and a cabin with four berths and a skylight. The middle section of the lower deck was divided to make room for troops while the crew quarters were under the forecastle. John Dennis, the shipwright from York who was appointed the master builder at Point Frederick in 1803, took some liberties with Munn's design and increased the vessel's dimensions. Various surveys taken by individuals in the Royal Navy more than a decade later showed it was 61ft (keel) by 23ft 8in by 7ft with a burthen of 168 tons.[24]

Like the *Duke of Kent*, the new vessel at Kingston spent two years on the stocks and was named (the *Earl of Moira*) well in advance of its launch on 28 May 1805. Originally intended to be either a schooner, snow or brig, the *Moira*, pierced for fourteen guns, was given three masts and a square rig, making it only the second ship-rigged vessel to be launched on Lake Ontario. Besides changes in hull design and rig, the construction of the *Moira* was notable for two reasons. One was the amount of thought that was given to the type of figurehead the vessel should have. The initial design, apparently depicting the Earl of Moira, a prominent British soldier and government official, pointing the way, telescope in hand, was drawn by the Canadien sculptor François Ballarge, but revised by William Robe, the assistant deputy quartermaster general at Quebec; even Lieutenant Hugh Earl, denying any artistic talent, submitted a sketch of how he thought the head of the vessel should look.

Whether a fancy ornament graced the bow of the *Earl of Moira* is not certain, but there is no doubt that an uncommon effort was made to stave off the decay that shortened the careers of freshwater vessels. This involved the purchase of 100 barrels of salt from the rich salt springs in the region of Lake Oneida, thirty miles southeast of Oswego. Based on the assumption that salt was a useful preservative, it was shovelled into the spaces between the frames of the *Moira* in the spring of 1805 as the interior planking was applied. There was no clear verdict on the experiment's effectiveness. One officer who examined the vessel in 1811 happily observed, 'I had occasion to unsheathe her in part on account of some necessary repairs and on examination found the timbers as perfectly sound and free from decay as the day they were first put in.' A year later, however, a second officer wrote that 'notwithstanding the process of salting, many of the timbers are rotten and must be taken out.'[25] The test of time did not clearly substantiate the value of the salting experiment because the *Moira*, which saw demanding service late in its career, was worn out ten years after its launch.

Preservation of the freshwater vessels continued to be a concern for the Provincial Marine as it always had been. The British harvested cedar, most notably on Lake Erie, but the use of that wood did not seem to ensure longevity and it was in relatively short supply; oak and pine were the

TABLE 14
Ship/HM Brig *Earl of Moira* (1805), *Charwell* (1814) – legend of particulars

Launched: 28 May 1805, Kingston
Altered to brig: 1813
Original draught by: Alexander Munn
Builder: John Dennis

HULL DIMENSIONS, 1815

Gun deck	70ft 6in
Keel/tonnage	56ft 3⅝in
Breadth extreme	23ft 8in
Depth of hold	7ft
Tons	168 59/94
Draught loaded	7ft 6in forward
	8ft 6in aft
Number of ports	14
Dimensions of ports	
height	2ft 7in
width	2ft 10in
between	6ft 6in
above deck	1ft 5in

SPAR DIMENSIONS AS A BRIG, 1815

Mast	Length	Diameter	Yard Length	Yard Dia
Fore	48ft	16½in	40ft 6½in	8in
Topmast	32ft	11in	31ft 7½in	7in
Topgallant	31ft 6in	6in	24ft 11in	5in
Main	44ft 6in	17in	45ft 9in	11in
Topmast	32ft	11in	31ft 7¾in	7in
Topgallant	31ft 6in	6in	24ft 10in	5in
Bowsprit	39ft 6in	16in	—	—
Jibboom	24ft	8½in	—	—
Driver boom	45ft 6in	11in	—	—
Gaff	32ft	6in	—	—

ORDNANCE

Date	Carronades	Long Guns
1812	10-18s	
1813, 1814	14-24s	2-9s
1814	12-24s	1-18

Source: NAC, MG 12, ADM 106/1997; RG 8, I, 729.

mainstays of the dockyards. Stocks of these woods were created in the dockyards, but they also decayed quickly. Frequent surveys, repairs and careenings were conducted to keep the vessels afloat, although they were often hampered by a lack of suitable artificers. One report blamed the source of decay on a want of cleanliness due to the neglect of shipboard discipline. The snow and ice of winter took their toll on the vessels, which were laid up each December. Their sails, spars and running rigging were removed and put in store, but the records lack a clear indication that standardised steps were taken to house the decks over and protect them from the ravages of freezing and melting. In short, during this period of wooden ships vessels on the lakes, no reliable cure was found for the rot that limited the careers of all but a handful of the vessels to seven or eight years.[26]

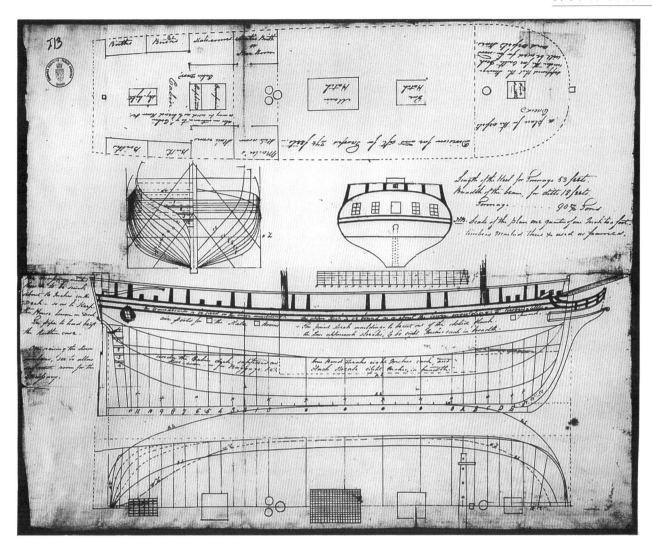

Alexander Munn, a Quebec shipbuilder, prepared this draught for a Provincial Marine vessel in 1802. Originally intended to be set up as a brig, the vessel's dimensions were increased and it was given three masts when it was launched in May 1805 as the *Earl of Moira*. (National Archives of Canada, RG 8, I, 725, p213)

There was considerable debate over the details in the figurehead of the *Earl of Moira*. Several different views of the earl were proposed, although which one, if any, of them was used is uncertain. (National Archives of Canada, C15227)

William Bell, the Provincial Marine master builder at Amherstburg, prepared this draught of the schooner *General Hope* in 1803. A recommendation was made to close in the open rail to create bulwarks along the full length of the deck, but whether it was followed is uncertain. (National Archives of Canada, RG 8, I, 726, p77)

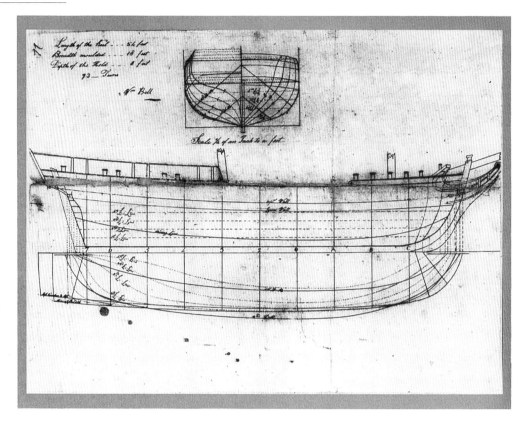

Captain William Robe, the assistant deputy quartermaster general at Quebec, drew this plan for sliding keels, based on Captain John Schank's model, for use in the *General Hope*. Robe suggested that the keels would improve the windward sailing qualities of the schooner, which needed to be shallow enough in draught to pass the shoals in the St Clair River before it could cruise on Lake Huron and beyond. (National Archives of Canada, RG 8, I, 726, p80)

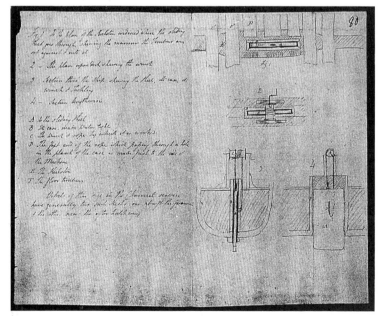

At the time of the *Moira*'s launch, the schooner *Hope* was in its initial full season of operation on Lakes Erie and Huron. Approved in 1803, it was the first vessel officially built by William Bell who had been the foreman of John Normand's crew during the construction of the *Earl of Camden*

and, as correspondence implies, was instrumental in completing that project. Bell was a native of Scotland who spent years in the dockyard at Quebec before finding employment at Amherstburg around 1799. Similar to the *Moira*, the *Hope* was to have a burthen of 93 tons and measure 54ft by 18ft by 8ft with a midships deadrise of about 12 degrees. It was also flush-decked, but, as Bell's draught shows, lacked the room to create comfortable accommodations since it was intended to draw only seven feet of water so it could pass over the shoals in the St Clair River that had always made transit to and from Lake Huron difficult.

Two improvements to the draught of the *Hope* were debated. The first, which appears to have been followed, was the extension of the railing the full length of the hull 'and fitted up strong for the reception of guns when needed.' [27] A second suggestion came from Captain William Robe of the quartermaster general's department at Quebec. He had been stationed in England during the 1790s and had seen gunbrigs outfitted with Captain John Schank's sliding keels, the widely known success of which prompted Robe to suggest that Bell's

Above: This model of the *General Hunter* is on display at Fort Malden, Amherstburg, Ontario. (Parks Canada, Fort Malden National Historic Site)

Below: Built to replace the *Hope*, wrecked in 1805, the *General Hunter* was very nearly identical in design to its predecessor. (Parks Canada, Fort Malden National Historic Site)

schooner would be 'in size and flatness of floor' very similar to the brigs and might benefit from such equipment.[28] To enhance his recommendation, Robe sketched the appearance of the innovative device, explaining its placement beside the keel, its water-tight box and the winch used to raise and lower it. He added that the brigs in the English Channel generally had two of the keels, one just behind the foremast and the second adjacent to the aft hatchway. Robe also advised the employment of lightweight 18pdr carronades (ordnance which, hitherto, appear not to have been employed on the lakes) in the waist of the *Hope* and a pair of 4pdr long guns in the bow. There is no evidence that Schank's centreboards were ever utilised in warships on the lakes during this period, nor that the *Hope* was ever armed.

The career of the *Hope* was brief. On 21 October 1805 Lieutenant James Fleet, who was alleged to have been thoroughly inebriated, ran the schooner onto a shoal ten miles from the British post of St Joseph Island on the northern fringe of Lake Huron. The vessel, cargo and one seaman were lost. An accident of harsher consequences had

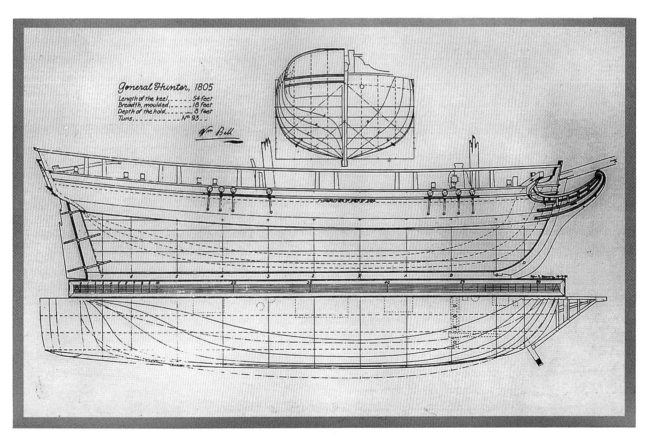

General Hunter, 1805
Length of the keel,_____54 feet
Breadth, moulded_____18 feet
Depth of the hold,_____8 feet
Tuns,_____Nº 93.

Wm Bell

occurred during a violent storm on 8 October 1804 when the schooner *Speedy* sank off the village of Presque Isle on Lake Ontario with all hands and a passenger list of prominent Upper Canadians.[29]

In 1806 plans were made to replace the *Hope* with the schooner *General Hunter*, and to build a schooner, the *Duke of Gloucester*, at Kingston.[30] The draught of the *Hunter* shows that it was essentially a copy of the *Hope* at 54ft on the keel by 18ft by 8ft for a burthen of 93 tons, while the Lake Ontario vessel, replacing the worn out gunboat-schooner *Swift*, was said to be only 65 tons in burthen. The *Gloucester* was later noted for its small size and inadequacy as a war vessel, so it seems likely that John Dennis followed his orders; of the actual construction only the estimate survives, showing that 4000 feet of oak, 1500 feet of pine and 80 oak knees were harvested from Wolfe Island to do the work. The *Hunter* and *Gloucester* both went into the water in 1807.

By that year the merchant fleets were dominating commerce on the lakes. About twenty vessels operated on Lake Ontario with a few more than that on the upper lakes, including Lakes Michigan and Superior. Approximately half the carriers were owned by American firms that had set up shop at Ogdensburg, Sackets Harbor, Oswego, Fort Niagara, Black Rock, Erie, Detroit and Mackinac. The craft were all fore-and-aft rigged, shallow of draught and busily occupied from spring to fall delivering essentials and fineries to the communities rapidly growing around the rim of the lakes and taking their produce for transhipment to Quebec, New York and beyond. The nature of the trade was typified by an advertisement placed in a York newspaper in 1807 by a prominent merchant:

> Mr. Q. St. George ... has arrived from Montreal and has brought with him an ample stock of Fall and Winter goods, also Crockery, Glass Ware, Cutlery and Ironmongery and a handsome and well chosen assortment of Furriery ... a variety of Beaver Bonnets ... and the most fashionable Ostrich Feathers. ... He proposes to receive in payment and barter for Goods, ... Flour, Wheat, Indian Corn, Oats, Pease and Pork. ... The pork must be well cured and packed in sufficient barrels and warranted for twelve months.[31]

Despite having taken over the southern shore of the lakes, the United States government made little effort to maintain public vessels on the lakes, perhaps, due to the cost and the paucity of settlements in that region. The sloop *Detroit* was purchased by the quartermaster's department of the US Army shortly after Major General Anthony Wayne took possession of Detroit in 1796. Two other craft were said to have been government property after 1800, the 60-ton schooner *Tracy* and the 35-ton sloop *Niagara*, both on Lake Erie, but they were eventually sold to private firms. The most active public vessel was the brig *Adams*, said to have been about 125 tons in burthen and built on the River Rouge, near Detroit, starting in 1797. One account reveals that the *Adams* preceded the *Earl of Moira* in being the first vessel on the lakes salted for preservation. Ten years after the brig's launch, a naval officer remarked that its floor timbers had been so tightly packed that bilge water would not melt the salt before it could permeate the adjacent timbers, and that during a repair after a decade of service the salt was found packed hard and dry between the frames. The *Adams* was launched by 1801, but, like the vessels just noted, it was operated by the US Army rather than the US Navy. During most of its career, the *Adams*'s captain was Lieutenant Henry B Brevoort of the 2nd US Infantry Regiment who commanded a meagre crew with a mission identical to their counterparts in the Provincial Marine, namely transporting public freight among the various outposts. Also similar to the British force was the practice of carrying private cargo in the *Adams*, and for the sake of maintaining regularity in the system Brevoort was instructed 'to clear your vessel, every trip, whether you have any private property on board or not; and, at all times, make such manifests as the case may require.'[32]

There were no American armed vessels on Lake Ontario prior to 1809. The events which changed that situation, however, began to unravel two years before and led eventually to the final, great escalation of shipbuilding on the Great Lakes during the age of fighting sail.

<table>
<tr><td>

CHAPTER 4

'Naval ascendancy'

1807 – JUNE 1812

</td></tr>
</table>

INTERNATIONAL HOSTILITIES again proved to be the catalyst for sudden changes in the nature of the freshwater warships. The rise in tensions between Britain and the United States prompted both sides to launch new and potent little warships, which would set the standard for the vessels that would fight in the opening stages of the eventual war.

The Napoleonic War led indirectly to a significant change in Great Lakes shipping because the combatants interfered with American commerce by shutting off free trade with European ports. The government of the United States, led by President Thomas Jefferson, complained to the British and French about the damage done to the nation's economy, but its arguments fell on deaf ears. As a result, Jefferson imposed the Embargo Act in 1807 as a means of getting back at the European powers by prohibiting trade between them and the United States. The policy had little effect abroad while causing a fiscal disaster at home among the countless Americans who had nurtured a lucrative business with British North America; their exports to the Canadian provinces had exceeded those sent from Britain prior to the imposition of the trade restrictions. American merchants protested to their government, but to no avail and when bankruptcy and starvation threatened them, the American businessmen turned to smuggling. Day and night, boats and rafts loaded with tea, tobacco, timber and potash swept north down the Richelieu River into Lower Canada, across the St Lawrence or along the southern shores of Lakes Ontario and Erie into the upper province; 30,000 barrels of American potash were estimated to have arrived illegally at Montreal in 1808 alone. When solitary customs collectors at the wilderness posts proved powerless to stop the traffic, Jefferson ordered a small military force to New York and asked the state's governor, Daniel Tompkins, to

The quality of the vessels built by Henry Eckford (1775-1832) in his shipyard at New York drew the attention of the US Navy and led to his involvement in building warships for the lakes. After the War of 1812, he served for a period as the chief constructor at the navy's Brooklyn yard. (US Naval Historical Center, NH66615)

call out the militia in aid of the collectors.[1]

As part of the effort to enforce the trade restrictions, Jefferson's cabinet decided to establish a naval presence on Lakes Champlain and Ontario and ordered the building of gunboats, the type of craft preferred by the current administration, two on Champlain and one on Ontario. The former vessels appear to have been of conventional gunboat design – long and low, propelled by oars and a simple rig, – but the craft on Lake Ontario became something quite different. 'I want her to be made sufficiently large and armed to cope with any vessel of war now in Lake Ontario or with a small sloop of war,' wrote Secretary of the Navy Robert Smith early in the summer of 1808.[2] He ordered a native of New York, Lieutenant Melancthon Woolsey, USN, to supervise the building of the vessel at Oswego with assistance from Captain Isaac Chauncey, commandant of the New York navy yard, and the navy agent there, John Bullus.

The navy advertised for bids on the Oswego project and accepted the offer made by the firms of Bergh and Eckford, well reputed shipbuilders in New York City. Christian Bergh, an American by birth, was 45 years old and had gained some prominence in the late 1790s as the master builder of the USS *Philadelphia*, 44, one of the navy's large warships. Henry Eckford, 33 years of age, was a Scot who had apprenticed with his uncle in a Quebec shipyard before setting up business at the turn of the century along the east channel of the Hudson River near the navy's dockyard at Brooklyn and adjacent to the Bergh yard. All the key shipbuilders at New York had been involved in the navy's gunboat programme during Jefferson's terms so men like Bergh and Eckford and Adam and Noah Brown were well known to the local naval officers. Another New Yorker, named John Winans, won the contract for the two 20-ton gunboats on Lake Champlain while Bergh and Eckford combined their resources to underbid their rivals with an estimate of $20,505 for the construction of the vessel at Oswego.[3]

The expedition to Lake Ontario began early in August 1808 and involved the transportation of all the necessary ship fittings and stores north on the Hudson and west along the Mohawk, the traditional route to the northern frontier. Lt

Woolsey took a small naval party, among whom was Midshipman James Fenimore Cooper, the future American man of letters, and a party of shipwrights under foreman Henry Eagle; a detachment from the 6th US Infantry Regiment also went to form a guard. Henry Eckford followed with more men, paced out his yard and laid the keel early in September using wood that had been cut the year before. At Christmas the hull was completely framed and planked and the upper deck in place, the principal timbers being of 'the best white oak and well seasoned', according to Woolsey.[4] The rigging, sails, cables and anchors were arriving along with the guns, sixteen 24pdr carronades and a single long 32pdr; Woolsey recommended the substitution of an additional pair of carronades for the ponderous cannon as its operation would require the construction of a topgallant forecastle and its weight would not 'make the Vessel work well [and] will render her extremely laborsome.'[5]

Labour continued on the vessel through the winter and involved the same type of preservation efforts that the British had utilised on the *Earl of Moira* – salting. Lt William Gamble, USN, suggested the process, telling Woolsey that he had seen the army's brig *Adams* at Detroit, its frames packed with salt prior to its launch, which was known to be in fine shape after a decade of service. Woolsey passed the information to the navy department and received permission to buy 240 barrels of salt which was shovelled between the frames as the ceiling planks were fastened.[6]

On 31 March 1809 the first United States Navy vessel on the Great Lakes was launched and Woolsey, having received no direction from Washington despite his queries, gave it the popular local name of *Oneida*. Meant to be rigged as a brig, the *Oneida* was 85ft 6in (between perpendiculars), 77ft 6in (keel) by 23ft by 8ft for a burthen of 262 tons. It had ports for sixteen carronades and a topgallant forecastle raised 2ft 9in above the upper deck on which a pivot-mounted carriage would move the long 32pdr around a circular track; Woolsey continued to complain that this arrangement would interfere with the brig's sailing qualities as well as the handling of anchor cables. The *Oneida* was in every sense a warship, its flush upper deck reflected the corvette-style employed in the large American sloops and was devoted to ordnance with crew quarters and storage space below. The wardroom and its cabins were cramped, the captain's cabin being little more than an alcove squeezed between the fashion pieces and lit only by a skylight. Despite the sparse accommodations, Lt Woolsey looked upon his command in Oswego Bay and declared: 'She is (I think) the handsomest vessel in the Navy.'[7]

Observers on the British side of the lakes saw the *Oneida* as something quite different. Relations between Britain and the United States had worsened, not only because of the persisting trade restrictions, but also because of the incident that occurred off Chesapeake Bay on 22 June 1807 when Captain Salusbury Humphreys of HMS *Leopard*, 50, opened fire on the ill-prepared US frigate *Chesapeake*, 40, after its senior officer, Commodore James Barron, refused to allow the British to search his ship for deserters. This humiliation to the US Navy, and British disrespect for the rights of American sailors, especially those pressed from merchant ships, further aggravated relations between the countries, as did tensions between American settlers and British-supported natives southwest of the lakes. By late 1808, war seemed imminent and in Upper Canada fears rose that the arrival of military and naval detachments at Oswego and on Lake Champlain showed the

Melancthon Woolsey (1780-1838) was the son of the revenue collector at Plattsburgh, New York. He joined the navy as a midshipman in 1800 and ended his career as commodore of the American squadron at Brazil between 1832 and 1834. (US Naval Historical Center, NRL11122)

This unattributed painting shows four vessels at Fort Niagara (*circa* 1792) which may be (left to right) the sloop *Caldwell*, one of the converted gunboat/schooners *Catherine/Buffalo* or *Sophia/Bear*, and the schooners *Onondaga* and *Mississauga*. (Old Fort Niagara Association)

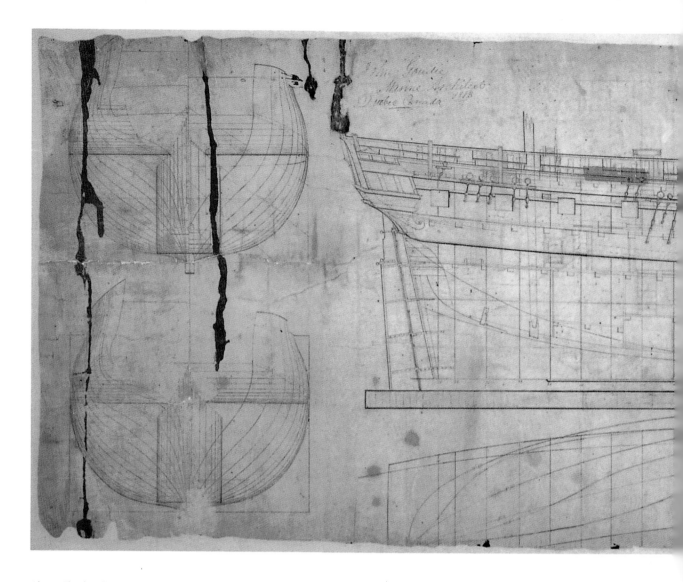

Above: The draught prepared by John Goudie appears to be a proposed plan for the frigate *Princess Charlotte*. However, its rounded hull with slight midships deadrise differs considerably from the appearance of the ship in the 'as-built' draught drawn by Thomas Strickland in 1815, so was probably rejected outright. (National Archives of Canada, NMC97256)

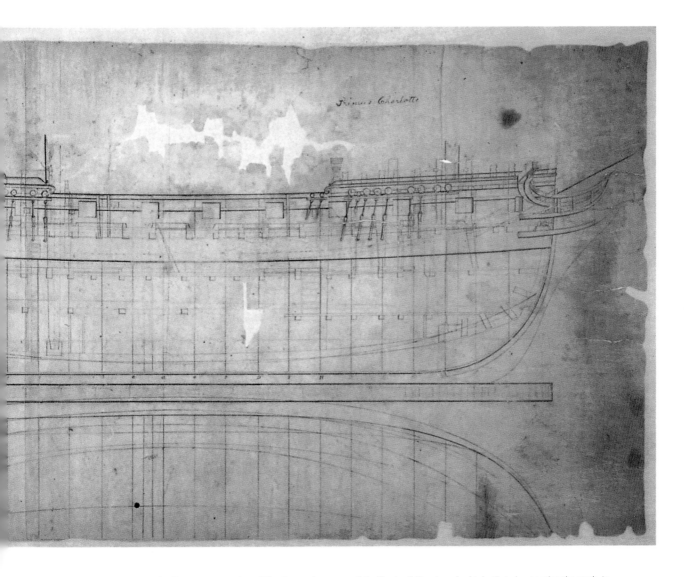

Princess Charlotte

Below: Commodore Chauncey had begun construction of First Rates when news of the Treaty of Ghent reached Lake Ontario, stopping the work. In September 1815 a British officer painted this scene of the squadron at Sackets Harbor. The vessels (from left to right) are the *Jones*, *Sylph*, *Pike*, *Lady of the Lake*, *Mohawk*, *Jefferson*, *Superior*, *Madison*, *New* Orleans, and *Oneida* (its topmasts visible above the *New Orleans*. The lugger-rigged craft in the right foreground is identified as a gunboat and may be one of the galleys built during the summer of 1814. (Royal Military College, Kingston, Ontario)

The second stage of the landing at Oswego, 6 May 1814: the vessels are (left to right) *Prince Regent*, *Star*, *Princess Charlotte*, *Charwell*, *Montreal*, *Niagara* and *Magnet*. Although part of the same series as the print on page 109, the original of this is said to be the work of Lt John Hewett, RM. (National Maritime Museum, neg A3914)

United States was mobilising its forces along the border. Richard Cartwright, a leading Kingston merchant, wrote: 'The ostensible object of [the arrival of such forces] is more effectually to enforce the Embargo; But the Vessel building ... is to carry eighteen guns besides a twenty-four Pounder in the Bow [which] is much less adapted to this service than Armed Boats would be.'[8]

Correspondence flew between Quebec and the outposts in the upper province. Sir James Craig was now the governor-in-chief of British North America and Francis Gore was the lieutenant governor of Upper Canada, but little had changed in regards to the Provincial Marine. It was still managed by the quartermaster general's department at Quebec (Colonel Alleyne Hampden Pye was the deputy quartermaster general responsible for the marine) and Alexander Grant and John Steel still commanded their weakly manned squadrons. The *Earl of Moira*, *Duke of Gloucester* and *Duke of Kent* sailed Lake Ontario, but the last was in a state of decay so advanced that proper repair seemed unlikely. The *General Hunter* and *Earl of Camden* on Lake Erie were without sufficient armament and when eight carronades from Fort George at Niagara were allocated for their use, it was revealed that the worn frame of the *Camden* might not support the extra weight. In January 1809 Governor Craig decided that a strengthening of the Provin-

cial Marine was needed and ordered new vessels constructed, one at Kingston and a second at Amherstburg.[9]

Records of the project at Kingston are scarce, although it is known that John Dennis oversaw the work assisted by a crew of eighteen in the Point Frederick dockyard, which Craig supplemented with twenty-five hands from Quebec. There was an ample supply of suitable timber available and on 21 February 1809 the keel was laid. By 21 April the hull was planked to the wales and in July it was launched; there is no evidence that salting for preservation was utilised. Christened the *Royal George*, the new vessel, like the *Oneida*, was built to fight, more so than any of its recent predecessors. It was termed a 'ship corvette' (square-rigged with a flush upper deck) and measured 96ft 9in on deck, 81ft 11½in by 27ft 7in by 11ft 1in for a burthen of 330 tons. With a midships deadrise of about 17 degrees, the ship had a sharper hull than previous British warships on the lakes and, drawing 10ft 10in forward and 13ft 11in aft, had about 3ft of drag. It had ports for twenty 18pdr or 24pdr carronades, a continuous berth deck (with 6ft 1in of height) and a 5ft space below that deck. Unlike the smaller *Earl of Moira*, however, the *Royal George* lacked a cabin with stern lights, having instead tightly confined accommodations for the officers, much like the *Oneida* had.

The launch of the *Royal George* marked a significant change in the type of vessels built by the British on the Great Lakes. John Dennis is given credit for the draught of the corvette, but its appearance suggests strongly that he was trying to imitate the lines of the class of British warships modelled after the popular brig-sloop *Cruizer* and the ship-rigged *Snake*, reducing the draught of water they drew to meet the demands of freshwater confines. More than 100 vessels of their class were built in British yards between 1803 and 1813, all of them featuring flush upper decks, batteries of twenty or so carronades and a burthen around 330 tons.[10]

Although launched within three months of the *Oneida*, the *Royal George* was not commissioned in 1809 because that spring Jefferson's embargo was repealed. With war tensions easing again and manpower shortages a continuing problem for

TABLE 15

British vessels launched, 1807- May 1812

Vessel	Launch	Place	Rig	Remarks
Lake Ontario				
Royal George (B), 20	1809	Kingston	ship	1814 renamed *Niagara*(B); 1816 condemned; 1820s rebuilt; 1830s sold, broken up
Lake Erie				
Queen Charlotte, 20	1810	Amherstburg	ship	1813 taken by Americans, sunk for preservation; 1835 sold as commercial carrier

TABLE 16

American vessels launched 1807-1811

Vessel	Launch	Place	Rig	Remarks
Lake Ontario				
Oneida, 18	1809	Oswego	brig	1815 in ordinary; 1825 sold as commercial carrier; 1837 unserviceable

the Provincial Marine, the *Royal George* was tied up at dockside on Point Frederick. Lt Woolsey received orders at Oswego to put the brig in ordinary since it was not needed to enforce customs regulations and in July he left the *Oneida* moored at stem and stern in the stream with all its rigging and sails stored on board.[11]

About the time of the *Royal George*'s launch, William Bell laid the keel at Amherstburg for the second vessel that Sir James Craig had ordered. Originally meant to have been built in 1809, the project was delayed due to a short supply of good timber and shipwrights. Officials spent most of the year preparing the lists of materials needed for the vessel, which was intended to be 'a large stout Corvette Brig to carry sixteen guns upon one Deck with good quarters for the men ... built exclusively for fighting and sailing and the navigation of Lake Erie, having at the same time as much accommodation as possible for the conveyance of Troops.'[12] In October Craig stated that he wanted the vessel constructed in spite of the changing diplomatic situation and approved a draught that William Bell had prepared for a ship rather than a brig. During the winter, local labourers hauled in stacks of timber and in the spring of 1810 the *Hunter* and *Camden* sailed to Pelee Island, forty miles east of Amherstburg, to collect cedar. Shipwrights left Kingston to join William Bell's gang and began assembling the hull, using oak for the large members and hull planking, cedar for the beams and 400 futtocks, and pine for deck planking; 270 knees and 200 'shores' went into the decks, head, stern and boats.

Launched late in 1810, the ship was named the *Queen Charlotte*. Bell's draught has not come to light, but two skilfully drawn scenes from 1813 show the *Queen Charlotte* resembling the lines of the *Royal George* except that it appears to have had stern lights and a railing around a raised quarterdeck. This description is supported by the comments of Commander Robert Barclay, RN, when he first examined the ship in June 1813: 'The *Queen Charlotte* is a fine vessel of her class and if well manned would be a very effective ship. ... She is like the vessels on Lake Ontario more fitted as a packet than a man of war.'[13] Measurements of the vessel taken in 1813 by Master Commandant Jesse Elliott, US Navy, after it had been cap-

tured, showed the *Queen Charlotte* as being '116 foot on Deck, 26 foot beam, 11 foot hold, well and substantially built.'[14] The length to breadth ratio of these figures (4.46:1) varies significantly from the norm of that period, however. The *Cruizer*, at 100ft by 30ft 6in by 12ft 9in had a length to breadth ratio of 3.33:1 while the *Royal George* had a ratio of 3.5:1. Measurements taken off the *Queen Charlotte* at the port of Buffalo during the 1830s (when it was used as a merchantman after being re-rigged as a brig) provides more reasonable figures for the ship: 92ft 2in (deck) by 26ft by 12ft for a length to breadth ratio of 3.54:1 and a burthen of 254 tons. It was also described at that time as having a scroll head, no galleries and a flush deck; whether the raised quarterdeck that appears in the Reynold's painting was removed after the war or was an artistic error remains to be confirmed.

After the launch of the *Queen Charlotte*, the *Earl of Camden* was retired from service, leaving the *General Hunter* as the only public vessel with shallow enough draught to sail into Lake Huron. A plan for the Provincial Marine establishment of 1811 listed Alexander Grant, three lieutenants, four warrant officers and forty seamen at Amherstburg. On Lake Ontario there would be John Steel, four lieutenants, six warrant officers and fifty seamen sailing the *Moira* and *Gloucester* (the *Duke of Kent* was alternating as a sheer hulk and winter barracks) while the *Royal George* remained in ordinary. At St Jean the derelict schooner *Royal Edward* had one aged seaman on board as a caretaker.[15]

Melancthon Woolsey returned to Lake Ontario in the summer of 1810 to commission the *Oneida*, a task made more difficult by the fact that ice had pushed the brig off its moorings and onto the shore during the previous winter. After two months of backbreaking labour, he managed to get the vessel into the water, refit it and lift it over the shallow bar at the harbour's mouth and with a crew numbering fewer than ten, sail down the shore to Sackets Harbor. He had chosen this tiny settlement as the only suitable harbour for a naval station on Lake Ontario; Fort Niagara was under the guns of Fort George and the mouth of the bay at Oswego was too shallow, especially as the navigation season wore on and water levels

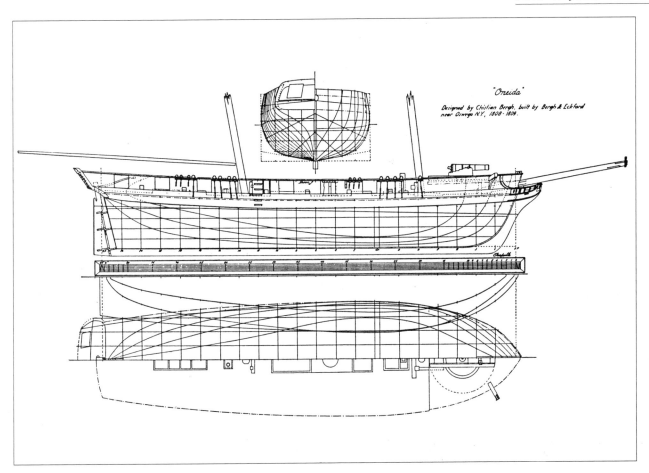

"Oneida"

Designed by Christian Bergh, built by Bergh & Eckford near Oswego N.Y., 1808-1809.

Above: Howard Chapelle prepared this draught of the US brig *Oneida* based upon Christian Bergh's original plans. It shows the 32pdr long gun mounted on the topgallant forecastle, although the brig appears to have been built without this gun and deck. (Smithsonian Institution)

Right: Chapelle also reconstructed this lofty sail plan of the *Oneida*. (Smithsonian Institution)

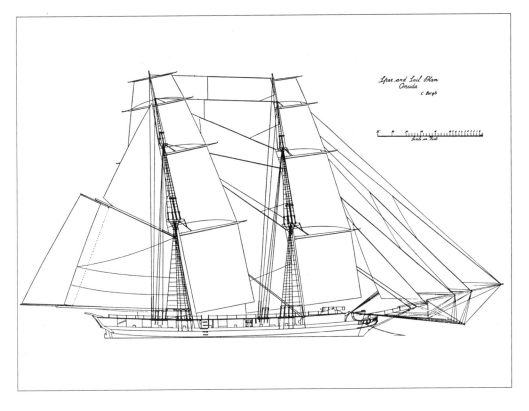

Spar and Sail Plan
Oneida
C Bergh

dropped. The little cove that had been named for its original settler, Augustus Sacket, was also partially obstructed by a bar, but the deep, thirty-acre basin protected by a narrow peninsula of sand and gravel was accessible. Located on the lip of Black River Bay at the easternmost end of the lake, Sackets Harbor was dangerously close to Kingston, only thirty-five miles due north by water, and it lacked the water connection to New York that had made Oswego so important in the past. On the American side, however, there were no better harbours on the lake and in November 1810 Lt Woolsey opened his nation's first Great Lakes naval station at Sackets.[16]

Relations between Britain and the United States soured during 1811 and apprehensions sprung up around the lakes again that war was near. Woolsey listened to rumours about the strength of the Provincial Marine squadron on Lake Ontario and sent a report to the new Secretary of the Navy Paul Hamilton that exaggerated the strength of the British force as consisting of the *Royal George* with twenty-two carronades, the *Earl of Moira* with fourteen 9pdrs, the *Duke of Gloucester* with twelve 6pdrs, the *Governor Simcoe* (the private merchant schooner) with fourteen guns and the *Toronto* with eight. Woolsey also compiled a list of eight American-owned merchant vessels that could be bought into the navy and armed if hostilities erupted. During the autumn of 1811, Secretary Hamilton sent Woolsey orders to improve the condition of his station and, consequently, he built barracks and opened an enlistment office. By the end of the year the crew of the *Oneida* numbered 96, just 21 short of a full complement.[17]

After years of friction with Britain (and to a similar degree with France), President James Madison clearly stated in his annual address to Congress in November 1811 that the time had come for preparing the United States for war. His words were met with celebration by the state representatives who had been recently elected to promote such policies and who were widely known as the 'War Hawks'. Their rhetoric was loud, but in the committees set up to turn propositions into legislation words proved to have little substance. For fear of alienating the public by raising taxes to fund a war machine, the American legislators approved only

half-hearted measures to put their country on a footing for doing battle with Britain. In the naval context, this meant that Secretary Hamilton's request for the construction of twelve ships of the line, ten frigates and a dry dock, the creation of timber stocks and purchase of naval equipment was pared down until money was only allocated for fitting out three existing frigates. As a result, the US Navy's entire 1812 fleet consisted of seventeen vessels and none of the naval expenditures went to increasing the armament on the lakes.

Some individuals urged the government to invest in a force on the lakes. Brigadier General

---

TABLE 17

HMS *Royal George* (1809), *Niagara* (1814) – legend of particulars

Launched: July 1809, Kingston
Original draught by: John Dennis
As built draught by: Thomas Strickland, 1815
Builder: John Dennis

HULL DIMENSIONS, 1815

Gun deck	96ft 9in
Keel/tonnage	81ft 11¼in
Breadth extreme	27ft 7in
Depth of hold	11ft
Tons	330 20/94
Draught loaded	10ft 10in forward
	13ft 11in aft
Number of ports	20
Dimensions of ports	
height	2ft 2in
width	2ft 10in
between	6ft 6in
above deck	2ft 3in

SPAR DIMENSIONS, 1815

Mast	Length	Diameter	Yard Length	Yard Dia.
Fore	56ft	20in	52ft 11in	12in
Topmast	41ft	12½in	40ft	11½in
Topgallant	35ft	7¼in	32ft	6¾in
Main	63ft 6in	21½in	54ft	12¾in
Topmast	41ft	12¼in	44ft	12½in
Topgallant	38ft	7¾in	31ft 8in	7in
Mizzen	54ft	17in	43ft 4in	12in
Topmast	33ft	9in	31ft 3in	9in
Topgallant	23ft	6in	22ft	5½in
Bowsprit	44ft 4in	19½in	—	—
Jibboom	40ft	11¼in	—	—
Crossjack	—	—	43ft	7¾in
Driver boom	46ft	11in	—	—
Gaff	28ft 7in	6½in	—	—

ORDNANCE

Date	Carronades	Long Guns
1812	20-32s	
1813, Spring	18-32s	2-9s
1813, Autumn	2-68s	2-18s
	16-32s	
1814	18-32s	1-24
		2-18s

Source: NAC, MG 12, ADM 106/1997; RG 8, I, 729.

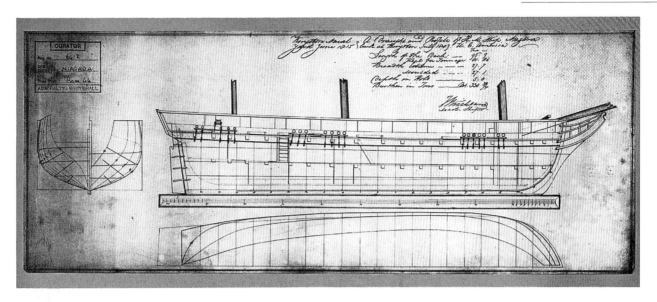

In response to the construction of the *Oneida* at Oswego, the British ordered a heavily gunned warship, the likes of which had not been seen on the lakes since the Revolutionary War, to be built at Kingston. Launched as the *Royal George* in July 1809, the 'ship-corvette' resembled in general layout the Royal Navy's small, flush-decked sloops of the *Cruizer/Snake* type. (National Maritime Museum, neg DR6412)

William Hull, governor of the Michigan Territory, wrote to Secretary of War William Eustis in March 1812: 'If, sir, we cannot command the Ocean, we can command the Island Lakes of our Country. ... We ought to have built as many armed Vessels on the Lakes as would have commanded them. We have more interest in them than the British Nation and can build them Vessels with more convenience.'[18] Another leading figure, Major General John Armstrong, also urged that 'no time should be lost in getting a naval ascendancy on both [lakes],' but while discussions were held in Washington in this regard nothing was done.[19] As the ice broke up in the spring of 1812 there were only two American armed vessels on the northern frontier, the ageing army brig *Adams* at Detroit and Woolsey's *Oneida*.

The British naval department on the lakes far exceeded the American force numerically, but three decades of weak management and the drowsy routine of a transport service had left the Provincial Marine ill-suited for fighting off an invasion. When estimates were made during August 1811 for the 1812 establishment no increases in manpower beyond the current 109 officers and men were expected. The threat of war influenced the suggestions made by Colonel A H Pye, however, when he reported on the state of the marine in December 1811. He identified the need to replace both the *General Hunter*, which was falling into decay and the *Duke of Gloucester*, which the civil government was using since

the schooner *Toronto* was lying unserviceable at York. Rather than suggesting the construction of larger warships like the *Royal George* and *Queen Charlotte*, both of which he criticised for being too deep of draught, Pye recommended the building of 'schooners from 120 to 160 Tons burthen built on the corvette plan and calculated when armed to carry 10 to 14 Guns and not to exceed nine and a half feet of water.' He preferred schooners because they had 'more capacity for their size than the larger Vessels ... [and] superior ease in manoeuvring and their small draught of water.'[20] He also addressed the matter of durability, stating the general rule that vessels wore out after eight years despite efforts having been made to season wood; he had seen examples of stacks of rotten lumber. Having examined the *Moira* and found it in good shape, Pye recommended salting as a key element of longevity. He also believed that Kingston lay too close to the American border and that the Lake Ontario headquarters for the marine department should be moved to York, as Lieutenant Governor Simcoe had preferred fifteen years before.

President Madison's speeches and the activities of the congressional committees in Washington caused concern for the military leaders in Canada. Changes in personnel had taken place again, owing to the return to England for health reasons of Sir James Craig and Francis Gore. Lieutenant General Sir George Prevost moved to Quebec from the post of lieutenant governor of Nova

Scotia to take on the duties of Captain General of the armed forces and Governor-in-Chief of British North America. His subordinate in Upper Canada was Major General Isaac Brock, who commanded the military forces and acted as president of the government's executive council in Gore's place. Early in December 1811 Brock initiated 'the adoption of such precautionary measures as may be necessary to meet all future exigencies.'[21] While most of his actions involved the reparation of garrisons, the movement of troops and activation of militia, Brock also attempted to better prepare the Provincial Marine for war, acknowledging that 'considering the state to which it is reduced, extraordinary exertions and great expense will be required before it can be rendered efficient.'[22]

The condition of the force was spelled out in hard terms by Captain Andrew Gray of the quartermaster general's department (who had taken over from Colonel Pye) in January 1812. After inspecting the dockyard at Kingston, Gray reported that the *Royal George* was still unarmed and that no one at the dockyard could figure out how to mount the carronades sent from Quebec because their slides had been built on a new design and there were no instructions for their assembly. The *Moira* he discovered to be badly decayed in places, contrary to what Colonel Pye had noted the year before, and a plan to lengthen the ship in order to increase its batteries was cancelled so that more essential repairs could be made. Gray favoured Colonel Pye's previous recommendation about moving the Provincial Marine headquarters to York and he criticised some of the officers of the department as being 'extremely inefficient, and, in short, totally unfit for the situations they hold.'[23]

Working in close consultation with Gray, Brock made a number of changes in the marine department in the following months. He ordered the enlistment of 100 seamen at Quebec and requested that companies of the Royal Newfoundland Fencible Regiment be sent up to act as marines on board the ships. Brock negotiated the retirement, with full pension, of 77-year-old Alexander Grant and the similarly aged commodore on Lake Ontario, John Steele; two veteran lieutenants in the marine were promoted

to replace them – George Hall on Lake Erie and Hugh Earl on Lake Ontario. Other officers were promoted to command vessels in existence and the schooners that were under construction at Amherstburg and York; the work at the latter place he considered an important step in the relocation of the Lake Ontario headquarters from Kingston. He wanted all the Provincial Marine vessels to winter at York at the end of the 1812 season and, with Gray and John Dennis assessed various sites for a dockyard that could launch warships. Governor-in-Chief Prevost approved Brock's actions and reported to the home government in April 1812 that 'considering a naval force properly constructed the most efficient and cheapest mode of defence, I have gradually increased the naval force on the lakes.'[24]

Despite the lack of fiscal support that the legislatures gave to developing a war machine, President Madison significantly heightened international tensions in April 1812 by invoking a ninety-day embargo similar to Jefferson's as a final warning to Britain that its restrictions on American carriers had to be lifted. Early the next month Lt Woolsey sailed from Sackets Harbor in the *Oneida* looking for violators of the new law. There had been no improvements to his force that spring, except for the arrival of a detachment of US Marines, but Woolsey was quite capable of performing his duties and on 5 June he seized the British merchantman *Lord Nelson* on the grounds that its master lacked certificates showing that it had properly cleared its last American port. Armed boats later brought in the American schooner *Julia* for the same reason from the upper St Lawrence River and, when word reached Sackets Harbor during the fourth week of June that Congress had approved the declaration of war (signed on 18 June), Woolsey immediately began fitting out the two schooners for duty as gunboats. Into the *Julia* he put the 32pdr long gun that he had never used on the *Oneida* and a pair of 6pdrs. With only one other 6pdr to spare, Woolsey wrote to Captain Chauncey at the New York navy yard for guns, ammunition and equipment.[25] The last great phase of naval escalation on the lakes had begun.

'Command of the lake'

Lake Ontario, June 1812 to December 1813

At the time of the American declaration of war in June 1812, the British held the upper hand on Lake Ontario due to the existence of the Provincial Marine squadron, headed by the 20-gun ship-corvette *Royal George*. Although the Americans would equip merchantmen for active service, and the British would improve their force, the ship-corvette became the critical element in each of the squadrons during the early stages of the war. This changed, however, when the frigate *General Pike* sailed, its battery of long guns posing a dangerous challenge to the carronade-dominated British force.

In the spring of 1812 Master and Commander Hugh Earl commanded the *Royal George*, *Earl of Moira* and *Duke of Gloucester* on Lake Ontario, to which was soon added the schooner *Prince Regent*, designed and built by John Dennis and launched at York in June and ready for service within a month. Pierced for ten guns, it measured 72ft 6in on deck, 59ft 10½in by 21ft 2in by 7ft 3in for a burthen of 143 tons and was exactly the type of small draught, manoeuvrable warship that Provincial Marine officials had called for just prior to the war. When one Royal Navy officer examined the *Prince Regent* in 1813 he wrote that it was 'a fine vessel for a despatch boat, but I do not think her capable of much severe active service.'[1]

It was not in British campaign goals to employ the Provincial Marine squadrons in an aggressive role. Governor-in-Chief Sir George Prevost wanted to reserve the limited troops he had in Lower and Upper Canada for the defence of the border as well as Montreal and Quebec and he was reluctant to provoke anti-British sentiments among residents in the northern states.[2] Major General Isaac Brock was eager to attack American garrisons, but accepted Prevost's plan which saw the Provincial Marine continue to perform its traditional function as a transport wing for the army. The addition of the *Prince Regent* on Lake Ontario combined the appointment of some new officers and fresh enlistments, including the arrival of detachments from the Royal Newfoundland Fencible Regiment, to make the squadron more effective in its role.

There were, however, several incidents during the early months of the war in which the guns of the Provincial Marine vessels saw use. The first occurred on 19 July when Earl led his squadron within range of Sackets Harbor and opened fire. This action seemed quite contrary to Prevost's policy, but Earl appears to have left no written explanation for his attack on the American base. Anecdotal evidence suggests that he sent in a message demanding that Lt Woolsey turn over the recently detained merchantman *Lord Nelson* and the *Oneida* or suffer the destruction of his post. Whatever Earl's intentions were, the assault was a failure because a small force of American sailors, army regulars and militia, returned fire on the British who soon turned tail and departed, having achieved nothing; Woolsey wrote to Secretary Hamilton: 'we hulled the *Royal George* three or four times … [and] from the confusion on board the *Royal George* I am induced to believe that some serious damage must have been done by our shot.'[3]

Later in July the *Earl of Moira* and *Duke of Gloucester* (still in service by necessity because of the outbreak of war) descended the St Lawrence about ninety miles to the British village of Prescott. Thinking this to be an attempt to capture American merchant vessels anchored under the guns of a battery at Ogdensburg, opposite Prescott, Woolsey sent Midshipman Henry Wells, USN, and a crew of volunteers in the schooner *Julia* to investigate. On 31 July Wells encountered the British vessels and engaged in a long range duel with them and a British shore battery until he slipped to safety at Ogdensburg under cover of twilight. Although the two Provincial Marine vessels remained in the river, the British made no attempt to attack the American shipping at Ogdensburg. A brief armistice at the end of August allowed the *Julia* and the merchantmen to proceed to Lake Ontario where some of them were added to the American naval force.[4]

In one other event Hugh Earl's squadron proved more successful. On 1 October he anchored the *Royal George* off the Genesee River and sent a raiding party composed of seamen and Royal Newfoundland troops to the village of Charlotte. They secured the village, confiscating provisions and two vessels, the 60-ton sloop *Lady Murray* and a large Durham boat (an open vessel somewhat similar to a batteau). A rare extant muster roll from that incident reveals that the crew of the *Royal George* was well below a full complement, numbering only 50 officers and seamen, supplemented by 64 soldiers.[5]

Apart from these few scrapes with the Americans, the Provincial Marine vessels were chiefly employed in transporting men and munitions among the key posts and carrying prisoners taken at Detroit and the battle at Queenston Heights (where Brock was killed on 13 October) down the system to detainment at Montreal. With its tradition as a fighting naval force removed by thirty-five years to the late 1770s, and Prevost's policy of non-aggression firmly in place, little more could have been expected from the freshwater navy. This transport role was an important one, as Lt James Richardson, PM, noted in his memoirs. 'Our little squadron ... managed,' argued Richardson, 'to keep open the communication between the Eastern and Western Divisions of the Army. ... The importance of such services in the then uninhabited state of the country, and the lack of land conveyance owing to the badness of the roads must be obvious.'[6]

By October 1812, however, the prevailing attitude on the British side was that the Provincial Marine was 'worse than nothing'.[7] Despite the fact that the defeats suffered by the Americans early in the war were, in part, due to their lack of dependable water transport, British citizens and officers undervalued the contribution of the Provincial Marine, expecting instead that it would suddenly take on the persona of the Royal Navy. Though it had not been linked to the Royal Navy since the late 1770s and Prevost's strategy included no plans for operations like the campaigns on Lake Champlain at that time, the marine department was harshly criticised. Prevost complained to his superiors in England about the inadequacy of the Provincial Marine 'officers [who] are deficient in experience and particularly in the energetic spirit which distinguishes British seamen.' To replace them, he requested 'that tried

officers of the rank of lieutenants and trusty men from the [Royal N]avy should be ... sent to me as early as possible next spring.'[8] Besides transmitting his despatches to the home government, Prevost also wrote to Admiral Sir John Borlase Warren at Bermuda for a detachment of personnel. Lacking in Prevost's correspondence, however, was any admission that he and Brock (who had been familiar with the Provincial Marine since arriving in Canada in 1802) should have realised the limitations of the squadrons and sought assistance from the Royal Navy from the vessels at Quebec or Halifax in the months prior to the war.

Prevost informed the home government of a second reason for improving the naval force on the lakes, namely that the American government was making a determined effort to establish a presence on the lakes. Having seen their fond hope of a quick and victorious conquest of Upper Canada squashed by Brock and his army, President Madison and his senior ministers realised the importance of seizing control of the northern waterways and decided to devote resources to achieve that goal. At the end of August, Secretary of the Navy Paul Hamilton sent orders to Captain Isaac Chauncey, commandant of the navy yard at New York, to proceed to the lakes as commodore of an inland navy which he would have to create on the spot. To attain the goal, Chauncey was given a free hand to use all the resources available at New York and to make requisitions to Navy Agent John Bullus for any other thing he lacked. He was 'to purchase, hire or build' whatever vessels he needed, to take 'upon this Service any of the officers or men of the *John Adams* or on the New York station,' and to set up enlistment 'rendezvous for entering additional men if necessary'. The undertaking was to be initiated immediately with men and materiel being sent to Sackets Harbor and to Buffalo, one of which would become Chauncey's headquarters.[9]

At forty years of age, Isaac Chauncey was among the senior naval officers in the United States Navy. A competent seamen, he had limited war experience, having served several tours of duty during the Quasi-War with France and the Tripolitan conflict, but he had earned a reputation as an energetic and thoughtful administrator and was well chosen for the task of building

Isaac Chauncey (1772-1840) was an experienced seaman when he joined the US Navy in 1798 as a lieutenant. He saw limited action during the war with Tripoli and commanded the navy's station at New York from 1807. His career continued afloat and on shore after the War of 1812 and he was president of the navy's board of commissioners when he died in 1840. (After a painting by J Woods: from Benson J Lossing, *The Pictorial Field-Book of the War of 1812*, New York 1868)

a navy where only one vessel existed. Chauncey quickly proved his worth by putting into motion a supply train the likes of which had not been seen since the days of the American Revolution. Within hours of receiving his instructions from Washington, he wrote to Lt Woolsey ordering him to obtain whatever merchant craft were available for conversion into gunboats, to choose a site at Sackets Harbor for building a vessel of 300 tons and to construct accommodations for 400 men. He wrote letters to Major General Henry Dearborn, the senior military officer on the northern frontier, and to Governor Tompkins informing them of his mission and asking for their support and advice. On 5 September the first detachment of shipwrights sailed up the Hudson River for Albany, followed over the next three weeks by Henry Eckford and 100 more artificers, about 600 naval officers and seamen, 100 US Marines, more than 100 guns and carronades and the vast mountain of equipment and provisions necessary to sustain such a force. Chauncey departed from New York on 26 September and after a brief stopover at Albany to confer with Dearborn and Tompkins he proceeded westward along the turnpike that followed the Mohawk River. While the largest and most burdensome of the ordnance and equipment went up the Mohawk to the narrow canal that had been dug at Rome in the 1790s to form a link with Wood Creek and Oneida Lake and the route to Oswego, many of the personnel and the lighter provisions left the river at Utica or Rome for the overland haul along weather-ruined roads to Sackets Harbor. This is the route that Chauncey took and when he arrived at Sackets on 6 October he was delighted to see that Lt

TABLE 18

The British squadron on Lake Ontario, August 1813

Vessel	Total Guns	Carronades 68s	32s	24s	18s	Long Guns 24s	18s	12s	9s	Crew Seamen	Marines	Total
Wolfe	23	4	10			1*	8			175	49	224
Royal George	20	2	16				2			155	49	204
Lord Melville	14		12				2			60	38	98
Earl of Moira	16			14					2	92	35	127
Beresford	12				10				2	70	28	98
Sir Sidney Smith	12		10					2		80	29	109
Totals	97		78				19			632	228	860

* pivot gun.
Source: NAC, MG 11, CO 42/51, p100; *DHC*, Vol 6, p281.

TABLE 19

The American squadron on Lake Ontario, August 1813

Vessel	Total Guns	Carronades 32s	24s	18s	Long Guns 32s	24s	18s	12	9s	6s	4s	Crew Seamen	Marines	Total
General Pike	26				24 / 2*							392	40	432
Madison	24	20						4				240	34	274
Oneida	18		16							2		132	14	146
Julia	2				1*			1*				35	1	36
Scourge	10									4	6	32	1	33
Conquest	3					2*		1				57	9	66
Growler	5				1*						4	30	1	31
Pert	3				1*					2		26	9	35
Tompkins	6		2		1*	1*			2			53	11	64
Fair American	2				1*	1*						52	11	63
Hamilton	9			8				1*				44	9	53
Ontario	2				1*			1*				26	3	29
Asp	2					1*		1*				27	0	27
Totals	112		46							66		1146	143	1289

* pivot gun.
Source: 18 July 1813 and 17 July 1814, Chauncey Letter Book.
The schooners *Lady of the Lake* and *Raven* were not with the squadron continuously during this period, while the prize *York* remained at Sackets.

Woolsey and Eckford had things well in hand.[10]

The keel for a ship-corvette to mount twenty-four 32pdr carronades was laid down in the yard, with its stem, stern and some frames already in place. The appearance of the *Oneida* pleased Chauncey and he was also relieved to find that Woolsey had been active in obtaining merchant-men since Chauncey knew his initial forays on the lake depended upon his ability to outfit such vessels as quickly as possible. Five schooners, the *Julia, Lord Nelson, Genesee Packet, Experiment* and *Collector*, lay at Sackets Harbor, while four more, the *Charles and Ann, Fair American, Diana* and *Ontario* were at Oswego.

The *Julia* (burthen 53 tons and purchased for $3800) was the only schooner that was armed and ready while work proceeded to modify the others. The *Lord Nelson* was smaller than the *Julia*, measuring about 60ft on deck and 45 tons in burthen. It had been built near the village of Niagara for British merchants James and William Crooks and launched in 1811; its career as a British carrier had been cut short when Woolsey seized it for revenue violations in June 1812. Ned Myers, the lone American able bodied seaman to leave a detailed record of his experiences on the lakes, remembered the schooner as 'unfit for her duty, but time pressed and no better offered.'[11] The vessel's conversion involved planking in the open bulwarks, the mounting of four 4pdrs and four 6pdrs (the delayed delivery of which slowed the preparation of the schooner) and the alteration of the hold into crew quarters, which Myers described as 'bad

enough'. Chauncey paid $2999 to acquire the vessel from the prize court and commissioned the schooner with a new name, the *Scourge*.

The three other schooners at Sackets were the *Genesee Packet* (burthen 82 tons, bought for $5500), the *Experiment* (53 tons, $3200) and the *Collector* (50 tons, $3700). They were renamed the *Conquest, Growler* and *Pert* respectively and each armed with a single 32pdr long gun, with the exception of the *Pert* which, though smaller than the others, was sturdy enough to also house a pair of 6pdrs. Some, if not all, the single, large pieces of ordnance in these vessels were mounted on pivots, referred to as 'circles' and consisted of slides that rotated on circular tracks laid down on the centreline, in the bow or stern.

Of the craft at Oswego, the *Charles and Ann* ranked among the largest commercial vessels on the lake, having a burthen of 96 tons. It was built at Oswego in 1810 by Jacob Townsend and Alvin Bronson, two East Coast merchants who had grown weary of the problems involved in the West Indies trade and had ventured north in search of less aggravating markets. Chauncey bought the schooner for $5800, renamed it the *Governor Tompkins* and outfitted it originally with a 32pdr long gun and a 24pdr long gun on circles and four 32pdr carronades as broadside guns. The *Fair American* (82 tons, $5250) and the *Diana* (76 tons, $5250) were owned by Mathew McNair of Oswego. Chauncey renamed the latter vessel the *Hamilton* in honour of the naval secretary and put ten 18pdr carronades along its open bulwark rails while he kept the name of the *Fair American*, eventually arming it with two circle-mounted guns, a 32pdr and a 24pdr. The last of the schooners at Oswego, the *Ontario* (burthen 81 tons), owned by the firm of Porter, Barton and Company, was purchased for $4000 and given a single 32pdr long gun as its ordnance.[12]

Alteration of the schooners into warships was delayed by an aspect of the Great Lakes command that would hound Commodore Chauncey throughout his term on that station. While his officers and men and provisions marched or rolled into Sackets Harbor during October, the ponderous ordnance, carriages and cables had to be transported the full length of the water connection from Albany. Low water in the upper reaches of the

TABLE 20

British gunboat flotilla on the Upper St Lawrence River, July 1813

Gunboat No	Carronades	Long Guns	No of Oars	Crew
1	1-24	—	36	40
2	—	1-18	36	40
3	—	1-18	36	40
4	1-24	—	24	27
5	1-24	—	24	27
6	—	1-6	24	27
7	—	1-6	24	27
8	—	1-6	24	27
9	—	1-9	26	30
Totals	3	6	254	285

Source: NAC, RG 8, 1, 730, p52.
Commodore Yeo prepared this plan on 21 July 1813 for a gunboat flotilla to operate between Kingston and Prescott.

On 10 November 1812, Commodore Chauncey's squadron, consisting of the *Oneida* and six converted merchantmen, chased the *Royal George*, flagship of the Provincial Marine, nearly catching it before it found safety in Kingston Harbour. C H J Snider drew this speculative illustration for his *In the Wake of the Eighteen-Twelvers* published in 1913 (Toronto Reference Library, T15239)

Mohawk and the Wood Creek Canal slowed the arrival of the heavy equipment, causing Chauncey to wait through most of October until it could be run down the Oswego River. Late in the month he asked Secretary Hamilton not to blame him if he failed to 'accomplish the wishes of the government this fall [as] I cannot do it without the means and I have exerted myself to the utmost to get these means forward but have been frustrated in all my endeavours.'[13] The ordnance arrived in time, however, and by the end of the month Chauncey was writing hopefully of making his presence felt on the lake by the first of December.

When originally formulating his plans for the lakes, Commodore Chauncey had intended to develop a base at Buffalo at the same time as he built up the squadron at Sackets Harbor. The difficulties of transporting heavy ordnance and the like across New York State led him to decide early in October that it would be impractical to attempt any significant operation at the Lake Erie port before winter. Although he declared his intention to build two 20-gun brigs on Lake Erie, Chauncey sent only a small detachment of naval personnel to the post at Black Rock, one mile down the Niagara River from Buffalo, while he concentrated his efforts on Lake Ontario.[14]

Commodore Chauncey achieved, in the autumn of 1812, what no other American commander on the northern border was able to do; he confronted his British adversaries and put them to flight. After a couple of short patrols during which British vessels were sighted, he departed from Sackets Harbor on 8 November, steering a course to an anchorage at the Duck Islands, twenty-five miles west of the port. His squadron consisted of the *Oneida*, now armed with sixteen 24pdr carronades and a pair of long 12pdrs, the *Governor Tompkins, Hamilton, Conquest, Pert, Julia* and *Growler*. The next morning, as the squadron crept north toward the British shore, the Americans sighted the *Royal George* heading for Kingston and gave chase. Through the rest of that day and into the next, Chauncey's vessels followed the Provincial Marine flagship until it anchored in Kingston harbour. Under fire from land batteries and the *Royal George*, the Americans crept forward in an uneven line to engage the British ship at close range. As the light of day failed and storm conditions threatened, Chauncey called off the attack, anchoring after dark near the western tip of Wolfe Island. Although damage and casualties were light in this, the first significant encounter of this new conflict between British and American naval forces on the lakes, Chauncey's attack showed the British how quickly American naval strength had escalated.

At dawn on 11 November, while Chauncey fought to gain the lake against a rising head wind, he spotted the schooner *Governor Simcoe* and made chase. Like the *Royal George*, the *Simcoe* evaded captured, but ran too closely over a shoal and sank at its berth in Kingston from the damage it had incurred. With the weather worsening,

Chauncey laid a course for Sackets, which he reached late on 12 November. Early the next morning he was off again, in search of the *Earl of Moira*, reported en route to Kingston. The ship was sighted just as it reached the safety of Kingston, but Chauncey's disappointment at being unable to capture one of the British warships was somewhat compensated by the destruction of a British schooner, the *Two Brothers*, at a village above Kingston (on 10 August) and the capture of two merchantmen, the schooner *Mary Hatt* and the sloop *Elizabeth*. Renamed respectively the *Raven* (burthen 50 tons, bought for $2500 from the prize court) and the *Asp* (57 tons, $3500), Chauncey had the vessels armed and commissioned.[15]

The November patrols introduced the US Navy to how severely weather conditions on Lake Ontario would test the fabric of their vessels. Seaman Myers and some of his mates volunteered to serve on the *Oneida* since the *Scourge* was still being converted, and Myers recalled that the *Oneida* was 'a warm little brig … but as dull as a transport. She had been built to cross the bars of the American harbours, and would not travel to windward.'[16] After failing to catch up to the *Moira*, the squadron sailed into a gale 'with a Severe Snow-Storm, the small vessels labouring

This unattributed watercolour shows the US Schooners *Hamilton*, *Governor Tompkins* and *Julia* pursuing the British merchantman *Governor Simcoe* toward Kingston on 11 November 1812. The *Royal George* can be seen in the upper right coming out from Kingston. (Courtesy of the New York State Office of Parks, Recreation and Historic Preservation, Sackets Harbor State Historic Site)

Although designed by Henry Eckford in 1819, this draught (re-drawn by Chapelle) for a ship-corvette may provide an indication of what the *Madison*, launched at Sackets Harbor late in November 1812, looked like. (Smithsonian Institution)

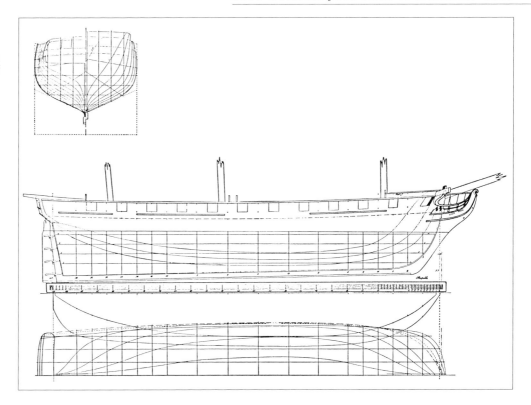

extremely, and the ice making so fast on the Slides of our Carronades that we could not have made use of them.'[17] Several days later, as the *Growler* maintained a blockade off Kingston with other gunboats in heavy weather, its foremast suddenly went by the board, tearing up the deck and splitting the keelson; the commanding officer, Sailing Master Mervine Mix, was barely able to navigate the schooner to a safe anchorage.

The American cruises in November 1812 also had a significant effect on the course of the war. After only two and a half months in command of the Lake Ontario station, Commodore Chauncey had outfitted a squadron that ran the Provincial Marine off the lake. This ended any further voyages to York by the British, interrupting their supply line and frustrating the plan to congregate the warships at a new marine headquarters at that port during the winter. The British were now faced with a hitherto unknown threat. 'I think I can say with great propriety,' Chauncey wrote to the navy secretary, 'that we have now the command of The Lake and that we can transport Troops and Stores to any part of it without any risk of an attack from the Enemy.'[18] While the lateness of the season prohibited such expeditions, the consequences of

Chauncey's energy and efficiency would be just as pertinent in the ensuing spring.

The Americans were allowed one more celebration before a hard winter set in. On 26 November the USS *Madison* was launched at Sackets Harbor; 'a beautiful Corvette-built ship,' wrote Chauncey, 'of the following dimensions – 112 feet keel: 32½ feet Beam: 11½ feet Hold: 580 Tons, and will mount 24 – 32 pounders, carronades.'[19] Henry Eckford had performed the task of creating a ship twice the size of Chauncey's original plans in only forty-five days; his draught of the *Madison*, as with all his lake vessel designs, was apparently not preserved. A document from October 1812 showed that sixty barrels of salt were purchased in order to pack their contents among the ribs of the hull, as had been done with the *Oneida*, in the hope of extending the vessel's life as long as possible.

The sudden appearance of a potent American naval squadron on Lake Ontario caused much alarm among British officials. Major General Roger Hale Sheaffe, who had taken over military and civil command in Upper Canada following Brock's death at Queenston, wrote that it would 'require exertions of the most energetic kind to enable us to contend with them in the spring for the ascendancy of the lakes.'[20] Prevost had once more sent the assistant quartermaster general, Captain Andrew Gray, to the province to assess the situation and make recommendations for a winter building programme. Gray proposed, with Sheaffe's full agreement, that 'a ship corvette, mounting 30 32pd. carronades, should be laid down at York, and two vessels of the class of the *Royal George* built, one at Kingston and the other at Amherstburg.'[21] While Gray admitted that York was virtually defenceless, he continued to promote the idea of splitting the available resources on Lake Ontario between two major building projects. Prevost concurred with this flawed idea and created further difficulties when he failed to assign the task of designing the ships

to John Dennis, who had been building ships for the Provincial Marine for ten years. Intent on injecting new blood into the system, rather than taking advantage of Dennis's knowledge of local materials and personnel, Prevost contracted Thomas Plucknett, a builder at Quebec, to design the two Lake Ontario vessels and to personally superintend proceedings at York; Gray hired a builder from Montreal named James Morrison to manage the project at Kingston.

Problems plagued the British shipyards through the winter. The frame of the ship at Kingston was erected by the first week of February, but Morrison proved so incompetent and dilatory that Gray fired him and put the foreman of the yard, Daniel Allen, in charge; short of artificers, however, Gray soon hired Morrison back to fashion the ship's spars. Allen lasted less than five weeks on the job, losing his place after inciting the shipwrights to strike on the grounds that their provisions had not been properly delivered to them; Gray replaced him with a shipwright named George Record.[22]

In spite of such setbacks, the ship on Point Frederick neared completion by the end of March even though it was no longer the only project under construction. The *Earl of Moira* was receiving an extensive repair which included the reduction of its rig from a ship to a brig. The British conducted surveys on two merchantmen early in March, the *Governor Simcoe* and the *Lady Gore,* in order to determine if they could bear the weight of guns and the strain of hard duty. They rejected the *Gore,* but advised that the *Simcoe,* if altered, would be serviceable. The survey revealed interesting information about the *Simcoe,* which appears to have been the oldest vessel on the lakes at the time, its launch having been in 1794. The board measured the schooner at 74ft (on deck) by 18½ft by 12ft. It had 'an old appearance', was rotten in places, needed its stern altered and its tiller 'placed abaft the Rudder Head', but its masts and rigging were in good repair and the hull was strong enough to support ten 18pdr carronades and a pair of 6pdr long guns.[23] To carry such guns, the board recommended that the *Simcoe's* deck be lowered three feet so that five gunports could be made on each side with two more each at bow and stern.

While work began on refitting the *Simcoe,* the

TABLE 21

HM Schooner *Prince Regent* (1812), *Lord Beresford* (1813), *Netley* (1814) – legend of particulars

Launched: July 1812, York
Original draught by: John Dennis
Builder: John Dennis

HULL DIMENSIONS, 1815

Gun deck	72ft 6in
Keel/tonnage	59ft 10½in
Breadth extreme	21ft 2in
Depth of hold	7ft 3in
Tons	142 67/94
Draught loaded	7ft 6in forward
	9ft 4in aft
Number of ports	8
Dimensions of ports	
height	2ft 2in
width	2ft 10in
between	6ft 6in
above deck	2ft 3in

SPAR DIMENSIONS, 1815

Mast	Length	Diameter	Yard Length	Yard Dia.
Fore	58ft 6in	15½in	40ft	8in
Topmast	24ft	7½in	34ft	6¾in
Topgallant	13ft	4in	21ft 6in	4¾in
Main	64ft	15½in	40ft	8in
Topmast	23ft 6in	7in	34ft	5¾in
Topgallant	13ft	4in	17ft 6in	3½in
Bowsprit	28ft	16¾in	—	—
Jibboom	25ft	7½in	—	—
Driver boom	50ft 4in	11½in	—	—
Gaff	26ft	6½in	—	—

ORDNANCE

Date	Carronades	Long Guns
1812	10-12s	2-6s
1813	10-18s	2-9s
1814	8-18s	1-24s

Source: NAC, MG 12, ADM 106/1997; RG 8, I, 729.

TABLE 22

British vessels launched and acquired on Lake Ontario, 1812-1813

Vessel	Launch	Place	Rig	Remarks
Prince Regent (A)	June 1812	York	schooner	1814 renamed *Netley*; 1817 in ordinary; *Lord Beresford*,12; 1830s sold, broken up
Sir Sidney Smith, 12†	1793	Kingston	schooner	ex-*Governor Simcoe*; 1814 renamed *Magnet*, destroyed to avoid capture
Sir George Prevost/Wolfe (A), 23	28 April 1813	Kingston	ship	1814 renamed *Montreal*; 1817 in ordinary; 1830s sold, broken up
Lord Melville, 14	22 July 1813	Kingston	brig	1814 renamed *Star*; 1817 in ordinary; 1830s sold, broken up
Confiance (A), 2	1811	Oswego	schooner	ex-*Julia* ‡; 1813 recaptured by Americans*
Hamilton (B), 5	1809	Ogdensburg	schooner	ex-*Growler* ‡, 1813 recaptured by Americans*

† private vessel hired or purchased for government service.   ‡ prize vessel.   * see Table 23.

TABLE 23

American vessels acquired and launched on Lake Ontario, 1812-1813

Vessel	Launch	Place	Rig	Remarks
Julia, 2†	1811	Oswego	schooner	1815 sold *
Scourge, 10†	1811	Niagara	schooner	ex-*Lord Nelson* ‡; 1813 upset in storm
Conquest, 3†	1810	Ogdensburg	schooner	ex-*Genesee Packet*; 1815 sold
Growler (A), 5†	1809	Ogdensburg	schooner	ex-*Experiment*; 1815 sold
Pert, 3†	1809	Ogdensburg	schooner	ex-*Collector*; 1815 sold
Governor Tompkins, 6†	1810	Oswego	schooner	ex-*Charles and Ann*; 1815 sold
Fair American, 2†	1804	Oswego	schooner	1815 sold
Hamilton (A), 9†	1809	Oswego	schooner	ex-*Diana*; 1813 upset in storm
Ontario (C), 2†	1809	Lewiston	schooner	1815 sold
Raven,1†	1810	Oswego	schooner	ex-*Mary Hatt* ‡; 1815 sold
Asp, 2†	1808	Mississauga	sloop	ex-*Elizabeth* ‡; 1815 sold Point, Upper Canada
Madison, 24	26 Nov 1812	Sackets Harbor	ship	1815 in ordinary; 1825 sold as commercial carrier
Lady of the Lake, 1	5 April 1813	Sackets Harbor	schooner	post 1817 in ordinary; 1825 sold; 1826 sank
York (A), 6	1807	Kingston	schooner	ex-*Duke of Gloucester* ‡; 1815 sold
General Pike, 26	12 June 1813	Sackets Harbor	ship	1815 in ordinary, 1825 sold, broken up
Sylph, 10	18 August 1813	Sackets Harbor	schooner	1815 in ordinary, 1825 sold, broken up

† private vessel hired or purchased for government service   ‡ prize vessel   * see Table 22.

The Provincial Marine naval base on Point Frederick at Kingston had been in existence for nearly thirty years when the War of 1812 broke out. Despite the facilities already in place, the British were not able to match the industry of the US Navy in the first year of the conflict. ('Plan of Kingston Harbour', Plate IV in William James, *Military Occurrences ...* London 1818)

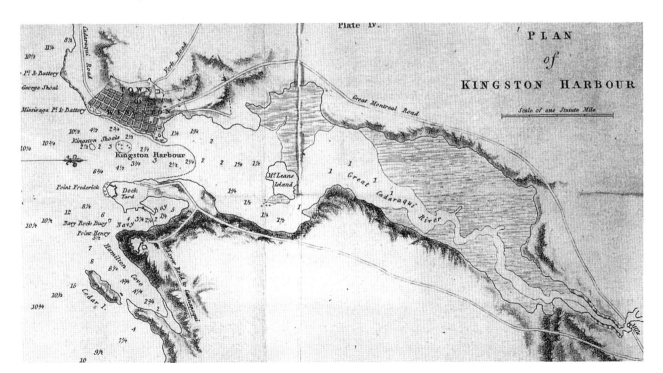

British undertook another project at Point Frederick. After appraising the two merchantmen and the materials in stock at the dockyard, they realised they had enough timber on hand to build a schooner like the *Lady Gore* and that the work would cost about the same as modifying that vessel for service. Consequently, George Record prepared a draught for a new schooner, the keel of which was laid in mid-March. In addition, part of the work force at Point Frederick commenced the construction of several gunboats meant to carry single 9pdr long guns or 12pdr carronades.[24]

The situation at York was a disaster in comparison to the progress made at Kingston. From the minute that Thomas Plucknett made his appearance in the province's capital there had been trouble, beginning with his refusal to build the 30-gun vessel at the site which Gray, John Dennis and Lt William Fish, PM, had selected. Owing to shallows adjacent to the construction site, they proposed the fabrication of a launching slipway measuring 800ft by 100ft that would extend into deep water, an idea that Plucknett found preposterous and refused to support. After discussing the matter with General Sheaffe, Plucknett had his way and proceeded at a site he had chosen, but so slowly and in such a disorganised manner that one of the local military officers soon complained: 'Whether Mr. Plucknett is a regular professional ship builder or not, it is not in my power to determine, but that he wants system and arrangement, I feel no hesitation in asserting.'[25] Governor-in-Chief Prevost arrived shortly thereafter on a quick tour of the upper province and when he expressed disappointment at the slow pace of the building, Plucknett blamed the delays on John Dennis, who had been hired as the foreman. It was only through the vigorous defence of Dennis by local officials, who claimed the situation would have been worse if it had not been for

Work on the *Isaac Brock* faltered due to poor management and the difficulty of getting materials up to York during the winter. This watercolour by Owen Staples shows the ship being planked with the dismantled *Duke of Gloucester* pulled up on shore and the masts of the schooner *Prince Regent* in the distance. (Toronto Reference Library, T15211)

This chart, drawn in 1816, shows the configuration of the bay at York with soundings that indicate the shallowness of the harbour. In 1813 the garrison stood across the creek and northeast of the large fortification shown here. (National Archives of Canada, NMC17441)

Dennis's efforts, that the former master builder's job was saved. In spite of all the complaints made about Plucknett, he retained his position at York without improving his inefficient methods so that by the middle of April the hull of the new ship, which had already been named the *Sir Isaac Brock*, had only eleven strakes of plank on one side and none on the other. Captain Gray, long a proponent of setting up the York dockyard and replacing experienced hands with the likes of Thomas Plucknett, was forced to admit that 'as matters now stand it is very doubtful when [the *Brock*] will be ready.'[26]

Across the lake at Sackets Harbor there had been problems with personnel, sickness and supplies, but the dockyard had managed to function effectively under the management of Henry Eckford and the industrious support of Commodore Chauncey. Only one vessel rose in the dockyard, but the hands were also busy preparing the components of a ship intended at first to resemble the *Madison*. The labourers cut the ice at the foot of the slipway in the basin on 5 April and launched the schooner *Lady of the Lake* the next morning.

Like most of Eckford's Lake Ontario vessels, little is known about the *Lady*, other than it was about 65ft on deck, 89 tons in burthen and, modelled after the pilot boats at New York, built for speed.[27]

Chauncey's main concern during the early months of 1813 was to build another ship to match the growing British squadron. The day after the launch of the schooner, the new keel was laid and, due to Eckford's preparations, the frames were up and planking had begun by 23 April. In consultation with Eckford and the new secretary of the navy, William Jones, the commodore increased the dimensions of the ship to nearly match those of the US Frigate *Essex*; launched in 1799, the *Essex*, 32, measured 141ft 9in (gundeck) by 37ft by 12ft 3in. Chauncey also meant to arm his ship exclusively with twenty-six long guns, but aware that conventional cannon might overburden the shallow draught hull, he requisitioned 'the old 24 Pounders that were landed from the Constitution. … They are short and light – the ship here will bear them with great convenience.'[28] Replaced afloat by longer and heavier weapons, the guns (measuring about 8ft in length)

were in use in land batteries and in the USS *John Adams*, 28, at New York; navy agent John Bullus was able to collect them and all their appurtenances for shipment to Oswego. A second reason for installing long range weapons instead of carronades was that Chauncey believed 'we shall have to encounter some heavy batteries at Kingston [so] we require heavy metal.'[29] As it turned out, Chauncey's decision to arm his new ship with long 24s would significantly influence events on the lake that summer.

While the new ship rose in the dockyard, Sackets Harbor was abuzz with activity as the military force that had gathered there was preparing to launch the spring campaign in co-ordination with the navy. Commodore Chauncey, Major General Henry Dearborn and the principals in Washington had long considered Kingston as the first objective of the year, but they suddenly changed their target to York. Reasons for the change were numerous, among them being the fact that Kingston would be blocked by ice until the end of April. As well, sources had informed the Americans that the British were building two 18-gun brigs at York and that the *Prince Regent* and the *Duke of Gloucester* (carrying 18 and 16 guns respectively, Chauncey was told) were moored there. 'By possessing ourselves of these vessels,' Chauncey wrote to Secretary Jones, 'and taking or destroying all the public stores and munitions of war at York, [it] will give us a decided advantage in the commencement of the campaign.'[30] On 22 April, 1700 troops began embarking on the squadron which now consisted of the *Madison*, 24, *Oneida*, 18, *Governor Tompkins*, 6, *Conquest*, 3, *Ontario*, 2, *Fair American*, 2, *Asp*, 2, *Pert*, 3, *Growler*, 5, *Julia*, 2, *Hamilton*, 9, *Scourge*, 8, and *Raven*, 1; the *Lady of the Lake*, 1, was carry-

This watercolour by Owen Staples portrays the general layout of events on 27 April 1813 when the Americans attacked York. Although misleading in proportions and the number of vessels in Chauncey's squadron, it indicates that the *Madison* and *Oneida* anchored in deep water off shore while the schooner-gunboats covered the military operations on land. (Toronto Reference Library, T10271)

ing messages to Fort Niagara. Heavily burdened as they were, the vessels struggled to gain the lake on 23 April and were forced back to Sackets by a gale that Chauncey feared would upset his smaller craft. They were off again on 25 April and after a quick passage appeared within sight of York the next evening.

The attack on York, 27 April 1813, was the largest joint operation that the US Army and Navy had performed in their short history. Under the cover of the naval guns, the infantry went on shore led by Brigadier General Zebulon Pike and pushed back the British troops, who they outnumbered by more than two to one, after a severe skirmish at the landing point. Realising the situation was lost, Major General Sheaffe, who happened to be in York on government business, gathered up his remaining regulars and withdrew toward Kingston, leaving behind orders to set fire

to the *Sir Isaac Brock* and to detonate a well-stocked magazine at the garrison. The resulting explosion killed and wounded more than 200 Americans (Pike was fatally injured) and the loss of the new ship and naval stores nearby deflated Chauncey's prime reason for attacking York. He was able to confiscate twenty guns of various calibres, ammunition and some supplies, but the *Prince Regent* was not there (it had sailed to Kingston several days before) and the *Duke of Gloucester* proved to be a decaying schooner that Chauncey renamed the *York*, but never employed as more than a floating magazine at Sackets.[31]

The attack on York was followed by more than a week of chaos during which army and naval parties ran amok in the town and then rode out a storm that pinned the squadron to its anchorage. The squadron finally got away on 8 May to deliver the troops to the Four Mile Creek anchorage near

Fort Niagara and to return to Sackets for reinforcements and provisions. In spite of these unexpected turns of event, Chauncey's control of Lake Ontario allowed the Americans the time needed to recuperate from their expedition to York and to prepare for their next objective, capturing Fort George and occupying the Niagara Peninsula. This attack took place on 27 May with Chauncey's squadron escorting three waves of batteaux and laying down a barrage that took out British batteries and facilitated the capture of Fort George. The British army escaped, however, and marched to a position at Burlington Heights at the western extreme of Lake Ontario which was commonly referred to as the Head of the Lake. While a plan was under consideration to catch the British between two wings of the army, one of which Chauncey would transport to a spot east of Burlington, word reached Niagara that the British had attacked Sackets Harbor. With visions of his headquarters destroyed and his new ship consumed by flames, Chauncey departed immediately for Sackets.

While the Americans operated unchallenged in the western reaches of Lake Ontario, Kingston had been the scene of considerable activity. On 28 April the *Sir George Prevost* was launched at Point Frederick, prompting Captain Gray to claim that it was 'as fine a vessel of her class as ever sailed under the British Pendant.'[32] At the request of the governor-in-chief, the ship's name was soon changed to the *Wolfe*. It measured 101ft 9in (on deck), 86ft 1½in by 30ft 6in by 11ft with a burthen of 426 tons, making it larger than the *Royal George* after which it had been patterned. With a midships deadrise of 16 degrees, slightly less than the *Royal George*'s, the *Wolfe* also drew less water (9ft 10in forward, 12ft 4in aft), thereby overcoming a complaint that the former ship sat too deep in the water. The *Wolfe* also carried more ordnance than its predecessor, having twenty-two ports at which were initially mounted two 68pdr carronades, eighteen 18pdr carronades and two long 12pdrs.

Within days of the *Wolfe*'s launch, Commander Robert Barclay, RN, arrived at Kingston with two other commanders and several lieutenants, the first of the Royal Navy personnel to reach the lakes in response to Prevost's requests the previous autumn. Barclay and his small party had been

On 27 May 1813 Commodore Chauncey's squadron played an important role in supporting the US Army landing at Niagara by escorting the flotilla of batteaux and then subduing the British batteries at Fort George and along the shore. This view inaccurately shows the *Madison* with only four gunports. (Archives of Ontario, S1439)

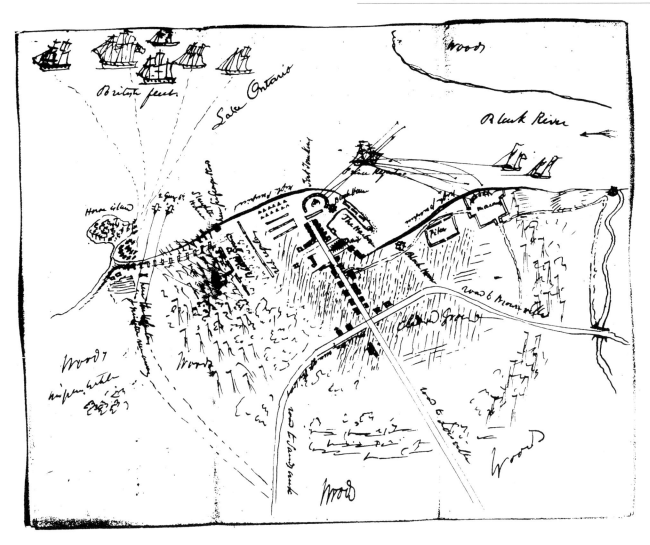

In this eyewitness sketch (but of unknown origin) the British squadron under Commodore Yeo is depicted standing off shore during the attack on Sackets Harbor on 29 May 1813. Only the schooner *Lord Beresford* (seen here under fire from the American batteries) was able to get within range of the shore. The ship *General Pike* is under construction in the dockyard where a fire, mistakenly started by navy personnel, nearly consumed it. (Library of Congress, 400434)

sent from Bermuda to the lakes by Admiral Sir John Borlase Warren and had gone overland from New Brunswick to Quebec to reach their destination as soon as possible. Through an order issued by Prevost, Barclay and his colleagues took full charge of naval operations at Kingston, superseding the officers of the Provincial Marine, many of whom took positions ashore or left the service. The remaining officers and men were soon transferred to Royal Navy musters and the Provincial Marine on Lake Ontario officially ceased to exist. In the view of the Royal Navy officers, this was no loss. Although they had been surprised to find vessels like the *Wolfe* and *Royal George* at Kingston, they considered them 'in such a wretched state with respect to discipline and furniture, that they would have reflected disgrace upon a maritime power of the lowest possible

grade; … they were under the command of the Military Commandant, and officered and manned by provincials, men of no experience whatever in Naval tactics.'[33]

On 15 May Commodore Sir James Lucas Yeo reached Kingston at the head of 465 Royal Navy officers and men from England and superseded Barclay, who soon left to take command of the Lake Erie squadron at Amherstburg. At thirty years of age, Captain Yeo was a twenty-year veteran of war at sea. He had gained prominence for service in the Mediterranean, Portugal and South America and his assignment to the Great Lakes was his first employment as commodore on a remote station. As with all such appointments, Yeo operated under orders from the Admiralty, but, due to his distance from London, he was expected to report to Admiral Warren and 'to co-operate most cordially with [Prevost], not undertaking any operations without the full concurrence and approbation of him or of the Commanders of the Forces employed under him.'[34] Building on the changes begun by Barclay, Yeo worked energetically to prepare the Kingston squadron for a quick meeting with the Americans and was ready by the fourth week of May when Prevost, having heard that Chauncey had sailed for Niagara, approved a raid on Sackets Harbor.

On 27 May a military force of 800 men embarked in the squadron which consisted of the *Wolfe*, 22, *Royal George*, 20, *Earl of Moira*, 18 (now a brig), *Lord Beresford*, 12 (formerly the schooner *Prince Regent*), *Sir Sidney Smith*, 12 (formerly the schooner *Governor Simcoe*), the merchantman *Lady Murray* and three gunboats, the *Black Snake*, *Glengarry* and *Quebec*. After an aborted attempt to land at Sackets the next day, the British went ashore early on 29 May and put the first wave of

James Lucas Yeo (1782-1818) entered the navy in 1792 and was promoted to lieutenant four years later. He was knighted in 1809 for his exploits in French Guiana while in command of HMS *Confiance*, 22. He was the commodore of the squadron on Africa's west coast in 1818 when he died of one of the prevalent fevers. (National Maritime Museum, PAD3283)

TABLE 24

HM Brig *Lord Melville* (1813), *Star* (1814) – legend of particulars

Launched: July 1813, Kingston
Original draught by: George Record
Builder: George Record

HULL DIMENSIONS, 1815

Gun deck	71ft 7in
Keel/tonnage	56ft 9½in
Breadth extreme	24ft 8in
Depth of hold	8ft
Tons	186 46/94
Draught loaded	8ft 6in forward
	9ft 9in aft
Number of ports	14

Dimensions of ports

height	2ft 6in
width	2ft 10in
between	7ft 3in
above deck	1ft 2in

SPAR DIMENSIONS, 1815

Mast	Length	Diameter	Yard Length	Yard Dia.
Fore	42ft	16¾n	40ft 6in	12¾in
Topmast	32ft	11in	31ft 7½in	7in
Topgallant	31ft 6in	6in	24ft 11in	5in
Main	45ft 6in	17in	46ft 9¾in	10¼in
Topmast	32ft 6in	11in	32ft 7¾ft	7¼in
Topgallant	32ft 6in	5¼in	25ft 10in	5¼in
Bowsprit	39ft 6in	16½in	—	—
Jibboom	24ft	8½in	—	—
Driver boom	46ft 6in	11in	—	—
Gaff	32ft	5in	—	—

ORDNANCE

Date	Carronades	Long Guns
1813, 1814	12-32s	2-18s

Source: NAC, MG 12, ADM 106/1997; RG 8, I, 729.

TABLE 25

HMS *Sir George Prevost*, *Wolfe* (1813), *Montreal* (1814) – legend of particulars

Launched: 25 April 1813, Kingston
Original draught by: Thomas Plucknett
Admiralty 'as built' draught by: Thomas Strickland
Builders: James Morrison, Daniel Allan, George Record

HULL DIMENSIONS, 1815

Gun deck	101ft 9in
Keel/tonnage	86ft 1½in
Breadth extreme	30ft 6in
Depth of hold	11ft
Tons	426 23/94
Draught loaded	9ft 10in forward
	12ft 4in aft
Number of ports	22

Dimensions of ports

height	2ft 8in
width	2ft 9in
between	5ft 10in
above deck	1ft 3in

SPAR DIMENSIONS, 1815

Mast	Length	Diameter	Yard Length	Yard Dia.
Fore	63ft	19½in	56ft	12¾in
Topmast	38ft	12in	39ft 4in	8¼in
Topgallant	21ft 6in	7in	28ft 8in	5½in
Main	70ft 4in	22in	63ft 2in	15in
Topmast	43ft	13in	45ft 4in	9½in
Topgallant	24ft 6in	8in	31ft 4in	6in
Mizzen	58ft	15in	—	—
Topmast	30ft 6in	9½in	35ft	7in
Topgallant	19ft 6in	6in	27ft	5¼in
Bowsprit	45ft	20in	39ft	8in
Jibboom	36ft	10in	—	—
Crossjack	—	—	45ft	9½in
Driver boom	47ft	9½in	—	—
Gaff	30ft	8in	—	—

ORDNANCE

Date	Carronades	Long Guns
1813, Spring	2-68s	2-12s
	18-18s	
1813, Autumn	4-68s	1-24
	8-32s	8-18s
1814	18-32s	3-18s

Source: NAC, MG 12, ADM 106/1997; RG 8, I, 729.

American defenders to flight. Much stiffer opposition awaited them on the plain west of Fort Tompkins and the blockhouses that covered the dockyard, and fierce fighting took place as the British tried to dislodge the Americans. Due to a lack of wind, only one of the British warships, the *Beresford* under Commander Francis Spilsbury, was able to get close enough inshore to support the landing, which deprived the land force of the kind of support that Chauncey's naval guns had given the American army at York and Niagara. The troops made several attempts to overwhelm Fort Tompkins, but failed, and when Prevost saw that a fire seemed to be engulfing the dockyard where Chauncey's new ship stood in plain view, he ordered a withdrawal, to the bitter disappointment of many of his officers. The battle cost the British heavy casualties, including the death of Captain Andrew Gray, and is said to have spawned an immediate friction in the relationship between Yeo and Prevost. What the frustrated British did not immediately know, however, was Chauncey's dismay at seeing his shipyard left inadequately protected by the army and his new ship nearly destroyed (it was saved from the fire). Ever after, the American commodore was hesitant to leave Sackets Harbor unless he was certain that his base was relatively safe from attack.

The arrival of the Royal Navy and the launch of the *Wolfe* led Chauncey to conclude that his force was inadequate to battle the British for control of the lake. Accordingly, he decided to remain at Sackets through most of June and July while his new ship was completed. This allowed Yeo freedom to support the army at Burlington, help-

Equipped exclusively with long guns, the USS *General Pike* had a significant impact on the naval contest on Lake Ontario. During the conflict the *Pike* had a poop deck and topgallant forecastle where single long 24pdrs were mounted on circles. This full sail plan was drawn post-war. (US National Archives, NH57006)

TABLE 26
USS *General Pike* (1813) – legend of particulars

Launched: 12 June 1813, Sackets Harbor
Original Draught by: Henry Eckford
Builder: Henry Eckford

HULL DIMENSIONS, 1813
Gun Deck	142ft
Breadth Extreme	38ft 6in
Tons	900
Number of Ports	26

SPAR DIMENSIONS, 1813

	Length		*Length*
Fore mast	77ft	Fore yard	68ft
Topmast	45ft	Topsail yard	49ft
Topgallant mast	23ft	Topgallant yard	36ft
		Royal yard	25ft
Main mast	85ft	Main yard	75ft
Topmast	50ft	Topsail yard	54ft
Topgallant mast	25ft	Topgallant yard	36ft
		Royal yard	27ft
Mizzen mast	74ft	Cross Jack	54ft
Topmast	40ft	Topsail yard	38ft
Topgallant mast	21ft	Topgallant yard	28ft
		Royal yard	19ft
Spanker	54ft		
Bowsprit	34ft		
Jib Boom	38ft		
Flying Jib	40ft		

ORDNANCE
Date	Carronades	Long Guns
1813, 1814	0	24-24s
		2-24s (pivots)

Source: 16 April and 18 July 1813, Chauncey Letter Book.

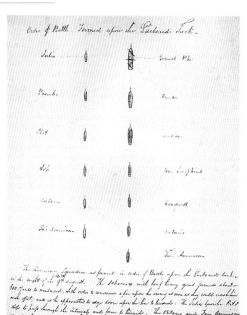

Commodore Chauncey used this sketch to show Navy Secretary William Jones his plan on the night of 10 August 1813 when he set his schooners in a line to windward in hopes of drawing the British squadron closer to the heavy guns in the rest of his vessels. The plan went awry when the *Julia* and *Growler* turned toward the British instead of edging toward the leeward line. (US National Archives, RG 45, M125, 30, p100)

ing it to push the American army back to Fort George and then harassing the American supply line along the southern shore of the lake. Just as Chauncey had been essential to the early success of General Dearborn's army, Yeo's commanding presence made it possible for the British land forces to turn the tide of the spring campaign, proving once again the necessity of holding supremacy on the lake.

On 12 June 1813 the USS *General Pike* was launched at Sackets Harbor, an event that drew crowds of onlookers who were eager to see such a grand vessel make its debut. A new arrival at Sackets, Master Commandant Arthur Sinclair, USN, who was to be Chauncey's flag captain, described the *Pike* in this way: 'She is 3 feet longer and 1½ wider than the *Essex* pierced with 28 ports, tons near 1000 and is a most beautiful ship – what an

From his viewpoint on the *Oneida*, Midshipman Peter Spicer sketched this view of the two squadrons on 10 August as the *Julia* and *Growler* (upper right) turn toward the British. The British vessels appear to be (centre from left to right) the *Beresford*, *Royal George*, *Earl of Moira*, *Sir Sidney Smith*, *Lord Melville* and *Wolfe*. The American vessels are (bottom and extreme right, left to right) the *Asp*, *Pert*, *Governor Tompkins*, *Fair American*, *Ontario*, *Conquest*, *General Pike*, *Madison* and *Oneida* (Naval Historical Center, NH75733KN)

On 11 September 1813, after being caught in a lull near the Genesee River for several hours, the two squadrons, propelled by gale force winds, raced northeastward to Kingston. Midshipman Spicer made this sketch of the limited action that was fought. The British squadron, above, consists of (left to right) the *Hamilton* (ex-*Growler*), *Earl of Moira*, *Sir Sidney Smith*, *Prince Regent*, *Royal George*, *Confiance* (ex-*Julia*), *Lord Melville* (shown here as a schooner, rather than a brig) and *Wolfe*. Chauncey's squadron is (left to right) the *Ontario*, *Fair American*, *Madison*, *Governor Tompkins*, *Oneida*, *Lady of the Lake*, *Sylph* (here rigged as a brig although accounts from the period list it as a schooner) and *General Pike*. (Naval Historical Center, NH75734KN)

elegant command on the attack. She has a poop and Topgallant Forecastle as far as the foremast forward and mizzen mast aft, and only wants it continued on and bulwarks above to make such a ship as the *Constellation*.'[35] Chauncey gave the deck's dimension as 142ft (and the burthen at 900 tons), which was close to the size of the frigate *Essex*, 32 (1799), which measured 141ft 9in on deck by 37ft by 12ft 3in. The frigate *Constellation*, 38 (1797), at 163ft 7in on deck by 40ft by 13 ft, was a considerably larger vessel, but both frigates had more extensive upperworks than Sinclair noted in the *Pike*. Ware's sail plan for the *Pike* shows its straight sheer, the stern galleries and thirteen ports rather than fourteen as Sinclair stated. On a broadside, however the ship could bring fifteen 24pdrs to bear, as two guns were mounted on circles, one on the topgallant forecastle and the other on the poop. The addition of the *General Pike* significantly strengthened the American squadron, which was now manned by 1146 officers and seamen and 143 US Marines.

While the *General Pike* was being fitted out, the British launched the vessel at Point Frederick

that George Record originally designed to be a schooner and laid down in March. By the end of April, however, 'timbers of a scantling that will enable her to carry <u>any</u> metal' were going into the hull so that it could be 'rigged a Brig ... [and] be fully competent to take her Station in our Line of Battle.'[36] The *Lord Melville* slid into Navy Bay on 22 July, in its final form measuring 71ft 7in on deck, 56ft 9½ in by 24ft 8in by 8ft for a burthen of 186 tons. Within nine days the brig was rigged and armed with twelve 32pdr carronades and two 18pdr long guns. Yeo had received all the ordnance and equipment sent from England and used it to reorganise the metal of his squadron, which was now crewed by 632 officers and men, supplemented by 228 infantry acting as marines. On 31 July Yeo set sail from Kingston in search of Chauncey who had headed up the lake several days before.

Now began the most intense phase of the contest for control of Lake Ontario. While the opposing armies remained in their stalemate on the Niagara Peninsula, both commodores were instructed to seek a battle that would resolve the issue of supremacy on the lake. Numerous conditions, however, complicated this seemingly simple solution, the foremost being the disparate nature in the armament of the two squadrons.

When Chauncey and Yeo finally came within sight of one another off Niagara at dawn on 7 August 1813, the American vessels had the potential to begin an action at a range of more than 1000 yards with nearly 800 pounds of iron in a broadside from their long guns, while the British long guns could respond with little more than 160 pounds. At the preferred 500-yard range of carronades the contest was better balanced since the British packed 1230 pounds of broadside iron in their carronades to the American 608 pounds. Yeo's daunting problem involved manoeuvring close enough to Chauncey to fight him on equal terms, especially since the *General Pike* loomed large with its broadside of 336 pounds of long range metal. To achieve his goal, the British commodore depended upon a strong, steady breeze and rapid shiphandling to place himself close enough to his foe so that his most powerful guns

could be effective. Chauncey anticipated Yeo's tactics and knew well enough to keep his distance, looking for the opportunity to wound the British with his long range capacity; a lull, for instance, would allow his schooner/gunboats to sweep down on Yeo and, virtually unmolested, hammer away at him. Everyone in the squadrons and on shore understood these parameters in the naval contest; a British military officer wrote 'Sir James, I am happy to observe, is fully impressed with the necessity of having a *commanding* breeze … [because] in a light one or calm the enemy's flotilla of small vessels would have an incalculable advantage.'[37] In the American camp, a witness to the action on the lake noted 'Sir James's object just now appeared to be to get ours in a position where he could attack the *Pike* with two vessels at once, but Chauncey manoeuvred too well for him.'[38]

There was also a significant difference in the sailing qualities of the two squadrons. After watching Yeo handle his command, Arthur Sinclair described the British squadron as 'six regular built vessels of war, all sailing alike and able

to support each other in any weather – capable of keeping the sea and acting efficiently when our Gunboats dare not cast their guns loose.'[39] Opinions on the British quarterdecks were less kind to their adversaries; Yeo considered the *Pike* 'a very fine large ship, but appears to be very unwieldy and unmanageable, and from the manner she is worked [I] should judge she is not complete with seamen. The *Madison* is about the size of the *Wolfe*, sails well and is managed better than the *Pike*. The *Oneida* is small and sails bad, and the schooners, though formidable in a calm, are very contemptible otherwise, as they have not the least shelter for their men.'[40] Chauncey agreed with Yeo, complaining about his 'dull Sailing Schooners' and the *Oneida* which, along with the slower schooners, he was forced to tow in order to keep them up with the better vessels.[41] In addition, it appears that the American crews lacked the kind of practical experience the British seaman had in shiphandling under pressing circumstances. On one occasion, Sinclair complained 'had our schooners done their duty we might have

had him. … but they are commanded by a set of boys without the least experience or judgement.'[42]

Ultimately, no climactic battle took place on Lake Ontario in 1813, although several notable incidents occurred. The best known is the loss of the *Hamilton* and *Scourge* in the early hours of 8 August near Twelve Mile Creek on the north shore of the Niagara Peninsula. Becalmed and hove to under partial sail in the dark after a frustrating day of sparring with the British, the schooners were upset by a sudden, violent storm and took seventy men to their deaths. Two nights later Chauncey contrived to lure Yeo within range of the *Pike*'s broadside by placing a line of schooners to windward as bait. As the British crept near, Chauncey ordered the schooners to ease down toward his leeward position, but the commanders of the *Julia* and *Growler* turned to windward instead whereupon Yeo signalled his squadron to close on them. Chauncey tacked in an attempt to engage the *Wolfe*, but Yeo ignored him to chase the misguided schooners. Fearful that some of his other schooners would go astray in the dark,

This watercolour by Owen Staples depicts one of the pivotal moments in the Lake Ontario contest when broadsides from the *General Pike* (right centre) dismasted HMS *Wolfe* (extreme left) on 28 September 1813. Commander William Mulcaster, RN, sailed the *Royal George* in between the flagships and engaged the *Pike* which gave Commodore Yeo enough time to recover and make off toward the anchorage at Burlington. (Toronto Reference Library, T15238)

Chauncey reversed his course in order to consolidate his squadron, although all eyes were on the *Julia* and *Growler* as they were captured and a few tongues whispered criticism of the commodore for failing to defend them.[43]

For several weeks Yeo employed the *Julia* (renamed the *Confiance*) and *Growler* (renamed the *Hamilton*) in his squadron, but eventually turned them into transports as he found them to be slow and unwieldy, a hindrance to the smooth operation of his line. He adjusted the armament of his squadron to increase its long gun strength in hopes of being able to confront Chauncey more effectively, especially since the American had lost four of his schooner/gunboats during his early August cruise. Their loss had proven to be insignificant, however, because Henry Eckford had begun work on another vessel as soon as the *General Pike* was launched. It splashed into the basin at Sackets Harbor on 18 August, a 340-ton schooner, pierced for twenty guns. Chauncey named it the *Sylph* and advised Secretary Jones that 'from her construction she must sail fast, [and] she will add very much to my present force, and in point of force fully counterbalance the vessels which I have lost.'[44] Beyond those facts little is known about the dimensions and qualities of the *Sylph*, although as the commodore predicted, it proved to be a quick vessel. Rather than fill its ports with smaller ordnance, Chauncey had only three 6pdrs mounted on each broadside, so that he could give the schooner four 32pdr long guns on circles.

In September 1813 Chauncey came close on two occasions to catching Yeo. The first occurred on 11 September when the British squadron fell into a lull near the mouth of the Genesee River for several hours as the Americans struggled to get close enough to bombard them. The *Pike* got within range and inflicted some damage on the British vessels, but before the rest of Chauncey's squadron – most notably the schooners which were supposed to have been perfectly suited for such conditions – could close on the British, a rising breeze swept off the land and propelled Yeo to safety near Kingston. On 28 September, in gale conditions ten miles south of York, the guns of the *Pike* knocked down the *Wolfe's* main and mizzen topmasts and left Yeo as an easy prey, struggling to regain control. Captain William

Mulcaster came to his commodore's rescue, however, by steering the *Royal George* between the two flagships and confronting the *Pike*. While Yeo made his getaway downwind with every scrap of canvas set on his foremast, Mulcaster peppered the *Pike*, slowing its advance. Chauncey's attack was further hampered when a gun on the *Pike's* forecastle burst, causing more than two dozen casualties and disrupting his forward batteries. A pell-mell engagement ensued over the next couple of hours with the British racing for an anchorage at the head of the lake and Chauncey's widely dispersed squadron in pursuit. As the lee shore rose and the weather worsened, Chauncey called off the chase and attempted to gather his squadron together. Under miserable conditions, the British skilfully anchored without a disaster on the north shore of Burlington Bay, while the Americans spent the next forty-eight hours clawing to windward. Again, Chauncey was criticised for not having pressed the attack, but more than the weather had constrained him. An American expedition against Montreal was in the works and he had been ordered to cover the flank of an army division that was about to sail in a flotilla of batteaux from Niagara to Sackets Harbor, thus making the preservation of his squadron essential to that campaign. While performing that duty in the first week of October, Chauncey succeeded in intercepting a convoy of seven British transports, for which Yeo had failed to provide proper coverage, capturing five of them near Kingston, including the *Confiance* (nee *Julia*) and *Hamilton* (nee *Growler*).[45]

Only on a rare occasion did the two commodores again view each other through the rest of the navigation season of 1813, but the experiences they had endured in trying to bring one another to battle during August and September had taught them some stiff lessons about waging war on Lake Ontario. Since weight of long range metal had proven to be the critical issue in their struggle, it was obvious that the commander who could float the strongest warships early the next spring could seize control of the lake. To that end, Yeo and Chauncey focused their attentions on their dockyards where resources had already been assembled to build ships the likes of which had never been seen on the lakes.

CHAPTER 6

'Only required for one battle'

LAKE ERIE, 1812-1814

WHEN THE AMERICANS declared war in June 1812, they were even less prepared to deal with Britain's naval strength on Lake Erie and above than they were on Lake Ontario. The weak Provincial Marine squadron dominated the lakes until the United States Navy began converting merchantmen and building gunboats and brigs. Similar in form to the ship-corvettes launched by the British, these shallow-draught warships played the key roles in achieving the first decisive naval victory of the war on freshwater.

In the early months of 1812, the British leaders, Prevost and Brock, took steps to improve the strength of the Provincial Marine squadron at Amherstburg by retiring Alexander Grant (after a career that dated back to 1759 with Loring and Amherst on Lake Champlain) and replacing him with Master and Commander George Hall, who had been in the service for more than a decade. Hall's original command consisted of the *Queen Charlotte*, 20, and the *General Hunter*, 6, (originally a schooner, but altered to a brig) to which was added in June the schooner *Lady Prevost*, 12. Like the *Prince Regent* on Lake Ontario, the new

schooner had been built in anticipation of imminent hostilities. William Bell's draught of the vessel has not survived nor has much dependable detail about its construction, apart from a postwar American bill of sale that showed its dimensions to be 68ft on deck by 18ft 6in by 9ft 3in. The schooner was also measured by Master Commandant Jesse Elliott, USN, in 1813 and shown to be '90 foot on Deck, 21 foot-beam, 9 foot hold', but these dimensions yield a length to beam ratio of 4.28:1, which is out of proportion to other similar lake vessels of the period; Elliott's dimensions for the *Queen Charlotte*, described in chapter four, were similarly disproportionate.[1] The *Lady Prevost* significantly improved Hall's squadron and when Commander Robert Barclay, RN, first went on board the schooner in June 1813, he remarked, 'I was agreeably surprised in her being a fine strong vessel.'[2]

Prior to the war, William Hull, the governor of the Michigan Territory, had warned President Madison and his ministers about the need for the United States to establish a naval presence on the upper lakes, but his advice went unheeded and the old army brig *Adams*, armed with six 6pdrs, remained the sole government vessel on the upper lakes. For their negligence, the Americans paid dearly in the opening phase of the war. On 17 July a small British force of regulars, fur traders and native allies seized the American post on Mackinac Island in a bloodless but significant action that secured British communication with the western native nations; through the rest of the conflict strategic planning by Madison's cab-

TABLE 27

The British squadron on Lake Erie, August 1813

Vessel	Total Guns	Carronades 24s	18s	12s	Long Guns 24s	18s	12s	9s	6s	4s	2s
Detroit	19	1	1		2	1*	6	8			
Queen Charlotte	17	14			2 1*						
Lady Prevost	13			10				2 1*			
General Hunter	10			2					2	4	2
Little Belt	3	—						1	2		
Chippewa	1	—						1*			
Totals	63	28									35

* pivot gun.
Source: NAC, MG 12, ADM 1/5445, p15.

TABLE 28

The American squadron on Lake Erie, August 1813

Vessel	Total Guns	Carronades 32s	Long Guns 32s	24s	12s
Lawrence	20	18			2
Niagara	20	18			2
Caledonia	3	1*		2*	
Ariel	4	—			4*
Scorpion	2	1*	1*		
Tigress	1	—	1*		
Porcupine	1	—	1*		
Somers	2	1*		1*	
Trippe	1	—		1*	
Totals	54	39			15

* pivot gun.
Source: Roosevelt, *Naval War of 1812*, p242.

85

Jesse Duncan Elliott (1782-1845) joined the US Navy as a midshipman in 1804 and was on board the USS *Chesapeake* when it was stopped by HMS *Leopard* in June 1807. Later in his career he commanded squadrons in the West Indies and the Mediterranean. (Enoch Pratt Library, US Naval Institute)

Daniel Dobbins (1776-1856) was a private merchant master on the upper lakes prior to the War of 1812. His report about British activity sparked President Madison to approve the building of gunboats at Erie before Commodore Chauncey could organise his Lake Erie command. (Courtesy Erie County Historical Society)

inet would always include a scheme to recapture the lonely garrison in the northern reaches of Lake Huron.[3] At Mackinac, the British confiscated several private American vessels, including the sloops *Erie* and *Friend's Good Will* and the schooners *Salina* and *Mary*. The latter two vessels sailed to Detroit as cartels bearing the prisoners taken at Mackinac and were recaptured, along with the brig *Adams*, when Major General Brock forced Hull's surrender at Detroit on 16 August; the British renamed the brig *Detroit*.

The loss of Detroit prompted officials in Washington to finally take Hull's advice by ordering Isaac Chauncey to develop an inland navy. Commodore Chauncey's responsibility was to establish a base on Lake Erie as well as one on Lake Ontario and, thinking at first that this was a readily achievable goal, he ordered men and munitions to Buffalo in September with the intent of buying merchant vessels into the service and building two 300-ton warships. When he became aware of the difficulties inherent in transporting the necessary equipment and personnel across New York State, however, Chauncey concentrated his resources on Lake Ontario and, for that reason, in the first week of October there was only a small naval detachment at Buffalo under the command of Lieutenant Jesse Elliott, USN. Elliott was eager for action and saw an opportunity on the night of 8 October when the *Detroit* and the 86-ton brig *Caledonia*, property of the North West Company and loaded with furs and armed with two guns, anchored off the British post at Fort Erie. Early the next morning Elliott launched a cutting out expedition, comprising his seamen and a company of regulars, and succeeded in carrying the *Detroit* and *Caledonia*. Due to the lack of wind and the rush of current at the head of the Niagara River, the Americans were unable to gain the lake and, under fire from British batteries, drifted downstream. The *Caledonia* reached safety below a battery at the village of Black Rock while the *Detroit* went aground at the southern tip of Squaw Island where Elliott finally ordered it burned when the British attempted to recapture it.[4]

While Chauncey was organising his expedition to the lakes in September, an experienced private mariner from the upper lakes named Daniel Dob-

bins made his way to Washington to report to the Navy Department about conditions in that quarter. He arrived at a perfect time because Madison and Navy Secretary Paul Hamilton were hungry for any information about the lakes and listened intently to what Dobbins had to say. Within days they gave him a warrant as a sailing master in the US Navy and sent him back north with orders to organise the building of four gunboats at Erie, Pennsylvania, about 100 miles west of the Niagara River, which was commonly referred to as Presque Isle after the peninsula that formed the large, protected bay there.[5]

Upon reaching Erie, Dobbins began work on the bank of Lee's Run at the tiny village and informed Lieutenant Elliott of his undertaking. Elliott quickly responded with criticism of Dobbins's building site, arguing that informants had assured him that Presque Isle Bay was indefensible and lacked the depth of water necessary to launch warships. He preferred to set up a dockyard beside Scajaquada Creek, which was shielded from the British by Squaw Island and less than a mile below Black Rock, and despatched that opinion and Dobbins's to Chauncey for his assessment. Shortly afterward, Lieutenant Samuel Angus, USN, took charge at the dockyard when Elliott left to join the Lake Ontario squadron; due to other pressing matters, Chauncey did not respond to the Dobbins-Elliott correspondence. Without positive instructions from the commodore, Dobbins proceeded cautiously at Erie, worried that Chauncey would disapprove of what he was doing and he would be stuck with the bills. He hired men on a daily basis, erected a work shed and blacksmith shop, bought materials and initiated contracts with forges at Pittsburgh. A local shipbuilder named Ebernezer Crosby prepared rough draughts for two gunboats measuring 50ft by 17ft by 5ft, and by the middle of December Dobbins's men had one of them framed and were setting up the keel for the second.[6]

Having secured his force at Sackets Harbor for the winter, Commodore Chauncey set off to inspect his Lake Erie command late in December. He reached Black Rock on 25 December and found the post in disorder, the responsibility for which he attributed to Lieutenant Angus. Besides the *Caledonia* (purchased for $3700), there were

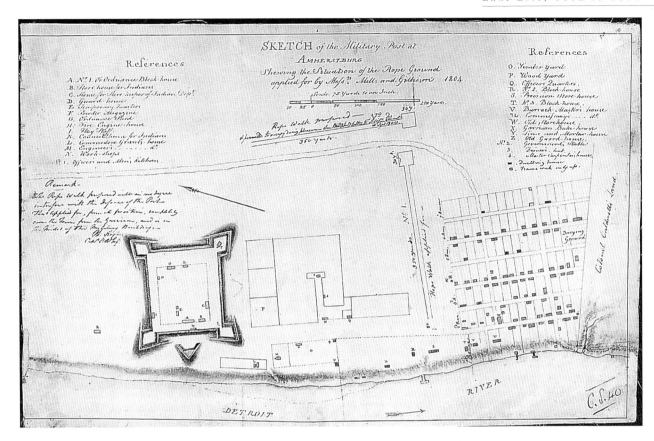

The British post at Amherstburg included Fort Malden and the dockyard of the Provincial Marine. Two local residents had set up a ropewalk adjacent to the village (No 1 on the plan) where rigging for vessels on the upper lakes was manufactured. (National Archives of Canada, C52252)

three private schooners, the *Catherine* ($5500), *Ohio* ($4000) and *Amelia* ($6900) and the sloop *Contractor* ($5000) moored in Scajaquada Creek, all of which Elliott or Angus had purchased into the service. During his time at Black Rock, Elliott had ordered their decks and sides torn up so that they could be refitted, but Chauncey stopped this work as he did not think they could be employed until the British were chased from their batteries on the other side of the river and he did not want to waste time and money needlessly. The commodore then set out for Erie where he arrived on 1 January 1813. He considered the two gunboats that Dobbins had started on the banks of Lee's Run too small for their expected duties, but also too far advanced in their building to be altered. Instead, he instructed Dobbins to increase the length of the next two gunboats by ten feet. Chauncey saw that the bar at the mouth of the harbour, presented a problem, but he agreed with Dobbins that Erie was the best available location for a dockyard and decided to build a brig of 300 tons there.[7] Soon after returning to Sackets Harbor, Chauncey learned that William Jones

had replaced Paul Hamilton as Secretary of the Navy. Jones opened correspondence with Chauncey on 27 January, indicating immediately that acquiring command on the upper lakes was a priority for the upcoming campaign. He approved the plans and progress made at Erie and ordered the construction of a second brig, promising to supply the Lake Erie squadron with every necessity so that the naval 'force would facilitate beyond calculation the operations of Genl [William Henry] Harrisons Army [which was moving into place to recapture Detroit], and in the event of the fall of Malden and Detroit, would enable you to detach part of your force to Lake Huron … to take Michelmacinack and command the waters of Lake Michigan.'[8]

Chauncey moved quickly to execute Jones's instructions. At New York in the third week of February he consulted Noah Brown who, along with his brother Adam, ranked among New York's foremost shipbuilders, and contracted him to build '2 Brigs capable of mounting 18-32 pounders carronades and 2 long 9s … made to draw not exceeding 6½ or 7 feet of water, and at

TABLE 29

British vessels launched and acquired on Lake Erie, 1812-1814

Vessel	Launch	Place	Rig	Remarks
Lady Prevost, 13	June 1812	Amherstburg	schooner	1813 taken by Americans at Put-in-Bay; 1815 sold as commercial carrier
Detroit (A), 6	1801	River Rouge	brig	ex-*Adams*‡; 1812 taken by Americans, destroyed to avoid recapture
Little Belt, 3†	1810	Black Rock	sloop	ex-*Friend's Good Will*‡; 1813 taken by Americans at Put-in Bay, later destroyed by British at Buffalo
Chippewa (B), 1†	1810	Maumee River	schooner	1813 taken by Americans, at Put-in-Bay, later destroyed by British at Buffalo
Erie, 2† ‡	1810	Black Rock	sloop	fate uncertain
Detroit (B), 19	July 1813	Amherstburg	ship	1813 taken by Americans at Put-in-Bay; 1815 sunk for preservation; 1835 sold as commercial carrier; 1841 wrecked at Niagara Falls
Surprise (B), 2	1813	Erie	schooner	ex-*Scorpion*‡; 1817 in ordinary, decayed *
Confiance (C), 1	1813	Erie	schooner	ex-*Tigress*‡; 1817 in ordinary, decayed *
Sauk, 1	1810	Cleveland	schooner	ex-*Ohio*‡; 1817 in ordinary, decayed *
Huron (B), 2	1809	Black Rock	schooner	ex-*Somers*‡; 1817 in ordinary, decayed *

† private vessel hired or purchased for government service. ‡ prize vessel. * see Table 30.

TABLE 30

American vessels acquired and launched on Lake Erie, 1812-1813

Vessel	Launch	Place	Rig	Remarks
Somers, 2†	1809	Black Rock	schooner	ex-*Catharine*; 1814 taken by British *
Ohio, 1†	1810	Cleveland	schooner	1814 taken by British *
Amelia, 1†	1801	Detroit	schooner	nee-*General Wilkinson*; fate uncertain
Trippe 1†	1803	Black Rock	sloop	ex-*Contractor*; 1813 destroyed by British at Buffalo
Caledonia, 3† ‡	1807	Amherstburg	brig	1815 sold as commercial carrier
Porcupine, 1	May 1813	Erie	schooner	1815 sold as commercial carrier
Tigress, 1	May 1813	Erie	schooner	1814 taken by British *
Scorpion, 2	May 1813	Erie	schooner	1814 taken by British *
Ariel, 4	May 1813	Erie	schooner	1813 destroyed by British at Buffalo
Lawrence, 20	May 1813	Erie	brig	1815 sunk for preservation
Niagara (A), 20	June 1813	Erie	brig	1820 sunk for preservation; 1913 recovered and rebuilt; 1988 remains of brig used in new *Niagara*

† private vessel hired or purchased for government service. ‡ prize vessel. * see Table 29.

the same time possess the qualities of sailing fast and bearing their guns with ease. Their frame, etc, will be entirely left to yourself.'[9] Noah Brown soon departed from New York with a gang of prime shipwrights and Chauncey's promise that he would order all the materials Brown needed delivered to Erie quickly. Master Commandant Oliver Hazard Perry, USN, also entered the picture at this time, having petitioned Chauncey in January for a command on the lakes and promising to bring with him a hundred or more seamen from his gunboat station at Newport, Rhode Island. Chauncey accepted Perry's offer, explaining to Jones that Perry could 'be employed to great advantage, especially upon Lake Erie.'[10] After spending several weeks with Chauncey at Sackets Harbor, Perry travelled to Erie where he arrived late in March.

Noah Brown had reached Erie a month earlier, but his efforts were delayed by bad weather, a lack of hands and building materials. He did what he could to advance the work on the three gunboats Dobbins was now constructing at Lee's Run and set up a second yard for the brigs and the fourth gunboat at Cascade Creek, a mile west of the village where there was a deeper launch basin. By mid-March the keels for the brigs were laid while the first two gunboats were getting in their beams. Perry assessed the progress when he arrived and soon set out for Pittsburgh where he contracted for most of the ironwork and rigging, the balance being sent from Philadelphia. Delivery of these materials was slow and unreliable, causing Perry and Brown to scour the vicinity of Erie for every scrap of iron and fittings they could find. Their efforts included salvaging the schooner *Salina* which had been carried out of the Detroit River in an ice flow and miraculously appeared off Erie. More shipwrights and artificers arrived from the east, the rate of building improved and the four gunboats were launched early in May, followed within a few weeks by the brigs. The slow supply train from Pittsburgh delayed the fitting out of the six new vessels with their rigging and guns until July.

Following the capture of Fort George at the end of May, Chauncey sent Henry Eckford and a large party of shipwrights to Black Rock to prepare the five vessels there for service. They com-

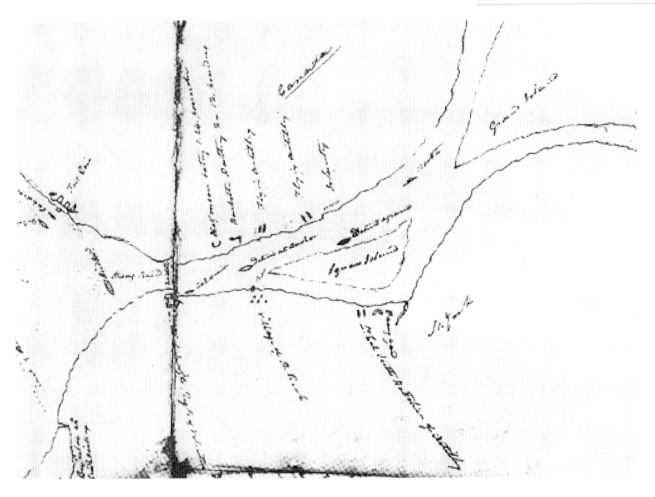

The villages of Buffalo and Black Rock are shown here across the head of the Niagara River from the British post at Fort Erie. Lt Elliott sketched this map for enclosure with his report of the capture of the British vessels *Detroit* (ex-*Adams*) and *Caledonia*. (US National Archives)

pleted the work in a short time and, with help from the local military and without hindrance from British batteries which had been evacuated following the loss of Fort George, hauled the vessels out of the Niagara River and into Lake Erie. Perry then sailed them up to Erie, narrowly missing a confrontation with the British squadron under Commander Barclay due to a fog bank that obscured the flotillas from each other.

When armed for battle, and finally manned to Perry's satisfaction (he and Chauncey had clashed bitterly over the supply of seamen sent to Lake Erie) at the end of July, the American squadron at Erie numbered eleven vessels in all.[11] The mainstays of Perry's squadron were the twin brigs, named *Lawrence* and *Niagara*, which measured 110ft between perpendiculars by 29ft (moulded breadth) by 9ft for a burthen of 493 tons. Noah Brown's draughts of the vessels have not survived, but some of his construction techniques were revealed when the *Niagara* was raised and recon-

structed in 1913. Brown employed a variety of woods fresh cut from the mixed forest around Erie; oak, ash and poplar for the frames, white and black oak for hull planking, white pine for the decks and red cedar and black walnut for uprights. A combination of treenails and iron fastenings held the components together and there was a scarcity of knees in the hull. As Chauncey had ordered, the brigs were very shallow in draught of water and had a midships deadrise of about 17 degrees, but they still had to be raised by camels and laboriously kedged over the bar in order to reach the lake. Howard Chapelle and others who examined the remains of the *Niagara* in 1913 speculated that Brown gave the brig a plain stem, but a contemporary portrait shows that the *Lawrence*, and presumably the *Niagara*, had a conventional beakhead. The brigs were armed with eighteen 32pdr carronades and two long 12pdrs in the bows of their flush upper decks, while the crews (numbering 130 or more)

89

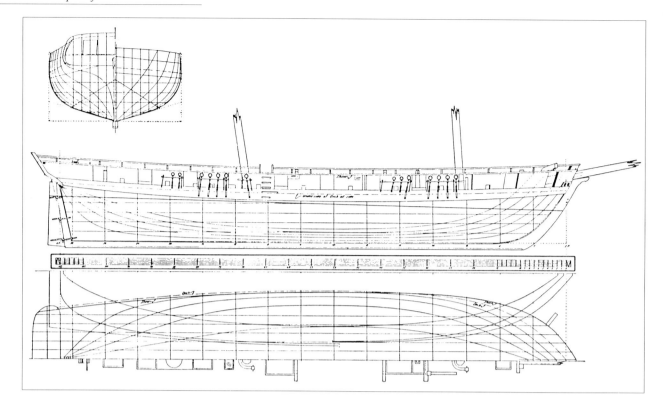

Howard Chapelle
reconstructed this draught
of the brigs built by Noah
Brown at Erie, Pennsylvania
using measurements taken
from the hull of the *Niagara*
when it was retrieved in
1913. Speculatively,
Chapelle gave it a plain bow
and an open rail atop the
bulwarks, but Robert Irvine's
portrait of the Lake Erie
warships showed that the
brigs did not have these
features. (Smithsonian
Institution)

crowded into tight quarters below. Under the pressure to build quickly and hampered by a lack of suitable materials and sufficient workers, Brown built the brigs without decoration. He is reputed to have remarked: 'we want no extras; plain work, plain work is all we want. They are only required for one battle; if we win, that is all that will be wanted of them. If the enemy are victorious, the work is good enough to be captured.'[12]

Of the gunboats built at Erie less in known. The two smaller craft designed by Ebernezer Crosby and begun by Dobbins in the autumn of 1812 were launched as the schooners *Porcupine* and *Tigress.* Their burthens were given as 52 tons and each carried a single 32pdr long gun mounted on a pivot. British records show that the *Tigress* (captured in 1814 and renamed *Confiance*) measured 60½ft on the deck by 17¾ft by 5¼ft. The schooner *Scorpion* was one of the vessels Chauncey ordered lengthened during his visit to Erie in January 1813. It carried a 32pdr long gun and a 24pdr carronade, both on pivots, and had a burthen of 63 tons. Like the *Tigress,* it was also captured in 1814 (renamed the *Surprise*) and as surveyed by the British measured 68½ft on deck

by 18½ft by 5½ft. The fourth gunboat was altered by Noah Brown to become, as he described it, a 'sharp schooner for a despatch vessel, and to look out, as she could outsail anything in the English fleet.'[13] Named the *Ariel*, this schooner had a burthen of 75 tons and was armed with four 12pdr long guns.

At Black Rock, the largest of the five vessels was former British merchantman *Caledonia.* According to Dobbins, it was built at Amherstburg in 1807 and had a burthen of 86 tons; Perry outfitted it with a pair of 24pdr long guns on pivots and a single, pivoting 32pdr carronade. The schooner *Catharine* was launched in 1809, the property of Sill, Thompson and Co of Black Rock. Perry renamed it the *Somers* and gave it two guns on circles, a long 24pdr and a 32pdr carronade. During August 1814 the *Somers* fell into British hands (renamed the *Huron*) and was found to be 53ft 6in between perpendiculars, 41ft 3⅝in by 17ft 3½in by 8ft for a burthen of 65tons. The sloop *Contractor* had a burthen of 60 tons and was built by Porter, Barton and Co of Black Rock in 1803. Before being purchased by the navy, the vessel had spent part of its career supplying the US Army on the upper lakes. Perry renamed the sloop *Trippe* and gave it a single 24pdr long gun on a pivot. Perry did not change the name of the schooner *Ohio*, which was launched at Cleveland in 1810 by merchants named Murray and Bigsbey. He mounted a single long gun on board and Perry appointed Dobbins master of the vessel. It was also captured by the British (renamed the *Sauk*) in 1814 and was surveyed to be 59ft between perpendiculars, 45ft 10⅝in by 18ft 11in by 7ft 2in for a burthen of 87 tons.[14] The schooner *Amelia*, which began its life as the *General Wilkinson* in 1801, was found to be too decayed for active service in Perry's squadron.

With Perry's pendant aloft in the *Lawrence*, the American squadron departed from Erie on 12 August, setting a course for Sandusky, fifty miles southeast of Amherstburg, where a rendezvous with Major General Harrison's army had been arranged. From that day forward, the Americans

controlled the upper lakes because the British had failed to co-ordinate a building and supply programme to match theirs. Only one vessel had been built at Amherstburg during the winter and it would eventually be forced to sail with a hotchpotch of weaponry and a motley crew.

In November 1812 the British knew that the Americans meant to gain mastery of not just Lake Ontario, as Commodore Chauncey did that month, but also the upper lakes. Consequently, the same plan that led to the construction of the *Sir Isaac Brock* and the *Wolfe* also produced a new warship, the *Detroit*, at Amherstburg. This placed an additional burden on the British supply line, which would soon be strained to meet the needs of the separate shipyards at Kingston and York.

Like the *Wolfe*, the ship at Amherstburg was to be 'of the Class of the *Royal George*', although early references also compared it to the *Queen*

After occupying the eastern half of the Niagara Peninsula in the spring of 1813, the Americans gained control of the Niagara River which allowed them to haul converted merchantmen over the swift rapids and shoals between Black Rock and Lake Erie. (National Archives of Canada, MG 11, CO42/157, p23)

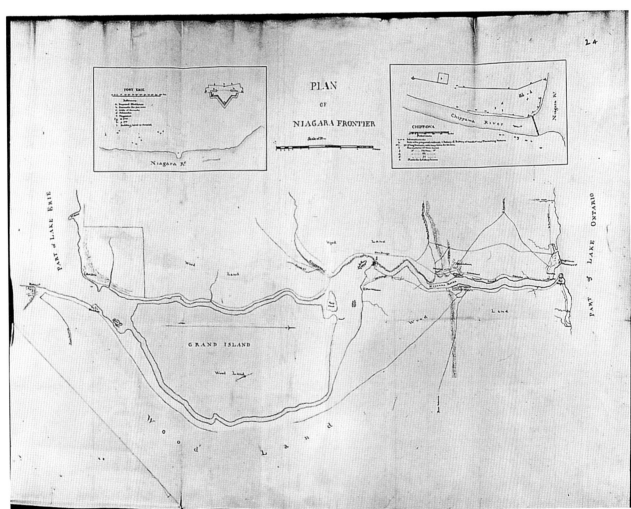

Charlotte.[15] Some consideration had already been given to building another schooner like the *Lady Prevost* at Amherstburg and plans had been made to strip the out-of-service *Camden* of its iron work, but the call for a larger warship yielded the preparation of new estimates and requisitions. The project would need 15,000 feet of oak timber, 200 oak knees, over 7000 feet of pine timber and boards, only a small portion of which was in store. While there were plenty of nails at Amherstburg, there were virtually no bolts and no sheaves or deadeyes. The rigging, it was calculated, could be fashioned from hemp at a rope-walk in town run by two local men, but there was a shortage of fabric for sails. The *Detroit* would carry sixteen 24pdr carronades and four long 12pdrs, although there were few such guns at Amherstburg. To build the ship, it was estimated that 6600 man-days of labour were required, but master builder William Bell complained that he had too few skilled workman in his gang, some of whom lacked skill. In spite of shortages, Bell began the project in January and, later reinforced by shipwrights sent from Kingston, gradually raised the frames. By the first of April he had started planking the bottom when the local military commander, Brigadier General Henry Procter ordered his shipwrights to work on two small

gunboats (the *Mary Eliza* and *Myers*) for the army, which took nearly a month to complete, further delaying the ship's progress. At the end of April Bell was still fitting the wales on the *Detroit*.

Commander Robert Barclay, RN, arrived at Amherstburg during the first week of June 1813 with several officers and two dozen Royal Navy and Provincial Marine seamen Commodore Yeo had detached from his squadron. The *Detroit* was still on the stocks and William Bell was concerned about a lack of iron and other stores. Barclay found the ship *Queen Charlotte* 'very much smaller than I had an idea of ... more fitted as a packet than a man of war', armed with sixteen 24pdr carronades and four long 12pdrs, but crewed by only 75 men including infantry acting as marines.[16] Barclay viewed the brig *General Hunter*, as 'a miserably small thing' with four 12pdr carronades and two long 6pdrs and a 30-man crew made up mainly of soldiers.[17] He complimented the construction of the schooner *Lady Prevost*, armed with ten 12pdr carronades and two long 9pdrs and with 43 men on board, one third of them being from the infantry.

To augment the squadron, the British had converted three merchantmen, the *Chippewa*, *Friend's Good Will* and *Erie*, for service. The first had been built on the Maumee River in 1810 and was cap-

Presque Isle Bay was created by the Presque Isle Peninsula opposite the town of Erie, Pennsylvania. The winding channel at the entrance was choked by a shallow bar. This map was made by Commodore Arthur Sinclair in 1814 when he commanded the Lake Erie squadron. (US National Archives, RG 45, M125, 36, p23)

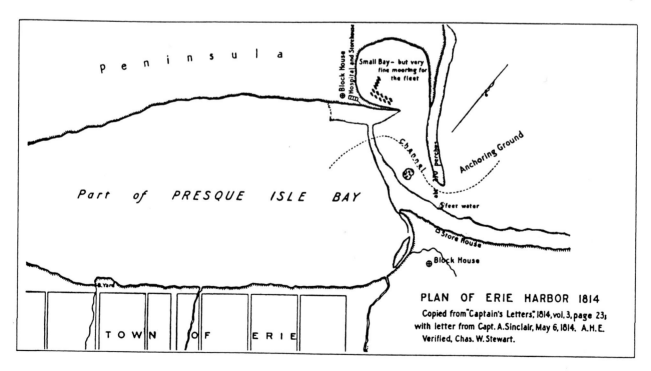

This watercolour by Margaret Reynolds shows the *Queen Charlotte* sailing up the Detroit River opposite Amherstburg where HMS *Detroit* stands painted and ready for launch in the dockyard. Two army gunboats, the *Mary Eliza* and *Myers*, are pulled up on the shore, while the vessel in the distance appears to be the brig *General Hunter*. (Fort Malden National Historic Site)

tured by the British shortly after the war started and initially armed with two 6in howitzers. The sloop *Friend's Good Will*, which was built at Black Rock in 1810, was also captured by the British, who renamed it the *Little Belt*, arming it at first with one 9pdr long gun on a pivot and a single 24pdr carronade. Master Commandant Jesse Elliott stated that the dimensions of both of these vessels were 59ft on deck by 16ft by 7ft for a burthen of 100 tons, but as with the statistics he compiled for the other British prizes, Elliott's measurements are suspect. Like the *Friend's Good Will*, the 60-ton sloop *Erie* was built at Black Rock on 1810 and captured at Mackinac. Armed with two long 12pdrs, one of which was on a circle, the *Erie* only remained with the squadron until the end of July.[18]

Barclay made several cruises in June and July to reconnoitre Perry's progress at Erie and to stop at Long Point where he hoped reinforcements and the guns and stores for the *Detroit* would arrive. He received little assistance despite the numerous requests he sent to Yeo, Prevost and local military commanders and when Perry made his laborious crossing of the Presque Isle Bay bar at the end of July, Barclay refrained from engaging him due to the weakness of his squadron. He withdrew instead to Amherstburg to await the launch of his new ship and the men and arms he needed.

The *Detroit* finally slid down the ways in mid-July. William Bell's draught of the ship has not come to light and there are very few dependable descriptions of the vessel. Contemporary portraits show that it had the *Royal George*'s flush, corvette-style upper deck pierced for twenty guns and was similar in appearance to the *Cruizer/Snake* class of warships. An enrolment completed for the *Detroit* in 1836 when, like the *Queen Charlotte*, it was converted into a merchantman, gave its dimensions as 96ft 2in on deck by 26ft by 11ft 1in, which very closely matched the *Royal George*'s dimensions of 96ft 9in on deck, 81ft 11½in by 27ft 7in by 11ft 1in. As noted in regards to other vessels of the British Lake Erie squadron, Jesse

THE DETROIT FRONTIER.

Pointe du Lac

Riu Delude

Commodore's Creek

Riu Crete

Pine River Fort St Clair

RIVER ST CLAIR

Riv aux Cygnes

Riu au Loutre
Riu Saline
Riu au Vasa

Riu aux Hurons

LAKE ST CLAIR

Pt aux Ginnialet

Grosse Pointe

Tremblay Creek

DETROIT
Springs
Sandwich

Here Gen'l Brockland

Riv aux Canards

Maguaga

Ft Malden
Amerstburg

Huron R.
Brownstown

Pidgeon Bay

LAKE ERIE

Variation 5° E
Point South
Peles or Portland

Frenchtown River Raisin

Middle Sister

Shoal reported near this place

East Sister

mud

Bird Island

Point Pel'e Island

Turtle Island

West Sister

St George Is

LaFleur Island

Shoal reported near this place

Miamis Bay

BATTLE OF LAKE ERIE

Shoal reported near this place

Buss Island

Maumee River

Ship Island

Cunningham Island

Ft Meigs

Sandusky Point

Sandusky Bay

Sandusky Riu

Yenice

Fort Stephenson.

Scale: 8 Miles to an Inch.

The British squadron sailed from Amherstburg on 9 September 1813 to confront the Americans who had taken up an anchorage at South Bass Island. Perry sailed out to meet Barclay and their engagement happened near West Sister Island. (From William Wood, *Select Documents of the Canadian War of 1812*)

Robert Barclay (1785-1837) joined the Royal Navy in 1797 as a midshipman and advanced to lieutenant in 1805. He was on board HMS *Swiftsure* at the Battle of Trafalgar. Sent to Halifax in 1809 to await an imminent promotion to commander, he had to wait until February 1813 when Admiral Warren made him a commander and sent him to the lakes. (Toronto Reference Library, T15259)

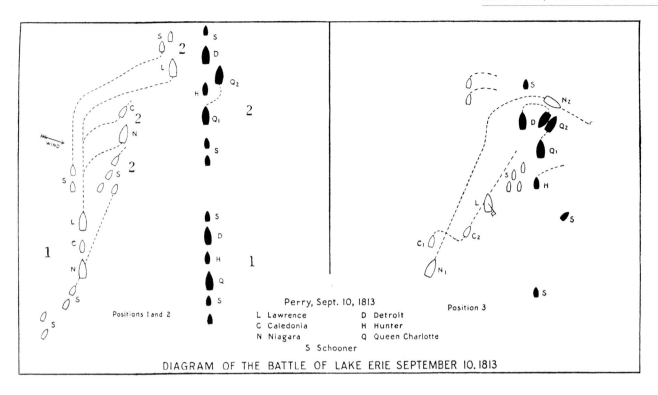

Positions 1 and 2

Perry, Sept. 10, 1813

L Lawrence   D Detroit
C Caledonia   H Hunter
N Niagara   Q Queen Charlotte
S Schooner

Position 3

DIAGRAM OF THE BATTLE OF LAKE ERIE SEPTEMBER 10, 1813

This diagram shows the early fighting in the Battle of Put-in-Bay when Perry's flagship *Lawrence* fought with little support against the *Detroit* and *Queen Charlotte*, and the last phase when Perry boarded the *Niagara* and cut the British line. (A T Mahan, *Sea Power in its Relation to the War of 1812*)

Oliver Hazard Perry (1785-1819) went to sea at fourteen years of age as a midshipman in his father's warship *General Greene*. He saw limited action in the war with Tripoli and held one independent command at sea, the schooner *Revenge*, before the War of 1812. (US Naval Academy Museum, 69.1.11)

Elliott's measurement of the *Detroit* (126ft on deck by 28ft by 12ft) produced disproportionate dimensions that may have been more concerned with submitting the largest possible tonnage to the prize court than with reporting fact. The 1836 *Detroit* enrolment mentions its lack of galleries and its scroll head while Barclay implies that Bell constructed the vessel to be as sturdy as possible; the commander described the *Detroit* as 'a fine Ship, but I fear with her shores (for she has one under every beam) she will sail heavily; but at all events fast enough to ensure a general action.'[19] One American observer wrote that the *Detroit* was 'a much finer vessel than either of ours, and built of the best materials; her quarters were grape proof – whereas ours would admit grape through both sides.'[20]

Perry's squadron blockaded the water route between Long Point and Amherstburg through August and in September, aggravating shortages in the British camp, especially the depletion of basic provisions. After discussing their dire situation, Barclay and Procter decided that, in spite of its incomplete state, the squadron would have to challenge Perry for control of the lake. The carronades and guns for the *Detroit* did not arrive at Amherstburg, so Barclay shifted ordnance

around his command and embarked ordnance from Fort Malden. Indicative of other short-comings was the fact that the *Queen Charlotte*'s sail lockers were emptied to provide canvas for the *Detroit*. On 9 September, just days after a reinforcement of 40 Royal Navy officers and men reached Amherstburg, Barclay left his Detroit River anchorage to seek Perry who was known to be at South Bass Island.

Barclay's total complement consisted of fewer than 60 Royal Navy personnel, about 110 Provincial Marine officers and men and more than 230 infantry from Procter's army. By way of comparison, about seventy per cent of Perry's crews were seamen, the rest being US Marines, infantry and volunteers. The American squadron significantly outgunned the British in weight of metal, but the battle, which commenced with a clear sky and light airs at noon on 10 September, was a closely run affair due to the fact that Perry's flagship, the *Lawrence*, was poorly supported by the rest of the line. For two hours, broadsides from the *Detroit* and *Queen Charlotte* hammered the *Lawrence*, inflicting heavy casualties, until Perry finally left his flagship to take command of the *Niagara*; Jesse Elliott, commanding the *Niagara*. would forever be under a cloud because of his inaction to that

The *Lawrence* is shown here (far right) shattered and drifting out of the action as the *Niagara* gets in among the British squadron with devastating effects. (National Maritime Museum, PAH8142)

point. In the British squadron, the commander and senior officers aboard each vessel except the *Little Belt* had been killed or wounded, and when Perry steered the *Niagara* to split the confused British line with its broadsides blazing, a surrender was quick in coming.[21]

All the British vessels fell into American hands and were towed or sailed to the Put-in-Bay anchorage at South Bass Island. Perry pressed the least damaged of the prizes into service within weeks when he transported Major General Harrison's army to a landing several miles below Amherstburg. General Procter was slow in deciding to evacuate the post and after a difficult retreat saw his army beaten by Harrison at the Battle of Moraviantown on 5 October.

Lt Robert Irvine of the Provincial Marine who served as second lieutenant on board HMS *Queen Charlotte* painted this watercolour of the principal warships of the Battle of Put-in-Bay at anchor at South Bass Island several days after the battle, providing what may be the most authoritative rendition of the (left to right) *Queen Charlotte, Niagara, Detroit* and *Lawrence*. (Royal Ontario Museum, 990.49.8)

and when a British force attacked and burned the village in December, the vessels were also set ablaze and destroyed.[22]

No further shipbuilding took place on or above Lake Erie through the rest of the war. The British discussed plans for building a new squadron at Long Point or on the southern shore of Georgian Bay, but nothing came of it before peace was signed in December 1814. Rumours of British intentions to open a shipyard in Georgian Bay reached American ears, however, and combined with a continuing commitment in Washington to recapture Mackinac, led to the development of a new campaign in the spring of 1814. Secretary Jones appointed Arthur Sinclair, who had left Sackets Harbor on sick leave late the previous autumn, commodore of the upper lakes squadron with orders to take control on Lake Huron, as well as supporting the army's planned invasion of the Niagara Peninsula.[23]

Sinclair arrived in Erie in April 1814 where he found the shipyard in a shambles and the squadron in a state of poor discipline and health.[24] After bringing order to the station, Sinclair set out for Lake Huron in June (rather than helping the army at Niagara) with the *Lawrence, Niagara, Scorpion, Tigress* and *Caledonia*, stopping at Detroit to embark nearly 1000 soldiers under Lieutenant Colonel George Croghan. The infantry soon came in handy because the larger vessels had to be hauled over the rapids and shallows at the head of the St Clair River before they could navigate Lake Huron.

Sinclair's campaign was a failure. Although he burned two British merchantmen and captured another, the joint attack on Mackinac was rebuffed and the exhausted military force was nearly lost during a stormy voyage back to Detroit. In addition, a small Royal Navy detachment under Lieutenant Miller Worsely, which had spent part of the summer supplying Mackinac in the merchantman *Nancy* (one of the merchantmen later destroyed by Sinclair) and examining locations for a future dockyard in Georgian Bay, captured the *Scorpion* and *Tigress* with help from several dozen regulars, native allies and fur traders. Worsely employed the schooners (respectively renamed *Surprise* and

The contest for control of Lake Erie having been decided, the issue of who held Mackinac and domination of the trade routes on the upper lakes was unresolved. Settling that matter had been one of the reasons for developing a naval squadron above Niagara Falls, but due to the lateness of the season and Perry's desire to leave Erie, no effort was made in 1813 to head for Lake Huron. Command at Erie passed to Master Commandant Elliott who secured the badly damaged *Detroit* and *Queen Charlotte* at Put-in-Bay and laid up most of the other vessels at Erie. Bad planning, however, led to the loss of four of the smaller warships. Sent with troops and supplies to Buffalo, the *Ariel, Trippe, Little Belt* and *Chippewa* were trapped there by winter weather

Confiance) for the rest of the season to supply Mackinac and then laid them up for the winter at the Nottawasaga River on the southern shore of Georgian Bay.

Upon returning to Erie, Sinclair learned that two of his other schooners, the *Ohio* and *Somers* had been captured in August off Fort Erie by another Royal Navy detachment under Commander Alexander Dobbs; the schooners (respectively renamed *Sauk* and *Huron*) were sailed down the Niagara River to an anchorage at Chippewa Creek, located about two miles above the falls. Sinclair sailed to Buffalo to support the army besieged at Fort Erie by the British and came close to losing more vessels. Beginning on 17 September, a gale rose out of the southwest and pounded the American vessels for several days as they attempted to escape the confines at the east end of Lake Erie. Sinclair, who had great difficulty in keeping the *Niagara* (in which he had raised his pendant) afloat and off the lee shore, attributed its suffering to:

The shallow construction of these vessels preventing their holding weight enough of such materials as we have for Ballast in their bottoms to counteract that of their Spars and guns and frequently lifting their rudders nearly above water; they lay broad off and lurch their whole topside under every Roll. The temporary manner in which they are built, without a knee in them, and the still more temporary manner in which they were repaired, by graving pieces, leaving their timbers unrenewed, made them leak more than out pumps could free.[25]

Late in November, Sinclair succeeded in getting the last of his warships over the bar at Erie, including the *Detroit* and *Queen Charlotte* which had been brought down from Put-in-Bay. He housed the vessels over for the winter and headed to Washington and his home in Virginia. The naval campaigns on the upper lakes were finished.

On 12 August 1814 a Royal Navy detachment under Commander Alexander Dobbs cut out from the Fort Erie anchorage the American schooners *Somers* and *Ohio* and sailed them to Chippewa Creek situated opposite Navy Island and behind British lines. (Toronto Reference Library, T15221)

Captain Arthur Sinclair (died 1831) served as Commodore Chauncey's flag captain on board the *General Pike* through the summer campaign on 1813. The following year he was appointed commodore of the Lake Erie squadron with orders to recapture Mackinac Island. (Naval Historical Center, NH44925)

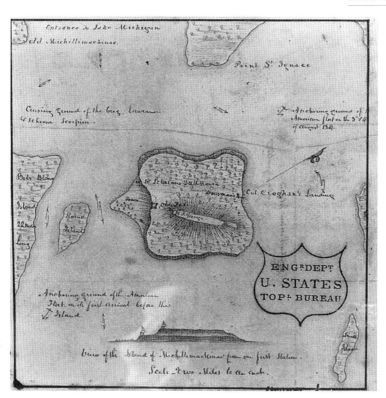

This map shows the location of the American landing on Mackinac Island in August 1814 as well as terrain of the island and the squadron's anchorages. (US National Archives)

'To look down all opposition'

LAKE ONTARIO, 1813 – 1814

THE EVENTS OF 1813 on Lake Ontario showed Commodores Yeo and Chauncey that firepower and manoeuvrability were crucial elements in their drive to gain supremacy over their theatre of operations. The battle between Perry and Barclay on Lake Erie also served to motivate them to seek the same kind of resolution to their contest. As a result, both officers oversaw ambitious building programmes in their dockyards beginning in the autumn of 1813 and continuing through the winter. Their mutual objective was to launch heavily armed frigates as soon as possible in the spring of 1814 and seize control of the lake. As the months passed, even frigates seemed inadequate and a First Rate was conceived to settle the question.

British discussion regarding vessels that would be larger than the *Royal George* and *Wolfe* were initiated prior to the launch of the *General Pike* in June 1813. Soon after arriving at Kingston during the first week of May, Commander Robert Barclay recommended building a ship to replace the *Sir Isaac Brock*, 30, which had been burned on the stocks at York in April. After the attack on Sackets Harbor at the end of May, during which he viewed the *General Pike* under construction, Yeo advised Governor-in-Chief Prevost to contract a master builder and workmen at Quebec to come to Kingston and construct a comparable vessel, 136ft on the deck, 129ft by 36ft by 13ft 3in. When news reached Yeo in July that master builder Henry Eckford was putting together what was thought to be a large brig (the schooner *Sylph*), the commodore called for another ship, one with a 160ft deck, 148ft by 42ft by 13ft.[1] After his encounters with Commodore Chauncey and his powerful flagship during August and September, Yeo, along with Prevost and their senior officers, agreed that control of Lake Ontario could only be won with ships that could outgun the heavily armed *Pike*.

The dockyard on Point Frederick at Kingston

had been a busy place during the summer of 1813. Commander Richard O'Conor, RN, who had volunteered to accompany Yeo to Canada, was appointed commissioner of the dockyard instead of being given a command afloat and was charged with the job of reorganising the yard to conform as nearly as possible with Admiralty standards. This proved to be an irksome task for O'Conor, but he managed to superintend successfully the completion of the brig *Lord Melville* and a number of large gunboats, and to erect storehouses, shops and barracks in the dockyard.

O'Conor's correspondence during the summer did not allude to the laying down of keels for new warships, although there is some evidence that the building of a large frigate commenced at Kingston in August 1813. In a memorial addressed to British officials after the war, a master builder from Quebec named John Goudie claimed to have been persuaded by Prevost to hire 100 shipwrights and proceed to Kingston in June, as per Yeo's initial suggestion. Goudie and his men spent most of July refitting the squadron and preparing the brig *Lord Melville* for service. After Yeo sailed on 31 July, Goudie wrote, he laid the keel for the large vessel that Yeo had proposed earlier in the month and which later became known as the frigate *Prince Regent*, 58. There were inadequate resources at Point Frederick to proceed very far on the hull, so Goudie left his shipwrights there in charge of his foreman, Patrick Fleming, and returned to Quebec; although he arranged for more artificers to travel up to Kingston, it appears that Goudie did not go back there in 1813.[2]

Commander O'Conor's correspondence revealed a ship, the *Prince Regent,* on the stocks early in October with its stem and stern up and a few floors across, the work being done by Goudie's men under Fleming. George Record, the master builder in the yard, had started another vessel by that time, also. Originally intended to be a transport brig, he modified the plans with Yeo and O'Conor's approval, to turn it into a frigate measuring 110ft by 36ft by 10ft. Named the *Vittoria* while comprising little more than a keel, this ship was eventually launched as the *Princess Charlotte*, 40.

By December the two frigates at Kingston

TABLE 31

The British squadron on Lake Ontario, spring 1814

Vessel	Total Guns	Carronades				Long Guns			
		68s	32s	24s	18s	24s	18s	9s	
Prince Regent	58	8	20			30			
Princess Charlotte	40		16			24			
Montreal	21		18				2	1*	ex-*Wolfe*
Niagara (B)	21		18			1*	2		ex-*Royal George*
Star	14		12				2		ex-*Lord Melville*
Charwell (A)	13			12				1*	ex-*Earl of Moira*
Netley	9				8	1*			ex-*Lord Beresford*
Magnet	11		10					1*	ex-*Sir Sidney Smith*
Totals	187		122			65			

* pivot gun.
Source: NAC, MG 12, ADM 1/ 2737, p78.

TABLE 32

The America squadron on Lake Ontario, summer 1814

Vessel	Total Guns	Carronades			Long Guns				
		42s	32s	24s	32s	24s	18s	12s	9s
Superior	58	26			30	2			
Mohawk	42		16			26			
General Pike	26		0			24	2*		
Madison	23			8			14	1*	
Jefferson	20	16				4			
Jones	20	18				2			
Sylph	18			16					2
Oneida	14	0						14	
Lady of the Lake	1	0							1*
Totals	222	100			122				

* pivot gun.
Source: 15 July 1814, Chauncey Letter Book; Crisman, *The* Jefferson.

TABLE 33

Particulars of the British gunboats on Lake Ontario and Upper St Lawrence River, 1814

No	Name	Rig	Dimensions	Carronades	Long Guns	No. of Sweeps	Where Built	Station in January 1814
1	*Nelson*	schooner	60ft × 13ft 6in	1-32	1-24	36	Pt Fred	C du Lac
2	*Quebec*	lugger	44ft × 8ft 3in	1-32		26	Quebec	C du Lac
3	*Kingston* (A)	lugger	60ft 9in × 13ft 6in	1-24		24	Pt Fred	C du Lac
4	*Glengarry*	sloop	48ft × 8ft 7in	1-24		24	Quebec	C du Lac
5	*Thunder*	lugger	40ft × 8ft		1-6	22	USA	C du Lac
6	*Retaliation*	sloop	44ft × 8ft 3in		1-6	24	USA	Prescott
7	*Brock* (A)	sloop	58ft × 8ft 2in		1-6	22	USA	C du Lac
8	*Black Snake*	lugger	44ft × 8ft 6in		1-6	22	USA	C du Lac
9	*York* (B)	sloop	36ft × 8ft	1-12		22	USA	C du Lac
10	*Cornwall*	sloop	58ft × 8ft 2in	1-12		24	USA	C du Lac
11	*Crysler*	Lugger	48ft × 12ft		1-24	30	Pt Fred	Pt. Fred
12	*Queenston*	lugger	48ft × 12ft		1-24	30	Pt Fred	Pt Fred
13	*Niagara* (C)	lugger	60ft × 14ft	1-32	1-24	36	Pt Fred	Pt Fred
14	*Buffalo*	lugger	58ft × 16ft	1-32	1-24	36	Pt Fred	Pt Fred
15-20	six gunboats	lugger	55ft × 12ft		1-24	36	C du Lac	C du Lac

Source: 26 Jan 1814, NAC, MG 11, CO 42/160, p320; April 1814, NAC, MG 12, ADM 1/ 2737, p78. *Ibid*, ADM 51/4096; *ibid*, ADM 106/1998. This table shows gunboats on station, under repair or construction during the winter of 1814. Details about vessels built in the United States are lacking; they were either small merchantmen captured by Yeo during the spring 1813 or part of General Wilkinson's flotilla in the autumn of 1813. The names of the *Crysler*, *Queenston* and *Niagara* were likely changed to *Nelly*, *Lais* and *Cleopatra*. Names of gunboats mentioned later in the year include *Muros*, *Helena*, *Sydney*, *Gananoque*, *Spitfire*, *Tecumseh*, *Prescott*, *Dreadnought*, *General Robinson* and *General Kempt*. Some of the Lake Champlain gunboats ended up on the St Lawrence in the autumn of 1814.

stood with their upper timbers nearly complete, their planking started and the sawmill going full tilt. Progress had been slow because of labour problems between Goudie's privately hired workers and the men on the public payroll under Record. William Bell, the master builder from Amherstburg who had fled with General Procter's army after the American invasion, reached Kingston about this time, and O'Conor hoped to settle the labour strife by putting him in charge of both projects. He changed his mind, however, and kept Bell for other work, hoping to avoid worsening the already tense situation and choosing instead to make a contract like Goudie's with Record who then resigned as master builder to complete the job privately. This decision seemed to solve problems in the dockyard and by January 1814 the new ships were nearly complete. O'Conor predicted: 'The *Prince Regent* promises to be as fine and formidable a Frigate as any Sailing on the Atlantic. The *Princess Charlotte* (late *Vittoria*) has every appearance of being a most desirable vessel in size equal to our small Frigates, but in force superior from the heavy metal she is intended to carry.'[3]

The design of the *Prince Regent* was attributed to Patrick Fleming, although his plans have not come to light and it seems likely that, being Goudie's foreman, Fleming worked from a draught made by his employer. The ship's 'as built' draught depicts a vessel very similar in form to the two '50-gun' frigates ordered by the Admiralty in April 1813 and launched at the Wigram yard in England the following November. These were the *Leander* and *Newcastle*, built to carry thirty 24pdr long guns below and twenty-eight 42pdr carronades, plus a pair of long 24s, above. They were bigger than the *Prince Regent*; the *Newcastle* measured 177ft on the deck, 150ft 2¼in by 44ft 4½in by 14ft 11in, for a burthen of 1572 tons, while the *Prince Regent* was 155ft 10in on the deck, 131ft 1in by 43ft by 9ft 2in, for 1293 tons. The *Prince Regent* lacked the deep hull of the ocean fighters and had a sharp midships deadrise (about 20 degrees), but it possessed the same type of spar deck, straight sheer and reduced tumblehome of the *Leander* and *Newcastle*. Whether Fleming's design was influenced by the latest reports from the Admiralty is uncertain, but the three ships clearly reflected the influence that the heavy American frigates (the US Ships *Constitution*, *President* and *United States*) were having on ship design. They were all built to function as speedy gun platforms, the *Prince Regent* being outfitted originally with thirty 24pdr long guns, twenty 32pdr carronades and eight 68pdr carronades.[4]

Admiralty documents attribute the design of the *Princess Charlotte* to George Record, although an extant draught in the National Archives of Canada bears the name of the ship and was signed by John Goudie in 1813. Goudie's *Princess Charlotte* is very similar in overall appearance to typical Admiralty Fifth Rates of an earlier age (roughly the 1760s), and comparable in size to the *Princess Charlotte* as completed, listed as 121ft on the deck, 100ft 0½in by 37ft 8in by 8ft 8½in with a burthen of 755 tons. Goudie's plan, however, depicts a vessel with a deep hull and little deadrise while the 'as built' draught of the *Princess Charlotte* reveals a shallow hull with a very sharp midships deadrise (about 30 degrees) that would fit the conditions of Lake Ontario. Therefore Record's ship has nothing to do with Goudie's draught, the relevance of which to the eventual *Princess Charlotte* is unclear. As completed the frigate was armed with twenty-four 24pdr long

guns and sixteen 32pdr carronades.[5]

Recent archaeological investigations reveal that the remains of the *Prince Regent* and *Princess Charlotte* are probably the wrecks lying in Deadman Bay, adjacent to Navy Bay at Kingston; the dimensions of the submerged structures closely match the records of the frigates as does the deadrise of the remaining frame components. A limited number of samples taken from the timbers show that oak was the prevalent wood of choice, which appears to have been fastened throughout with iron spikes, nails and bolts. On the wreck believed to be the *Princess Charlotte* the floors each consist of a short gusset, or cross chock, sitting across the rising deadwood to which a half floor is scarphed and bolted on each side. Alternating with the floors are the two first futtocks which also meet at the midpoint of the keel. On the other wreck (*Prince Regent*) more conventional floors are formed, each from two timbers crossing the keel and alternating with pairs of first futtocks meeting on the rising deadwood. Along both keels there is no evidence of limber holes. The masts of the *Prince Regent* were stepped into spaces in the rider keelson with longitudinal members bolted into the keel and keelson providing lateral support, while the *Princess Charlotte* had conventional mast steps straddling the keelson, formed from large blocks of shaped wood.[6]

Fitting out the new frigates at Kingston required the import of equipment from Quebec and Halifax. HM Ships *Æolus* and *Indian* which had arrived at Quebec in the autumn were stripped of their sails, rigging, guns, ironwork and ballast to the extent that the captain of the *Indian* feared his sloop would capsize for want of ballast. He had hoped to fill casks with water to make up the deficit, but his cooper had been sent to Kingston; two local coopers were sent to his aid.[7] Royal Navy detachments, numbering nearly 500 officers and men, had reinforced Yeo's original establishment by the end of 1813, and another 210 were marching overland from Saint John, New Brunswick. Their arrival, along with a battalion of Royal Marines, would make it possible for Yeo to man a greatly enhanced fighting force by the time the ice broke up in the spring.

The British built three gunboats at Point Frederick during the early months of 1814, named

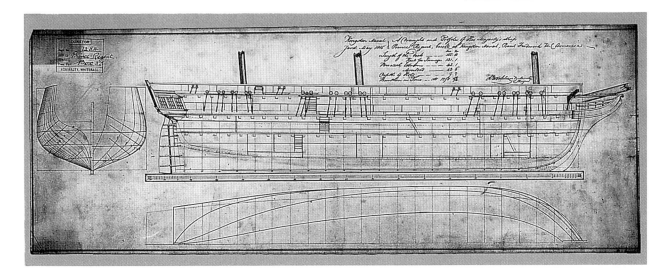

At its launch, the frigate *Prince Regent* was the largest ship ever built on the Great Lakes. Though shallower in draught than its seagoing cousins, its 58 guns provided significant firepower. (National Maritime Museum, neg DR1284)

originally the *Crysler*, *Queenston* and *Niagara*, and later the *Nelly*, *Lais* and *Cleopatra*. All of them were rigged as luggers, with the largest measuring 60ft long and 14ft wide, pulling 36 oars and armed with one 24pdr long gun and one 32pdr carronade, and the other two measuring 48ft by 12ft for 30 oars and a single long 24pdr. Six other un-named gunboats were built in 1814 at Coteau du Lac, twenty miles southwest of Montreal, measuring 55ft by 12ft, pulling 36 oars and armed with a single long 24pdr each. Another half dozen, identical gunboats (60ft by 14 ft, 36 oars, one long 18pdr, one 32pdr carronade) were reported to be in service on the St Lawrence River escorting flotillas of batteaux up from Montreal which was the primary employment of the British gunboats in 1814.[8]

The Americans had been much slower out of the gate in the race between the dockyards. Secretary of the Navy William Jones informed Commodore Chauncey in September 1813 that he had discussed with Adam and Noah Brown the idea of building three sloops at Sackets Harbor identical to the 22-gun *Peacock* they had just finished for the government at New York. Chauncey replied that he admired the Browns but favoured Henry Eckford and his proven record of being able to build good ships quickly. The commodore also informed Jones that he had reliable information about the British building a large frigate and two brigs at Kingston, but this ominous news did not prompt the Americans to take urgent steps to counter the British escalation of the naval

---

TABLE 34

HMS *Prince Regent* (1814), *Kingston* (1816) – legend of particulars

Launched: 14 April 1814, Kingston
Original draught by: Patrick Fleming, John Goudie
Admiralty 'as built' draught by: Thomas Strickland
Builder: Patrick Fleming

HULL DIMENSIONS 1815

Gun deck	155ft 10in
Keel/tonnage	131ft 1in
Depth of hold	9ft 2in
Tons	1293 50/94
Draught loaded	16ft forward
	17ft aft
Number of ports	56
upper deck	28
Dimensions of ports	
height	2ft 10in
width	3ft 0in
between	8ft 2in
above deck	2ft

SPAR DIMENSIONS 1815

Mast	Length	Diameter	Yard Length	Yard Dia.
Fore	91ft 5in	30½in	60ft	18⅞in
Topmast	54ft 11in	8½in	57ft 2in	11⅞in
Topgallant	31ft	9in	40ft 3in	8in
Main	103ft	34in	91ft 6in	19in
Topmast	61ft 10in	20½in	65ft 6in	13¾in
Topgallant	34ft	10in	44ft 6in	9½in
Mizzen	65ft 10in	22½in	57ft 11in	11in
Topmast	46ft 4in	14¼in	40ft 7in	9¾in
Topgallant	24ft	7½in	29ft	5¾in
Bowsprit	61ft 10in	33in	57ft	11in
Jibboom	46ft 11in	13in	36ft 2in	6⅝in
Driver boom	65ft 6in	11⅞in	—	—
Gaff	46ft	10in	—	—

ORDNANCE

Date	Carronades	Long Guns
1814	4-68s	28-24s
	24-32s	

Source: NAC, MG 12, ADM 106/1997, 1998.

war. It was not until the second week of January 1814, the delay having been caused by concerns over cost and the indecisiveness of President Madison's cabinet, that Eckford's shipwrights went back to work at Sackets Harbor.[9]

In line with Jones's suggestion, Eckford undertook to build a pair of brigs similar to the *Peacock*. This vessel was one of six ship-sloops, authorised by the US Congress early in 1813 and designed by William Doughty, the chief constructor at the Washington Navy Yard. It measured 117ft 11in (between perpendiculars) by 31ft 6in by 14ft 6in and carried two 12pdr long guns and twenty 32pdr carronades on its upper deck. With a steep midships deadrise (about 22 degrees), but a low drag (there was only a 1ft 9in difference in depth of water between the bow and the stern), the *Peacock* was reputed to be a fast ship.

Not surprisingly Eckford's plan for his version of the *Peacock* did not survive, but an extensive archaeological survey of one of the pair of brigs

that Eckford built at Sackets in the winter of 1814 has yielded some interesting revelations. The vessel, named the *Jefferson* (its twin was the *Jones*) measured 122ft 11in between perpendiculars, 108ft 9in by 33ft 2in by 10ft 5in.[10] Under normal conditions, it probably drew about 8ft 9in of water forward and 12ft 9in abaft. It had a very steep midships deadrise (about 25 degrees) and was sharp at both ends, making it a very swift vessel. Oak, mixed with some maple and elm, was the prime material used for the main structural members, with pine or spruce used for less critical components and for upperworks, probably to reduce weight. The keel was made of three pieces of oak, the forward half being composed of a main timber and a shoe that was added to create the dimensions of the latter half which came from a single tree. The keel was sided 11½in and moulded 1ft 11in. The frames were composed of a floor, two first futtocks, two second futtocks and two top timbers and were assembled along

Secretary of the Navy William Jones recommended to Commodore Chauncey that the *Peacock* class of sloops was proving to be very successful and might suit the rigours of Lake Ontario. The brigs built by Henry Eckford in 1814 were clearly influenced by these ships. (Smithsonian Institution)

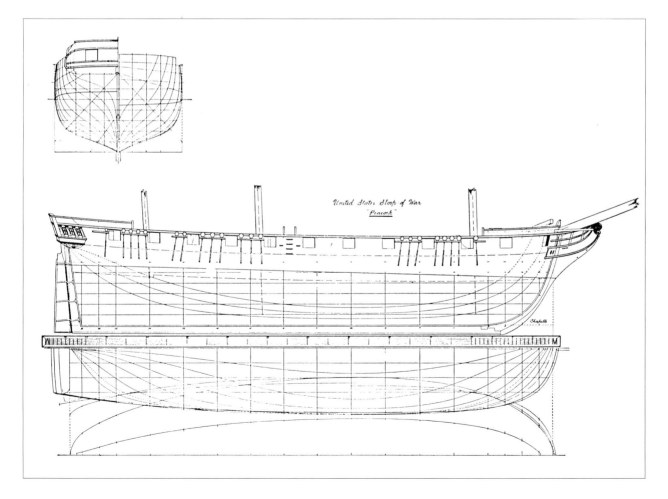

None of Henry Eckford's draughts for his Lake Ontario vessels have come to light, but this rare view of Sackets Harbor, painted by a British officer in September 1815, provides some insight into the appearance of the brig *Jones*. Only four of its 42pdr carronades are in the larboard battery and the topgallant masts have been struck down. (Courtesy of the Royal Military College, Kingston, Ontario)

conventional lines. A typical floor was 9in to 9½in sided and was moulded 13½in between keel and keelson, 16in at the rabbet and 9½in at the head. The first futtocks met over the centreline of the keel and were typically sided 7⅛in and moulded 16in at the rabbet and 7½ by 8½in at the head and were bolted laterally to the floor. All the fastenings appear to have been of iron, but the fine workmanship seen in the fitting of joints and scarphs indicates that time was taken to make things right. On the other hand, Eckford appears to have expedited construction by not installing knees. The weight of heavy ordnance on the upper deck required reinforcement, however, a problem Eckford solved by installing ten or eleven riders along each side of the hull, four ahead of the midframe angling forward and the rest angling aft. They varied in dimension from seven to ten inches square, were fastened by bolts to the ceilings and frames and extended from the keelson to the deck clamp. Besides supporting the gundeck, the riders added stiffness to the hull.

Like the ship-corvettes on the lake (*Royal George, Madison, Wolfe*), accommodations in the brigs (each had a complement of 160) were cramped and uncomfortable, but they were more powerful than the ships in terms of metal. Each

vessel was meant to carry eighteen 42pdr carronades, two 24pdr long guns and a pivoting 18pdr long gun on a topgallant forecastle. Brief trials conducted in June and July prompted the commanders of both brigs to alter the original arrangements, however. Master Commandant Charles Ridgely removed the *Jefferson*'s pivot gun and two of the carronades, replacing them with an additional pair of long 24s. In the *Jones*, Master Commandant Melancthon Woolsey also landed the pivot gun, but left the rest of his batteries intact. Both captains had the main mast re-stepped three feet further aft, which along with the ordnance changes, suggests that the brigs tended to plunge in a rising sea as their ponderous ordnance and heavy top hamper pressed down on their narrow bows. The vessels were meant to replace Chauncey's inadequate schooner-gunboats by carrying an impressive weight of metal and being able to hold their places in a line of battle. They were certainly capable of performing that task, but they demanded careful handling. The *Jefferson*'s crew learned that lesson at first hand in September 1814 when the same gale that nearly upset Commodore Sinclair's *Niagara* on Lake Erie managed to knock the *Jefferson* on its side twice in the western reaches of Lake

In 1814 Sackets Harbor became the most active naval station in the United States, with warships crowding its basin and more rising on the stocks. (US Naval Historical Center, NH001695)

Ontario. The pounding of the waves and movement of the brig opened the waterways on the forecastle, causing dangerous leaks. The brig drifted to leeward at a rate of nearly three knots and, with the British shore creeping closer, Ridgely jettisoned ten of his carronades. This eased the suffering of the *Jefferson* and it survived to limp back to Sackets Harbor.

At the same time that he undertook the work on the *Jefferson* and *Jones*, Eckford also began building a large frigate, destined to become the USS *Superior*, 58. Information about its partic-

ulars are virtually non-existent except for a reference Secretary Jones made to Eckford's plan to construct 'a Frigate 175 feet between perpendiculars and 40 feet abeam'.[11] The weight of metal it carried (thirty 32pdr long guns below and twenty-six 42pdr carronades, plus a pair of long 24s, above) also indicate that it was more heavily armed than HMS *Prince Regent*; Chauncey had acquired accurate information about the dimensions and nature of the British frigate before the *Superior* was designed. Two contemporary sketches also show the ship had the *Prince Regent*'s

TABLE 35
British vessels launched on Lake Ontario, 1814

Name	Launch	Place	Rig	Remarks
Prince Regent (B), 58	April 1814	Kingston	ship	1816 renamed *Kingston* (B); 1817 in ordinary; 1830s sank in Deadman Bay
Vittoria/ Princess Charlotte, 40	April 1814	Kingston	ship	1816 renamed *Burlington*; 1817 in ordinary; 1830s sank in Deadman Bay
three gunboats	April 1814	Kingston	lugger	
St Lawrence, 104	September 1814	Kingston	ship	1817 in ordinary; 1832 sold for use as a wharf
Psyche, 56	December 1814	Kingston	ship	1817 in ordinary, 1820s rebuilt; 1830s sold, broken up

TABLE 36
American vessels launched on Lake Ontario, 1814

Name	Launch	Place	Rig	Remarks
Jefferson	April 1814	Sackets Harbor	brig	1815 in ordinary; 1825 sold, sunk at Sackets Harbor
Jones	April 1814	Sackets Harbor	brig	1815 in ordinary, 1825 sold, broken up
Superior	May 1814	Sackets Harbor	ship	1815 in ordinary, 1825 sold, broken up
Mohawk (E)	June 1814	Sackets Harbor	ship	1815 in ordinary, 1825 sold, broken up
fifteen galleys	summer 1814	Sackets Harbor	lugger	

18

HMS Prince Regent
Captn June
Lake Ontario

Captain Henry Davies, RN, arrived at Kingston in June 1814 as part of the 900-man detachment sent to crew the frigates and brigs in frame. He was appointed Yeo's flag captain aboard the *Prince Regent* and painted this watercolour of his ship at anchor. (National Archives of Canada, C138986)

straight sheer and flush upper deck.

The *Jefferson* and *Jones* were launched on 7 April and 13 April respectively, with the *Superior* splashing into the basin at Sackets on 1 May. A week after the frigate cleared its slipway, Eckford laid down yet another keel, this one for a second frigate, the *Mohawk*, 42, that Chauncey later described as being 'something bigger than the *New York*'.[12] The latter frigate, launched at New York in 1800, measured 144ft 2in (between perpendiculars) by 37ft by 11ft 9in with a burthen of 1130 tons, the dimensions of which are the closest available description of the *Mohawk*. Launched on 11 June, just thirty-four days after the work had started, the *Mohawk* was armed with twenty-six 24pdr long guns and sixteen 32pdr carronades.

While the *Mohawk* was being fitted out, Eckford's shipwrights went to work to fill an order that had come directly from President Madison's cabinet. When the Americans finally formed their campaign objectives for 1814, they included the construction of fifteen gunboats at Sackets Harbor that Chauncey could use, with support from the army, to harass British supply lines on the St Lawrence. Little was recorded about these vessels, which were built at Sackets but never employed against the British. They were most likely based on the galley/barge design developed by William Doughty that measured 75ft by 15ft by 4ft and were rigged as luggers with a long gun in the bow and carronade in the stern.[13]

Despite the hectic activity at Sackets, the British won the race to control Lake Ontario in the spring of 1814. At Kingston the *Prince Regent* and *Princess Charlotte* were both launched on 14 April and ready for service by the end of the month. Beginning on 1 May, Commodore Yeo reorganised his command in accordance with instructions received from the Admiralty.[14] Originally the Lake Ontario squadron had functioned as a single establishment with co-operative ties to the military at Kingston and the civil department on Point Frederick. In January 1814, however, the Admiralty decided to put its Great Lakes detachment on a regular naval footing by creating an establishment for each ship and dockyard, by staffing the dockyard with Navy Board officials and by making Yeo Commander-in-Chief of His Majesty's Ships and Vessels on the Lakes of Canada. Among the many changes resulting from this decision was the renaming of the vessels in the 1813 squadron so that they could be entered properly onto the Navy List.

Yeo and the commander of military forces in Upper Canada, Lieutenant General Gordon Drummond, wanted to execute a full scale attack on Sackets Harbor in May, but Prevost opposed such ambitious plans. The two officers had to settle for a joint operation against Oswego on 5-6 May during which they confiscated a handful of guns, some rigging and up to 2000 barrels of provisions at the cost of heavy casualties.[15]

The raid on Oswego managed to interrupt Chauncey's supply line from New York briefly. Due to the industrious programme at Sackets, the train of ordnance, rigging, fittings, provisions and men boating up the Mohawk River had grown to an unprecedented extent. The late decision to build ships, the hassles of procurement and the miserable winter with its early thaw had turned the proceedings into a nightmare for Chauncey. At one point he protested: 'Figure to yourselves my situation and then judge whether I have not cause for anxiety and almost for mental derangement.'[16] Yeo's uncontested presence on the lake worsened Chauncey's situation, especially after the British squadron anchored within sight of Sackets at mid-May, effectively blockading the port. Chauncey redirected a larger portion of the supplies to be hauled overland from the Mohawk and waited for a good opportunity to run the heavy ordnance he needed down the shore from

The raid against Oswego on 5-6 May 1814 resulted in several detailed portraits of Commodore Yeo's squadron in action drawn by Captain William Steele of the Royal Marines. In this view, showing the approach to the American base, the ships are (left to right) the *Star*, *Charwell*, *Niagara*, *Montreal*, *Magnet*, *Princess Charlotte* and *Prince Regent*. The figure holding the telescope in the boat in the foreground may very likely be Commodore Yeo; the only contemporary illustration of him in action. (National Maritime Museum, PAG9085)

Oswego. When Master Commandant Woolsey left Oswego in a flotilla of batteaux on 28 May, Captain Stephen Popham of HMS *Montreal* (formerly the *Royal George*) imprudently attempted to capture the load of guns and cables and ran into an ambush at Sandy Creek which led to the loss to Yeo of 220 men killed and captured, as well as two of the gunboats (possibly the *Lais* and

Nelly) recently launched at Kingston.

Short-handed after Popham's defeat at Sandy Creek, Yeo raised his blockade of Sackets. He made one trip to Niagara to supply the British army situated there and then retired to the anchorage at Kingston for the rest of the summer, having detached his four smallest vessels to Niagara to support the army. In June the first of nearly 900 Royal Navy officers and men sent from England arrived at Kingston and filled the vacancies in Yeo's squadron, but he did not sail again to challenge Chauncey, convinced as he was that the new American warships would outgun his force. To play it safe, Yeo decided to wait until a new and formidable ship, HMS *St Lawrence*, rising in the stocks on Point Frederick, was ready for action.

The interruption to his supply line in May delayed Chauncey's preparations, although he informed Secretary Jones and Major General Jacob Brown who was preparing to invade Upper Canada at Niagara that the squadron would sail around 1 July. That date came and went as the last of the necessary equipment reached Sackets following which Chauncey fell ill for two weeks. Consequentially, the squadron did not depart until 1 August, by which time the commodore was being openly criticised by General Brown, who had expected naval assistance; Brown's drive into Upper Canada stopped after the Battle of Lundy's Lane on 25 July, leading to a British siege of Fort Erie that lasted into the autumn. Chauncey deflected the criticism aimed at him, stating that his main goal was to engage Yeo and gain supremacy on the lake. The closest he came to realising that objective was to provoke the destruction of the schooner *Magnet* (formerly, the *Governor Simcoe*/*Sir Sidney Smith*). This occurred on 5 August ten miles west of the mouth of the Niagara River when the commander of the *Magnet*, returning with munitions from York, drove his schooner ashore and blew it up to avoid being captured by Chauncey's squadron. Delegating some of his smaller vessels to blockade the Niagara River, Chauncey set a course for Kingston where he offered battle to his adversary to no avail. Cruising off the Kingston Channel, the Americans had to be content to watch the activity on Point Frederick as the gangs of shipwrights hur-

Thomas Strickland prepared this draught of the *Princess Charlotte* 'as built' in 1815. It reveals that George Record, master builder of the frigate, could not have used John Goudie's plan. Record's ship is clearly of a later generation, with flat sheer, a much sharper hull and fully berthed-up bulwarks on its quarterdeck and forecastle. (National Maritime Museum, neg DR6013)

TABLE 37

HMS *Vittoria* (1813), *Princess Charlotte* (1814), *Burlington* (1816) – legend of particulars

Launched: 14 April 1814, Kingston
Original draught by: George Record, John Goudie
Admiralty 'as built' draught by: Thomas Strickland
Builder: George Record

HULL DIMENSIONS 1815

Gun deck	121ft
Keel/tonnage	100ft 0½in
Breadth extreme	37ft 8in
Depth of hold	8ft 8½in
Tons	755 90/94
Draught loaded	14ft 4in forward 16ft 4in aft
Number of ports	42
gun deck	24
upper deck	18
Dimensions of ports	
height	2ft 10in
width	3ft 0in
between	7ft
above deck	2ft 2in

SPAR DIMENSIONS 1815

Mast	Length	Diameter	Yard Length	Yard Dia.
Fore	75ft 8in	22in	60ft 10in	15in
Topmast	45ft 8in	15¼in	45ft 5in	10in
Topgallant	24ft 3in	8in	33ft	6½in
Main	85ft	24¾in	74ft 4in	17⅞in
Topmast	51ft	15¾in	55ft	11⅜in
Topgallant	27ft 7in	9¾in	37ft 1in	7⅜in
Mizzen	62ft 8in	16¼in	55ft	10in
Topmast	38ft 3in	10⅜in	36ft 9in	6⅞in
Topgallant	28ft 8in	6⅞in	29ft 8in	5½in
Bowsprit	56ft 8in	25in	45ft 5in	11in
Jibboom	39ft	11in	33ft	6½in
Driver boom	55ft	10½in	—	—
Gaff	38ft 10in	9in	—	—

ORDNANCE

Date	Carronades		Long Guns
1814	2-68s	16-32s	24-24s

Source: NAC, MG 12, ADM 106/1997, 1998.

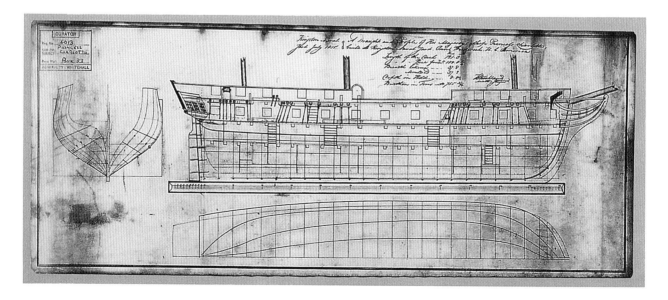

The assault having succeeded at Oswego, 6 May 1814, the *Star* and *Charwell* carry the reserve to shore while the *Montreal*, *Magnet* and *Niagara* venture into Oswego Bay. Note the soldier at the top of the flagpole about to strike the Stars and Stripes. (National Maritime Museum, neg A3915)

ried to put the finishing touches on the largest sailing warship to ever navigate the Great Lakes.[17]

The scheme to build the First Rate *St Lawrence* on Lake Ontario developed during early February 1814, when news reached Kingston that the Americans were building three ships at Sackets Harbor. In response to strategic discussions that took place thereafter, Commander O'Conor suggested that the Kingston yard could produce a small frigate in addition to the *Prince Regent* and *Princess Charlotte* by the spring. No final decision appears to have been made in this regard until March when the plans formed to build a vessel with the same straight sheer and sharp deadrise of the two frigates, but of much larger proportions. William Bell draughted the vessel with these dimensions: 198ft (gundeck), 170ft by 52ft 7in by 13ft 6in. By 12 April the keel was laid, its stem and stern up, the moulds were ready and the frames were being cut out and assembled, but the final strength of the ship had yet to be decided. During this period it seemed likely that an

armistice might be negotiated, in which case Yeo intended to make the new ship a two-decker. When peace talks failed, however, the British committed to building a First Rate of 102 guns, originally expecting it be armed with thirty-two guns on the lower deck, thirty-four on the middle deck and thirty-six on the upper deck. Commodore Yeo informed Prevost, 'the third ship now building is, I believe, of far great force than any the enemy can launch at Sackett's Harbor ... [and is] of a description to look down all opposition.'[18]

The extant 'as built' draughts of the *St Lawrence* include its lines, profile and a cross section plus views of its orlop, lower, middle and upper decks, which comprise the most extensive graphic record of any of the sailing warships built on the Great Lakes. They reveal how William Bell utilised the resources available to build a First Rate that could sail in the shallow confines of Lake Ontario.

The system that Bell employed to construct the frames of the *St Lawrence*, as revealed in the cross section and confirmed by a recent archaeo-

111

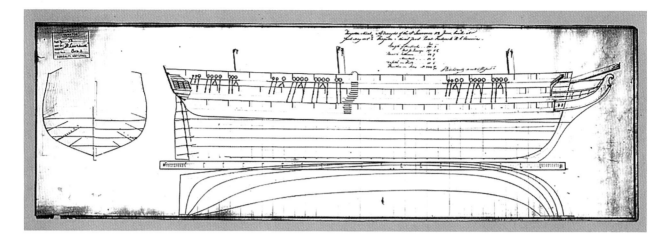

logical investigation, differed from conventional methods. To begin each frame, Bell joined a pair of half floors in a diamond-shaped scarph on the rising deadwood, fastening them together and to the keel by bolts. The scarphed floors were backed by, and fastened to, the first futtocks which also had a diamond scarph after which customary futtock assembly was employed. The keelson overlaid the lower structure, which was further stabilised by eleven riders spaced along the length of the keel. Bell's method of construction was not universally praised. Commodore Chauncey saw a glimpse of hope in a packet of captured British correspondence wherein was found a letter by a Kingston shipwright who expressed the commonly held apprehension that the ship would break its back upon launch because it had been so 'slightly built'.[19]

Apprehensions about the sturdiness of the ship might have also arisen because the *St Lawrence* appears to have been built with very few knees. Advertisements appeared in the *Kingston Gazette* through the summer announcing the navy's need for knees of oak, elm or spruce, sided to 10in, 6ft long with an arm of 3 or 4ft, but the draughts of the *St Lawrence* show sixty lodging knees installed on the orlop deck alone.[20] No hanging knees appear on the cross section, which shows all the beams mortised and tenoned to the frames and resting on clamps, one strake in size for each of the upper and middle decks and three strakes for the lower gun deck. The latter deck was also supported by a large shelf that was bolted to the frames and to the waterway. The orlop deck had a one-strake clamp and a wedge-shaped shelf.

TABLE 38			
HMS *St Lawrence* (1814) – legend of particulars			

Launched: 10 September 1814, Kingston
Original draught by: William Bell
Admiralty 'as built' draught by: Thomas Strickland
Builders: William Bell, Thomas Strickland

HULL DIMENSIONS 1815

Gun deck	191ft 2in
Keel/tonnage	157ft 8⅝in
Breadth extreme	52ft 6in
Depth of hold	18ft 6in
Tons	2304 90/94
Draught loaded	19ft forward
	20ft aft
Number of ports	102
lower deck	34
middle deck	34
upper deck	34
Dimensions of ports	
height	3ft
width	3ft
between	8ft
above deck	2ft 6in

SPAR DIMENSIONS 1815

Mast	Length	Diameter	Yard Length	Yard Dia.
Fore	108ft	36in	94ft	22½in
Topmast	65ft 6in	20¼in	67ft 6in	14in
Topgallant	30ft	11in	48ft 8in	10in
Main	118ft	40in	108ft	23¼in
Topmast	70ft	21¼in	77ft 6in	16in
Topgallant	33ft	11½in	54ft 11in	11¾in
Mizzen	83ft 6in	25½in	—	—
Crossjack	—	—	67ft	13in
Topmast	49ft	13½in	50ft 7in	10in
Topgallant	25ft 9in	5in	33ft 7in	7in
Bowsprit	73ft 6in	37in	67ft	13in
Jibboom	54ft 9in	15½in	—	—
Driver boom	77ft 6in	14in	—	—
Gaff	52ft 8in	11in	—	—

ORDNANCE

Date	Carronades	Long Guns
1814	2-68s	34-24s
	34-32s	34-32s

Source: NAC, MG 12, ADM 106/1997, 1998.

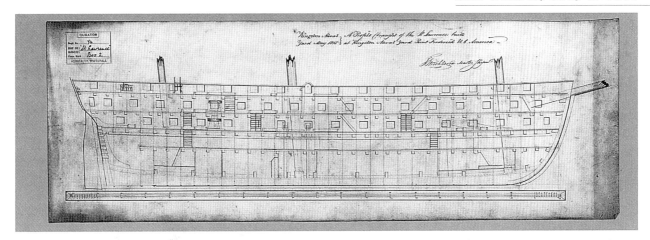

Above: The standard Navy Board inboard profile normally depicted the principle internal structural features like the knees and riders, but in the *St Lawrence*'s shown here the absence of hanging knees is evident. Even the shipwrights who worked on the ship doubted that the fastening techniques Master Builder William Bell employed would make it strong enough to survive its launch. (National Maritime Museum, neg DR74)

Right: The midship section of the *St Lawrence* shows the 'kneeless' system used on this ship. Although it seemed radically new to local shipwrights, the royal dockyards in England had been experimenting with similar arrangements for over a decade. (National Maritime Museum, neg DR79)

Below: Because the *St Lawrence* had only one tier of stern cabins, junior officers' accommodation had to be moved down to the orlop, as seen on this plan. (National Maritime Museum, neg DR75)

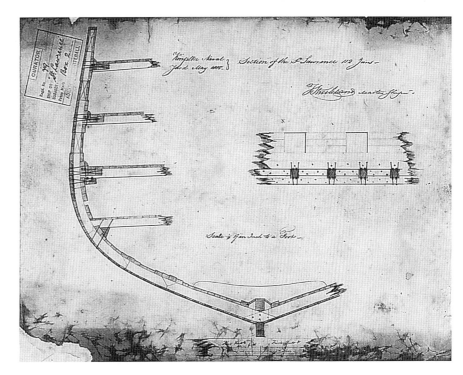

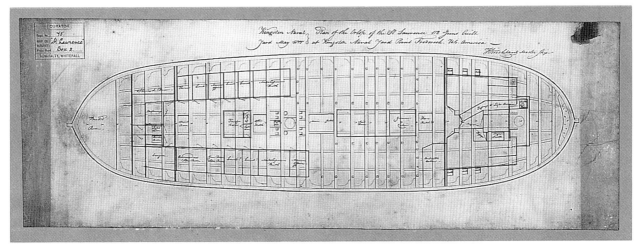

An unknown artist pictured the *St Lawrence* as it stood ready to be launched on 10 September 1814. Launches at Point Frederick were attended by throngs of people from Kingston and the surrounding villages. The launch of the *St Lawrence* must have caused a sensation. (Royal Ontario Museum, 74 CAN 258.967.106.1)

Between the beams on the upper three decks, Bell stiffened the assembly by installing three rows of carlines against each other and bolting them to the frame. A scarcity of suitable timbers likely contributed to Bell's decision to employ these techniques, as did the need to hurry the construction of the ship; besides the lack of knees the deck plans show that carlines replaced the conventional shaped, and labour intensive, half beams at the masts. Interestingly, similar techniques had been tried experimentally in the British home dockyards over the previous decade in order to circumvent the acute shortage of grown knees, so although they may have been new to local shipwrights Bell himself probably knew of these developments.

Worthy of note is the fact that Thomas Strickland, the master builder sent from England by the Navy Board to head up the yard at Point Frederick, arrived at Kingston early in the summer in company with Captain Sir Robert Hall, the new commissioner. Strickland officially superseded Bell, who soon went to England to clarify his status with the Navy Board, and Hall took over from Richard O'Conor, who had obtained a commission in Yeo's squadron. Hall and Strickland, it is assumed, would not have allowed the *St*

Lawrence to be launched if they had believed its construction was unsound, which suggests that Bell's techniques were not perceived as dangerously radical.

When launched, without incident, on 10 September 1814 the *St Lawrence* measured 191ft 2in on the deck, 157ft 8⅝in by 52ft 6in by 18ft 6in with a burthen of 2304 tons. On its maiden voyage it bore thirty-four 32pdr long guns on its lower deck, thirty-four 24pdr long guns on its middle deck and thirty-four 32pdr carronades plus a pair of 68pdr carronades on its upper deck for a total of 104 guns. Commodore Yeo considered the ship comparable to HMS *Caledonia*, 120, while the shipwright whose correspondence Chauncey read considered it akin to HMS *Nelson*, 120. Historians have similarly ranked the *St Lawrence* among Britain's most formidable warships of the period since it possessed an impressive weight of metal while being slightly smaller in dimensions that its largest contemporaries. Undeniably, however, there were some material differences that made the *St Lawrence* a unique First Rate. Most notable was its shallow hull and sharp midships deadrise (about 21 degrees) in place of a deep hold, a full-bottomed hull and a towering stern. Lacking a poop deck (or round-

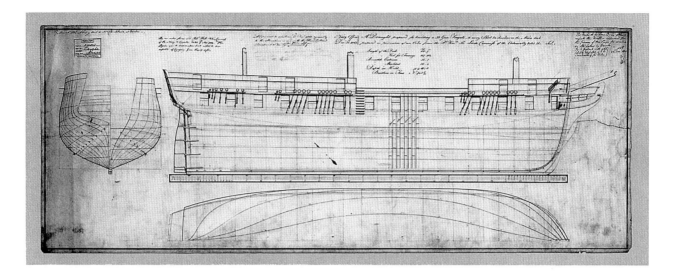

Discussions about the need for more warships to win the naval war on the Great Lakes led to the British government's decision to send two frigates and two brigs in frame for reconstruction in Canada. This is the draught prepared at the Chatham yard for the frigates *Psyche* and *Prompte*. The former vessel was eventually built at Kingston, its upper deck closed in so that it could carry additional guns. (National Maritime Museum, neg DR2409)

TABLE 39

HMS *Psyche* (1814) – legend of particulars

Launched: 25 December 1814, Kingston
Original draught by: Navy Board
Admiralty 'as built' draught by: Thomas Strickland
Builder: Thomas Strickland

HULL DIMENSIONS 1815

Gun deck	130ft
Keel/tonnage	108ft 0½in
Breadth extreme	36ft 7in
Depth of hold	10ft 3in
Tons	769 1/94
Draught light	8ft 10in forward
	9ft 8in aft
Number of ports	56
gun deck	28
upper deck	28

SPAR DIMENSIONS 1815

Mast	Length	Diameter	Yard Length	Yard Dia.
Fore	75ft	22in	60ft 10in	15in
Topmast	45ft	16⅛in	48ft 5in	10in
Topgallant	22ft 6in	7½in	29ft 6in	6½in
Main	86ft	26in	74ft 4in	17½in
Topmast	51ft	15½in	55ft 5in	11¾in
Topgallant	25ft 6in	8½in	33ft 6in	6⅝in
Mizzen	61ft	18¼in	—	—
Crossjack	—	—	55ft	11⅜in
Topmast	38ft 3in	10⅝in	36ft 9in	6½in
Topgallant	19ft 4in	6½in	25ft 6in	5¼in
Bowsprit	2ft 1in	25½in	43ft 5in	10in
Jibboom	26ft	10¾in	—	—
Driver boom	55ft	10½in	—	—
Gaff	38ft 7in	9in	—	—

ORDNANCE

Date	Carronades	Long Guns
1815	28-32s	28-24s

Source: NAC, MG 12, ADM 106/1997, 1998.

house), there was room for only one level of lighted cabins on the middle deck, as in the *Prince Regent*, *Princess Charlotte* and their American cousins, which required the junior commissioned and warrant officers to descend below the crew's berthing decks to cramped and stuffy quarters on the orlop.

Commodore Yeo was extremely pleased with the performance of the *St Lawrence* and asserted 'she sails very superior to anything on [Lake Ontario].'[21] The previous spring, however, he had predicted the ship would be ready for service early in the summer, an opinion that General Drummond and Sir George Prevost had shared, but as the work lagged over the summer and prevented the *St Lawrence*'s first cruise until 16 October, Drummond and Prevost became impatient with the delays. Yeo wrote: 'It is impossible to describe the prodigious labour and difficulty we have had in equipping this Ship from having to get all our supplies, from Quebec and Montreal.'[22] At a time when the British army on the Niagara Peninsula suffered from lack of supplies and reinforcements, the needs of the *St Lawrence* had taken up a good portion of the transportation resources on the St Lawrence River. Guns, ammunition, rigging, sails, fittings and every other imaginable necessity had been stripped from HM Ships *Centaur*, *Ajax*, *Warspite*, *Vengeur* and *York* at Quebec or had been sent from Halifax and moved up the St Lawrence in great flotillas of batteaux. In spite of the time this process took and the persistent calls for help from the army, Yeo refused to load his frigates with troops and provisions and sail to Niagara

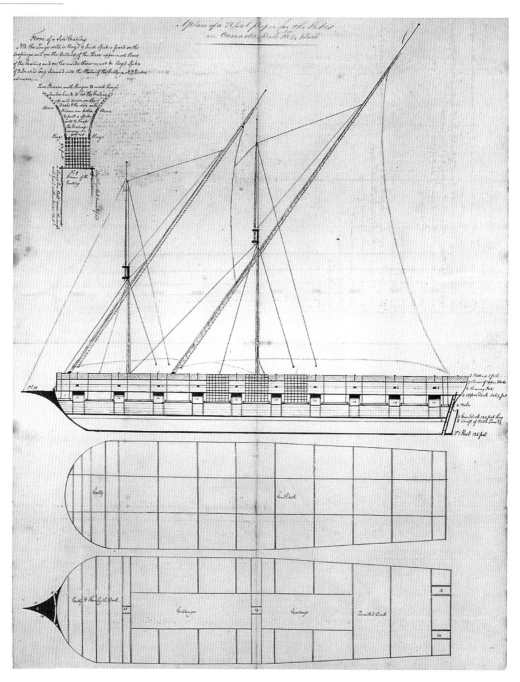

Several correspondents advised the British government to send warships in frame to the lakes. This plan for a 'xebec frigate' was devised in Canada by an individual named James Kerr and forwarded to the Admiralty for its consideration. (William L Clements Library)

because he was unwilling to risk a battle with Chauncey until his First Rate floated. By November Prevost was recommending to the home government that it send a rear admiral to oversee the entire Great Lakes theatre since a commander of an individual squadron faced conditions which 'might on some occasions give him a bias incompatible with the real good of the service.'[23]

The *St Lawrence* allowed Yeo to accomplish his main object, albeit too late to have a significant outcome on the events of the war. As the new ship's sailing date approached, Chauncey recalled his squadron to Sackets Harbor where he prepared to fight off an attack by the British. They left him alone, however, and the *St Lawrence* led the squadron on two round trips to Niagara to reinforce and provision the army before laying up for the winter at Kingston. Yeo had regained mastery of the lake, which is how the last of the naval conflicts on the Great Lakes ended when peace

When the American privateer *Fox* captured the British transport *Stranger* in September 1814, the Americans discovered guns and equipment for the vessels in frame in the transport's hold. The scheme was soon the subject of ridicule in American publications. (Beverley R Robinson collection, BRR 94.9.1)

was signed in Europe on 24 December.

Two more launches took place at Point Frederick after the *St Lawrence* sailed, the first happening on 14 November when the schooner *Julia* slid into the water. Only a few sparse records identify this schooner, showing its dimensions as 63ft 10½ (on deck), 52ft 3½in by 16ft 8½ by 8ft 7in for a burthen of 77 tons, but neither a draughtsman nor builder was identified for this vessel.

The second launch took place on 25 December 1814 when HMS *Psyche*, 56, glided down the ways into Navy Bay. Its story ranks among the most unusual tales about the freshwater fleets, because the *Psyche* was one of four vessels ordered by the Admiralty to be sent from England in frame to be erected on the lakes. The original suggestion for this venture was made in December 1812 by Sir Howard Douglas of the Royal Military College, who wrote to Lord Bathurst, the secretary for war and the colonies, about the need to gain supremacy of the lakes, especially Lake Ontario, in the war with the United States. The son of Commodore Charles Douglas, RN, he informed Bathurst about his father's accomplishments in the St Lawrence River and on Lake Champlain in 1776 and 1777 when a detachment from Dou-

glas's squadron had dismantled two schooners (the *Maria* and *Carleton*) in the commodore's squadron and a ship on the stocks at Quebec (later named the *Inflexible*) and hauled them up the Richelieu River to St Jean to be rebuilt. The British had also assembled a dozen gunboats sent in frame from England, but Douglas inaccurately asserted 'The vessels by which we maintained a superiority on Lake Champlain in 1776 were prepared in England.'[24] Although the gunboats had played only a minor role in the campaign against the Americans, Douglas went on to suggest that frames for large vessels could be prepared in England, sent to Canada to arrive at Quebec in the second week of May and transported up to Kingston by the first of June. At that place, they could be assembled, finished with native plank, masts and spars and ready for service by August. Uncertain about the value of Douglas's advice, Bathurst transmitted a copy to Prevost who rejected the scheme as being based on an outdated understanding of conditions in Canada.

The notion of sending prefabricated warships to Canada resurfaced in three different quarters late in 1813 not long after the loss of the Lake Erie squadron. In November a provincial legislator at Quebec forwarded to the Admiralty the ideas of an individual named James Kerr who believed the components for twelve 'xebec frigates' fashioned in a British shipyard could be sent to Canada where, in a month or six weeks, six of them could be constructed on Lake Ontario and six more on Lake Erie. Kerr's plan for the frigates showed a 23-gun vessel, based on the model of Mediterranean corsairs, measuring 125ft on the keel, drawing 3½ft and rigged with two masts carrying large lateen sails. A second proposal came from Admiral John Borlase Warren at Halifax on 1 December, who urged the Admiralty 'to construct three ships and three brigs in frame during the winter, to be set up at Long Point on Lake Erie or *Machedash Bay on Lake Huron* [actually on Georgian Bay].'[25] Lacking knowledge of the transportation problems in the Canadian wilderness, Warren concluded the job could be done fast enough to recover command on the upper lakes in the ensuing campaign. The third recommendation sent to the government was signed only by a 'Loyalist', whose concept closely paralleled Howard Douglas's original ideas.

The disturbing defeat on Lake Erie, combined with Yeo's inability to suppress Chauncey during their encounters in the summer of 1813, left the British government more amenable to innovative approaches to the Great Lakes war as the year ended. On 15 December the decision was made to build the components for a frigate and send them along with all the necessary equipment, arms and men to Canada in the first convoy in the spring. During the first week of January the plan was expanded to include a second frigate and a pair of brigs, all built of fir. The frigates would be named *Psyche* and *Prompte* to carry thirty 24pdr long guns and eight 32pdr carronades, while the brigs, rated as sloops, the *Colibri* and *Goshawk*, would be armed with eight 24pdr long guns, two 12pdr long guns and eight 24pdr carronades. The work was done at the Chatham dockyard and completed by the last week of February and early the next month transports began taking on the thousands of carefully marked pieces plus all the accessories needed to complete them. Of particular interest is the fact that the Admiralty sought to reduce the burden on the frigates by arming the vessels with 7½ft long 24pdrs, designed by Congreve; thirty of the guns, and a great deal of other stores, were found in the hold of the transport *Stranger* when captured by the American privateer *Fox* in September 1814. To build and man the ships and brigs in Canada, a large contingent of shipwrights and nearly 900 Royal Navy officers and men under Captain George Downie also embarked for passage to Canada.

Despatches announcing the government's plans to transport prefabricated vessels to Canada reached Quebec at the beginning of April. Immediately, Prevost sent the news to Yeo and others for their reaction and convened a board of officers to evaluate the scheme. With the *Prince Regent* and *Princess Charlotte* nearly ready for launch at the time and the keel of the *St Lawrence* set up, the universal opinion was that the plan was completely impractical as it would conflict with the current building programme and strain the over burdened transport system. The various reports and commentaries were sent to England six or seven weeks before the first of the transports carrying the 'fir frigates', as they were known, arrived at Montreal; transports with shallow draughts had been specially chosen so that they could carry the components as far up the St Lawrence as possible.

Faced with direct instructions from England, Prevost had the transports unloaded at Montreal and employed a private contractor named William Forbes to undertake the transportation to Kingston of 'Frigate B', the *Psyche*. The prodigious task stretched over the summer and into the autumn; Thomas Strickland laid the keel for the frigate on 31 October. As with other vessels at Point Frederick, the *Psyche* changed form on the stocks, its open waist being decked over so that the batteries could be increased from 38 to 56 guns, evenly split between twenty-eight 24pdr long guns and twenty-eight 32pdr carronades, making it almost as powerful as the *Prince Regent*. The ship was closer in size to the *Princess Charlotte*, however, measuring 130ft 6in on the deck, 108ft 0½in by 36ft 7in by 10ft 3in for a burthen of 769 tons. The *Psyche*'s slide into Navy Bay on 25 December 1814, marked the final launch of a warship on the Great Lakes during the War of 1812.

'Every man to do his duty'

LAKE CHAMPLAIN, 1812-1814

U NLIKE CIRCUMSTANCES during the Seven Years War and the Revolutionary War, the Lake Champlain region did not play a critical role in the War of 1812 campaigns until the final year of that conflict. This was due to the fact that military campaigns focussed on the Great Lakes region during the first two years of the conflict. Converted merchantmen played a key role in the first naval episodes, with shallow-draught brigs and ships (most similar to the vessels on Lake Erie) being launched to fight the battle that decided control of the lake.

In 1812 the American naval contingent on the lake consisted of the two gunboats built during the civil disturbances in 1808-9. There is uncertainty about their identity (they may have been the *Alwyn* and *Ludlow*) and it is believed there were 40ft in length and made to carry one long 12pdr each. In June 1812 the boats lay in disrepair on the shore of Basin Harbor near Vergennes, Vermont under the command of Lt Sidney Smith, USN. Smith managed to float the gunboats and

Thomas Macdonough (1783-1825) joined the US Navy as a midshipman in 1800. During the war with Tripoli he participated in the boarding and destruction of the USS *Philadelphia*, which had been captured. He served in several vessels as a lieutenant before assignment to the gunboat flotilla at Portland shortly after the War of 1812 started. (National Maritime Museum, PAD3377)

sail them to Plattsburgh; he manned one of them with locals and armed it with a 9pdr, but he received no direct instructions from the Navy Department about how to deploy his tiny command. Late in September, Secretary of the Navy Paul Hamilton ordered Lt Thomas Macdonough to leave his gunboat flotilla at Portland, Maine and take command on Lake Champlain. With the assistance of a small detachment of seamen en route from New York, Macdonough was to get both gunboats and six other craft recently purchased by the army ready for action.[1]

Macdonough reached Plattsburgh, New York in the second week of October and travelled south to the village of Whitehall at the southern tip of the lake, 100 miles from the border with Lower Canada, where the armed vessels were located. The army, under Major General Henry Dearborn, was in the process of building 160 batteaux at Whitehall as well as converting six former private sloops, the largest of which were the *President*, *Bull Dog* (renamed the *Eagle*) and *Hunter* (renamed the *Growler*). At first Dearborn balked at handing over the six merchantmen, but finally acquiesced to orders sent from Washington, and Macdonough, with twenty-five officers and men, took command of the vessels and began outfitting them to the navy standard. By early November his squadron consisted of the *President*, carrying his pendant and armed with six columbiads and two long 12pdrs, the *Growler* with two long 12pdrs, four long 6pdrs and a long 18pdr on a circle, and the *Eagle* with six long 6pdrs and a long 18pdr on a circle. He also mounted a 12pdr long gun in each of the two gunboats and sailed to Plattsburgh, where he employed his force in the transport of troops and munitions between Burlington, Vermont and Plattsburgh before taking up winter quarters at Shelbourne Bay, just south of Burlington.[2]

Of the sloops he originally outfitted, Macdonough said very little. They appear to have had raised forecastles and quarterdecks, typical of merchantmen on the lakes, which Macdonough strengthened to bear guns, and had these overall dimensions: *President* – 61ft; *Eagle* – 66ft 6in by 20ft 2in; *Growler* – 65ft by 20ft; the latter two were between 90 and 100 tons in burthen.[3] The columbiads that Macdonough employed in the

President deserve some special mention as this seems to have been the only example of their use on the lakes. The columbiad, supposed to have been named for the foundry in the District of Columbia where the guns were made, resembled a carronade in form and was developed just prior to the war by Lieutenant George Bomford of the US Army Ordnance Department as an alternative to the short guns designed by Congreve. It was a chambered weapon that could fire shot and shell; the single extant columbiad is a 50pdr measuring about 6ft 3½in long by 21½in overall diameter and 16¾in across the muzzle. Macdonough found his 18pdr columbiads at Whitehall where they had probably been sent for the use of the army.[4]

In Lake Champlain naval matters the British accomplished even less than the Americans did during 1812. The Provincial Marine post at St Jean had fallen into decay, its single schooner, the *Royal Edward*, launched in 1794, entirely useless. Military defences along the Richelieu River were also minimal as Commander-in-Chief Prevost at first concentrated his advanced defences of Montreal along the several key roads that crossed the border. News of naval preparations by the Americans, however, caused Prevost to select Isle aux Noix as the primary defence on the Richelieu, where he deployed a small force to man and improve its rundown fortifications. As well, Prevost ordered three gunboats in the St Lawrence to be hauled over the rapids above Chambly and sent up to Isle aux Noix. When Macdonough saw the gunboats in 1813 he described them as galleys carrying 'a long 24 pounder in the bow which fires only on a line with the keel and a 32 pr carronade in the stern which fires abeam or in any other direction as it traverses and carrying upwards of fifty men.'[5] British records fail to name these vessels although three gunboats in the 1814 flotilla, identified as the *Beresford*, *Popham* and *Brock*, were reported to have come from Quebec; their measurements were identical, 46ft by 11ft 2½in by 3ft 2in. Notice was made in September 1812 that a small gunboat had arrived at Isle aux Noix while a large one had yet to be conducted up to St Jean. The former might have been the smallest of the craft in the 1814 flotilla, the *Simcoe*, said to have been built in England and measuring only 32ft in length and 7ft 6in in breadth.

The Americans did little to augment their

squadron during the winter of 1813. Macdonough removed the raised quarterdecks of his sloops so he could increase their batteries from 7 to 11 guns, and that of the *President* from 8 to 12. As soon as the ice cleared, he sailed to Plattsburgh.[6]

The British decided to depend on gunboats in 1813 as protection along the approaches to Montreal and in April created a special marine corps to man flotillas at various points. The first division was to be stationed at Isle aux Noix and comprise two large boats and a small boat under Lieutenant William Lowe, but the actual strength of Lowe's unit is uncertain. Two of the gunboats in the 1814 flotilla were shown to have been built at Coteau du Lac, twenty miles southwest of Montreal, and they may have been sent up to Isle aux Noix about this time; they were identified as the *Murray* and *Drummond*, both measuring 62ft by 12ft 2½in by 3ft 8½in. Macdonough noted during the summer that the British force consisted of 'three galleys and two gunboats.'[7] Besides Lowe's unit, the fort at Isle aux Noix was now manned by a Royal Artillery detachment and six companies of the 100th Foot, commanded by Major George Taylor. They kept a close watch for enemy infiltrations and were ready to escort any small sailing craft and rafts that crossed the border carrying provisions and wood for shipbuilding to the British from private sources in Vermont and New York.

In an attempt to discourage such smuggling, Macdonough sent Lt Smith in the *Eagle* and *Growler*, the crews of which were reinforced by the gunboat men and a military company, to patrol near the border on 2 June. Smith injudiciously crossed the border the next morning and proceeded down the Richelieu despite warnings from his pilots that both wind and current would impede a retreat. When the sloops approached within two miles of Isle aux Noix, Major Taylor ordered Lowe to advance in three of the gunboats while he deployed his infantry on the banks of the river. Smith attempted to turn around, but as his pilots had warned, the narrowness of the channel (it was 100 yards wide, the river being 200 yards from bank to bank) made tacking nearly impossible. At close range the British poured in ball and shot, which the Americans returned for more than three hours, before the *Eagle*, hulled by a 24pdr, ran aground

Lake Champlain had served in the past as an invasion route into the heart of Canada. By 1812 a road system had developed along which armies could travel supported by a naval squadron. Part of a contemporary map reproduced in Sir Charles P Lucas, *The Canadian War of 1812* (Oxford 1906).

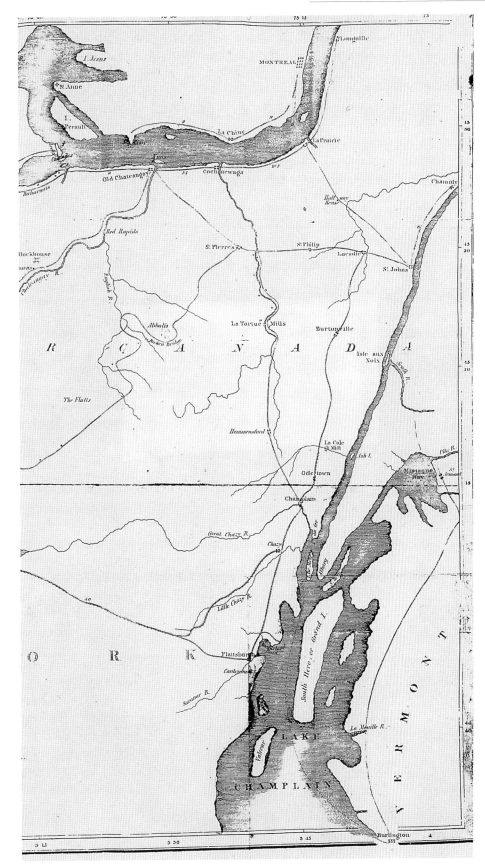

TABLE 40

The British squadron on Lake Champlain, 11 September 1814

Vessel	Total Guns	Carronades			Long Guns			Crew
		32s	24s	18s	24s	18s	6s	
Confiance	37	4	6		26			270
					1*			
Linnet	16	—			16			99
Chub	11			8			3	41
Finch	11			6			4	32
			1-18 columbiad					
two gunboats	4	1 each			1 each			82
one gunboat	2		1			1		41
one gunboat	2		1			1		35
three gunboats	3					1 each		99
four gunboats	4	1 each						100
Totals	90		33			57		799

* pivot gun.
Source: NAC, MG 12, ADM 1/5445, p78.

TABLE 41

Particulars of British gunboats on Lake Champlain, 11 September 1814

Vessel	Length	Beam	Hold	Carronades	Long Guns	Built
Yeo	62ft	12ft	—	1-32	1-24	Isle aux Noix
Prevost	64ft	12ft	—	1-32	1-24	Isle aux Noix
Blucher	57ft	12ft 6in	3ft 3in	1-32	1-18	Isle aux Noix
Beckwith	57ft	12ft 6½in	3ft 3in	—	1-18	Isle aux Noix
Wellington	53ft	12ft 2½in	3ft 5in	1-18	1-18	Isle aux Noix
Murray	62ft	12ft 2½in	3ft 8½in	—	1-18	Coteau de Lac
Drummond	62ft	12ft 2½in	3ft 8½in	—	1-18	Coteau de Lac
Beresford	46ft	11ft 2½in	3ft 2in	1-32	—	Quebec
Popham	46ft	11ft 2½in	3ft 2in	1-32	—	Quebec
Brock (B)	46ft	11ft 2½in	3ft 15in	1-32	—	Quebec
Simcoe	32ft	7ft 6in	—	1-32	—	England

Source: NAC, MG 12, ADM 1/5445, p15; *ibid*, pp5450; *ibid*, ADM 106/1997-8.
The *Simcoe* disappeared from lists after the battle, apparently renamed the *Cochrane*. The
Owen also appeared on later lists, measuring 63ft × 15ft 8in, carrying two guns and said
to have been built at Quebec; it was not mentioned in documents relating to the action
on 11 September 1814.

TABLE 42

The American squadron on Lake Champlain, 11 September 1814

Vessel	Total Guns	Carronades			Long Guns				Crew
		42s	32s	18s	24s	18s	12s	9s	
Saratoga	26	6	12		8				250
Eagle	20		12			8			142
Ticonderoga	17		3		4		10		115
Preble	9	—						9	45
six galleys:	12			1 each	1 each				100
Allen									
Borer									
Burrows									
Centipede									
Nettle									
Viper									
four gunboats:	4	—						1 each	210
Alwyn									
Ludlow									
Ballard									
Wilmer									
Totals	88		39			49			862

Source: NAC, MG 12, ADM 1/5445, p79.

and sank and Smith gave up the *Growler*.[8]

The action on 3 June was a sharp setback for Macdonough that suddenly improved the British force by adding two ready-armed sloops, renamed the *Broke* (ex-*Growler*) and *Shannon* (ex-*Eagle*) to their force. The next significant escalation of the naval contest was the appointment on 19 July of Commander Daniel Pring, RN, as commander of the Lake Champlain squadron. Pring was one of the officers Admiral Warren ordered to Canada from Bermuda with Commander Robert Barclay and had served briefly as Commodore Yeo's flag captain in HMS *Wolfe*. Lauded by Prevost as 'a most able and deserving officer,' Pring headed for Isle aux Noix around 20 July with half a dozen officers and men from Yeo's squadron.[9] Earlier in July Prevost had requested assistance from the Royal Navy ships at Quebec and succeeded in enticing Captain Thomas Everard, HMS *Wasp*, to undertake a two-week expedition to Isle aux Noix with 80 officers and men taken from his warship and several transports. Everard and Pring arrived there at the same time and found that Lieutenant Colonel John Murray was planning a series of raids on American positions on the lake. Embarking nearly 1000 soldiers in the armed vessels and batteaux, the British set sail on 29 July.

The British campaign, which became known as 'Murray's Raid', commenced on 31 July at Plattsburgh where public and private property and stores were destroyed and confiscated without opposition from local military units. The next day the army went north in two gunboats and the batteaux to destroy an army camp at Swanton, Vermont, while the naval contingent under Everard's command, looked for the American squadron. They found it anchored at Burlington. Given funding and promises of support in guns and men by Secretary Jones, Macdonough had purchased a pair of private sloops, the *Preble* and *Montgomery*, but had not been able to arm them. When Everard approached, Macdonough's vessels, including the two old gunboats and the *President*, were anchored in a line. An exchange took place at considerable distance, which ended after two hours when Everard concluded he could not lure Macdonough to meet him in open water and departed. Unimpeded by the American squadron, he captured or destroyed four or five merchant-

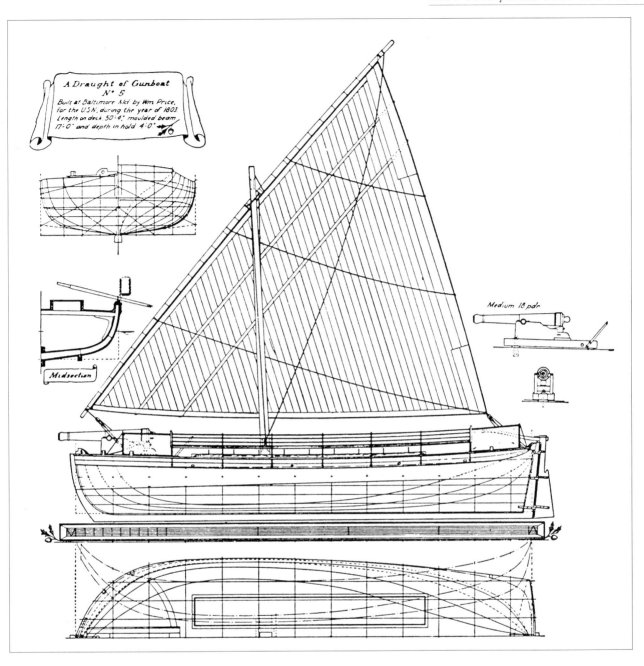

A Draught of Gunboat
N° 5
Built at Baltimore Md by Wm Price,
for the U.S.N. during the year of 1803.
Length on deck 50'-4", moulded beam
17'-0" and depth in hold 4'-0"

Midsection

Medium 18 pdr

Gunboats formed the only elements of naval force on Lake Champlain through most of 1812. The American government had ordered two built there in 1808. Their exact nature is unknown, but they may have been similar to this 50ft gunboat designed by Josiah Fox for the US Navy in 1803. (Smithsonian Institution)

men on the way back to Isle aux Noix which he reached on 4 August.[10]

The British made several other brief incursions into American territory in 1813 and Macdonough cruised near the border, but there were no further encounters of consequence between the combatants that year. Macdonough and Pring (the latter began his term as senior officer when Everard returned to HMS *Wasp*) both anticipated more significant engagements in the future, however, and worked to improve their squadrons.

Macdonough, promoted in July to master commandant, armed the *Preble* with seven 12pdr long guns and two 18pdr columbiads and the *Montgomery* with seven 9pdr long guns and two 18pdr columbiads. He acquired two other small sloops, the *Wasp* (three long 12pdrs) and the *Francis*, but they were unwieldy sailers and only temporarily in the line. Macdonough also had two new gunboats built (they were probably named the *Ballard* and *Wilmer*) and equipped them and the older gunboats with one long 18pdr each.[11]

In August Pring recommended to Prevost that a 370-ton, 16-gun brig and two gunboats be built at Isle aux Noix by William Simons, a builder who had been sent from Montreal to assess the two prized sloops. Pring informed Prevost that there was up to 5000 feet of oak plus a supply of pine in store at Isle aux Noix, but it took several more proposals before the commander-in-chief approved the construction midway through October. The British took down a redoubt on the east side of the island and laid out a dockyard where Simons could get to work on a brig that was supposed to carry 18 guns and to measure

110ft on the deck by 30ft 6in abeam with a hold of 8ft 6in; it would draw 8ft 6in of water at the bow and 9ft 6in aft.[12]

Simons spent most of the winter building the brig, which was launched about the middle of April 1814. Named the *Niagara* at first, then renamed the *Linnet*, the vessel ended up with a battery of 16 guns and seems to have been slightly smaller than Pring had originally wanted it to be. Although no draught of the brig has been found, sources indicate that it was probably 82ft 6in on deck by 27ft by 6ft 8in. A draught for brigs proposed to be built at Isle aux Noix in 1815 features dimensions very close to this and may offer a fair representation of the *Linnet*'s lines. If so, then the *Linnet* was flush-decked, had a plain stem, little sheer and a low midships deadrise of about 10 degrees. Preliminary archaeological investigations conducted in the 1980s of the remains of the *Linnet* support the notion of a low deadrise in the hull and revealed that Simons took advantage of the time available to him by putting good workmanship into the project, such as notching the keelson so it would fit snugly over the frames. The vessel's timbers were relatively small in size with the keel dimensions averaging 12in moulded by 8½in sided while the floors averaged 9½in moulded by 8 inches sided. The floors were short and to them were bolted the first

TABLE 43
British vessels captured and launched on Lake Champlain, 1812-1814

Name	Launch	Place	Rig	Remarks
Shannon ‡/*Chub*, 11	?	?	sloop	ex-*Eagle* *; 1814 taken by Americans at Plattsburg; 1815 sold
Broke ‡/*Finch*, 11	?	?	sloop	ex-*Growler* *; 1814 taken by Americans at Plattsburg; 1815 sold
Niagara (D)/*Linnet*, 16	April 1814	Isle aux Noix	brig	1814 taken by Americans at Plattsburg; 1815 in ordinary, decayed
Confiance (B), 37	August 1814	Isle aux Noix	ship	1814 taken by Americans at Plattsburg; 1815 in ordinary, decayed

The gunboats added to the British squadron have been omitted here due to the uncertainty surrounding their arrival, or construction, at Isle aux Noix.

‡ prize vessel.   * see Table 44.

TABLE 44
American vessels launched and converted on Lake Champlain, 1812-1814

Name	Launch	Place	Rig	Remarks
two gunboats	1808	Plattsburgh	lugger	1815 sold
President, 12 †	?	?	sloop	1815 sold
Eagle (A), 11 †	?	?	sloop	ex-*Bull Dog*; 1813 taken by British, renamed *Shannon* *
Growler (B), 11 †	?	?	sloop	ex-*Hunter*;1813 taken by British, renamed *Broke* *
Preble, 9 †	?	?	sloop	1815 sold
Montgomery, 9 †	?	?	sloop	1815 sold
Wasp, 3 †	?	?	sloop	fate uncertain
Francis (B) †	?	?	sloop	fate uncertain
two gunboats	1813	Burlington	lugger	1815 sold
six galleys	1813	Vergennes	lugger	1815 sunk for preservation
Saratoga, 26	April 1813	Vergennes	ship	1815 in ordinary, decayed
Ticonderoga, 17	May 1813	Vergennes	schooner	1815 in ordinary, decayed
Surprise (A)/*Eagle* (B), 20	August 1813	Vergennes	brig	1815 in ordinary, decayed

† private vessel hired or purchased for government service.   ‡ prize vessel.   * see Table 43.

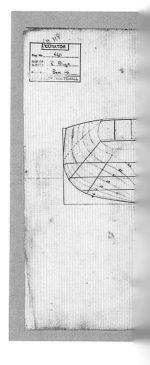

The British began construction of the brig that became the *Linnet* late in 1813. Although no draught of that vessel has come to light, the Admiralty design shown here for brigs to be built in 1815 bears some resemblance to the size and description of the *Linnet*. Dated Kingston Naval Yard 28 September 1815, the draught relates to 'Three brigs proposed to be built at the Isle au Noix'. (National Maritime Museum, neg DR6411)

futtocks which did not meet at the midway point of the keel, but were separated by a gap that left the heels of the futtocks several inches outside the keel. Iron fastenings were discovered throughout the wreck. Despite its apparently light construction, the *Linnet* was pleasing to the eye, as Thomas Macdonough noted when he saw it: '[the] brig is one of the first class and is a remarkably fine looking vessel.'[13]

At the same time as he granted Pring's request for a brig, Prevost also approved the building of five gunboats at Isle aux Noix. Simons did this work as well, producing the *Yeo, Prevost, Blucher, Beckwith* and *Wellington.* They varied in size, from the *Prevost* which measured 64ft long and 12ft abeam to the *Wellington* at 53ft by 12ft 2½in by 3ft 5in and each was heavy enough to carry an 18pdr or 24pdr long gun and a carronade.[14]

Late in 1813 Macdonough got wind of British preparations and wrote to Jones for permission to undertake the construction of a warship to match his opponent's growing strength. In particular, he was eager to counter the gunboats assembled at Isle aux Noix (he had heard there was upwards of a dozen of them) and proposed to Jones the building of twenty or twenty-five similar boats that would be shallow enough to be dragged down the rapids at Chambly in an eventual campaign against Montreal. Jones liked this idea and gave Macdonough permission to build fifteen 'galleys' in two classes, the first being '75 feet long and 15 wide, to carry a long 24 and a 42 pound Carronade, row 40 oars, and drawing but 22 inches water, with all on board'; the second '50 feet long and 12 feet wide, to carry a long 18 and 32 pd carronade, and row 26 oars; they have been tried, and are the most perfect of their kind.'[15] Jones thought highly of this type of galley, or barge as the craft were commonly known. They had been designed by William Doughty for use in Chesapeake Bay and suited the confinements of the lakes; boats of the same classes were built at Sackets Harbor during the summer of 1814.

In December 1813, Macdonough took his squadron up Otter Creek to a point below Vergennes, which was six miles from the lake. The village was a perfect location for a dockyard as it boasted eight forges, two furnaces and five mills of various types and the vicinity abounded with oak and pine. In mid-February Secretary Jones signed a contract with Noah Brown to do the work, and within weeks his shipwrights had keels laid for six large galleys which ultimately became the *Allen, Borer, Burrows, Centipede, Nettle* and *Viper.* The *Allen* went into the water late in April and, manned by 40 officers and men, served to cover Fort Cassin which had been erected at the mouth of Otter Creek.

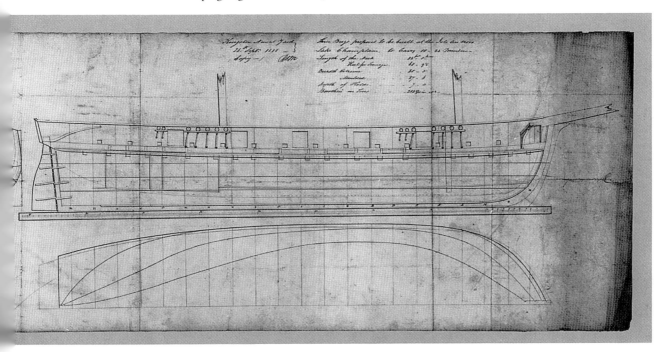

A recent archaeological study that focused on the remains of a galley believed to be the *Allen* showed that Brown improvised on William Doughty's plan. With a keel measuring between 68ft and 70ft long, the hull had a sharper deadrise, making it an easier vessel to handle under sail than Doughty's barges. The sternpost was straight rather than curved and battens appear to have been fixed to the ceiling planks to receive bulwarks that might have been used to create storage compartments. White oak, red oak, elm, white ash and white pine were randomly used to fashion the components without apparent concern for their function in the structure. The planks varied from 7in to 15in in width and the irregular sizes of individual frames and their spacing indicate that construction was hurried and lacking in quality control, as does the evidence that some bolts were found to have missed the members they were intended to join.[16]

Noah Brown also received a contract from the Navy Department to build a 26-gun ship, the keel for which he laid down on 7 March. With a large gang of shipwrights, readily available resources and apparently limitless industry, Brown completed the hull in forty days, launching it on 11 April. It was named the *Saratoga* and measured 143ft 6in between perpendiculars with a moulded beam of 36ft 4in, a hold of 14ft 6in,

and a burthen given at 734 tons. Its guns, mounted in 3ft square gunports spaced 7ft apart, comprised eight 24pdr long guns, twelve 32pdr carronades and six 42pdr carronades. A draught of the vessel, believed to have been penned by Noah Brown, shows that it was nearly identical in form to the Lake Erie brigs *Lawrence* and *Niagara*; it had a plain stem, little sheer, virtually no drag and about a 15-degree midships deadrise.[17]

The ship and galleys greatly enhanced Macdonough's force, but he added more strength to his squadron by converting to war service a vessel originally intended to become a steamship. Early in March 1814 Daniel Tompkins, the governor of New York State, informed Secretary Jones about a new vessel being built by the Steamboat Company of Lake Champlain at Vergennes that could be adapted for use as a warship. Macdonough and Brown examined the hull on the stocks and determined that it would serve the purpose; the Navy Department is believed to have paid $12,000 for the hull, $10,000 less than its owners wanted. Although the possibility of completing the hull as a steamship was contemplated, which would have made it the first steam-powered warship in the world, Macdonough chose to rig the vessel as a schooner, his reasons being to avoid the time lost in waiting for delivery and assembly of the necessary machinery and the fact that

These draughts show the two types of galleys built by William Doughty that Secretary of the Navy Jones recommended to Lt Macdonough. Six of the larger galleys were eventually built at Vergennes in 1814 and archaeological evidence shows that they were very similar to the Doughty design. (Smithsonian Institution)

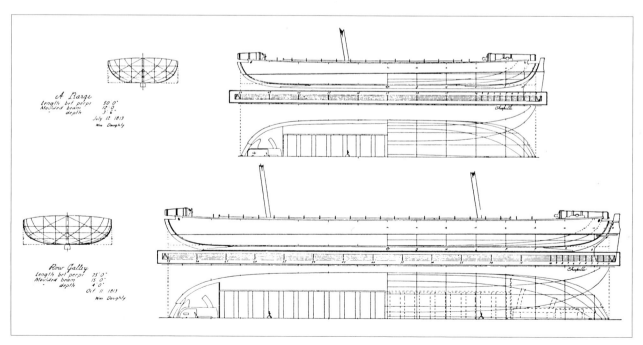

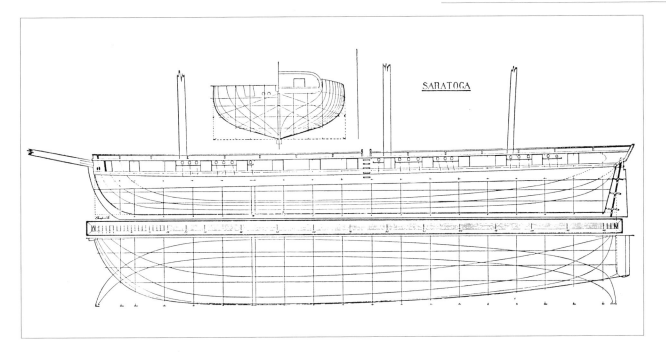

SARATOGA

Macdonough's flagship was the 26-gun *Saratoga* shown in this draught reconstructed by Howard Chapelle. (Smithsonian Institution)

the one steamboat then in service on the lake rarely completed a voyage without a breakdown. Once again Brown worked quickly, making the requisite changes to the hull and launching it on 12 May. Macdonough named the schooner *Ticonderoga*. It was 120ft on deck, 113ft 9in on the keel with an uncommonly narrow breadth of 26ft and a burthen of 350 tons. Macdonough took the ordnance from the sloops *Francis* and *Wasp* and the four gunboats to arm the vessel with eight 12pdr long guns, four long 18pdrs and five 32pdr carronades.[18]

Like the gunboat *Allen* and the *Linnet*, the *Ticonderoga* has been the subject of archaeological investigations. The keel and false keel measured just over 24in moulded by 13in sided on average, with the keel itself consisting of two long timbers and the false keel (which was 14in moulded) comprising five timbers, all of them of white oak. The vessel had a flat midships deadrise (about 10 degrees), typical of steamboats that could navigate without reliance on the wind and which also allowed for a more commodious hold. The remains of fifty-five frames revealed that the floors and first futtocks were set up in the same manner as William Simons used in the *Linnet*, that is, leaving a gap between the heels of the first futtocks, which were bolted to the floors. The floors and futtocks measured on average 8in

moulded by 7in sided. Careful workmanship was evident in the time taken to cut limber holes in the lower surface of the futtocks and floors, a step apparently omitted in most purpose-built freshwater warships. As well, attention was devoted to cutting and shaping frame timbers to take advantage of grain patterns and then skilfully finishing them to near perfect smoothness, although several pieces showed numerous tool marks, indicating hurry or carelessness. Iron spikes and bolts were used as fastenings with treenails reserved for cutwaters in the seams of the largest, exposed scarphs. The archaeologists concluded that Noah Brown added the false keel to make the long, narrow vessel stable enough to carry a heavy load of ordnance under sail. Brown's men probably did the planking inside and out, leaving most of the vessel's heavy components as its original builder, John Lacy, had constructed them for the steamboat company.

Two days after the launch of the *Ticonderoga*, the British squadron appeared off the mouth of Otter Creek. Having initiated dockyard activities earlier in the winter than the Americans, the British were able to commence their spring campaign before any of Macdonough's craft could get out of Otter Creek. Indeed, a prime objective of this first mission for the British was to choke off the creek by sinking two sloops in its mouth.

The opening of the battle at Plattsburgh on 11 September 1814 is shown here. The vessels are identified by the key below, the British vessels in italics. (National Maritime Museum, neg A3920 and PAD 5854)

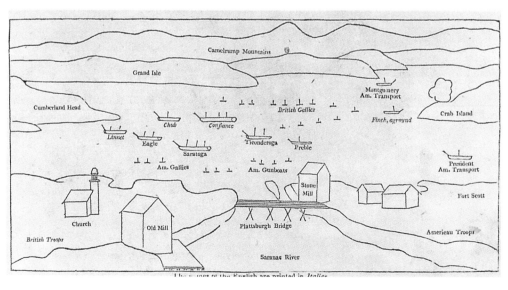

Americans sufficient warning to prepare a stiff defence against the British. Their resistance was strong enough that the attack was cancelled and Pring's squadron sailed off. After some minor activity along the American shore, the squadron took up a position about two miles south of the border.

Information that he picked up during the cruise about the extent of the building programme at Vergennes led Pring to conclude that Macdonough's force would soon outgun his squadron. Accordingly, he recommended to Prevost that a large warship be built at Isle aux Noix to achieve parity with the Americans. William Simons, whose talents Pring had praised, left Isle aux Noix for Montreal where he examined the two brigs sent in frame from England by the Admiralty. His conclusion was that they would draw 12-14ft of water which was impractical on Lake Champlain and he apparently echoed Pring's proposal by suggesting that a ship with a keel of 138ft, a breadth of 36ft and a draught of water of 7 or 8ft would better suit local needs. Prevost approved the project and by the end of May Simons was formulating plans and collecting shipwrights from Montreal and Quebec for the work.[19]

Macdonough sailed from Otter Creek with his squadron late in May and approached the British near the border on 12 June, prompting Pring to withdraw to the safety of the Richelieu. The Americans took up a position off Pointe au Fer, effectively blockading the river and interrupting the smuggling of Vermont timber to the British base, seizing large spars and 13,000 feet of plank in two instances alone. This first cruise gave Macdonough a chance to assess his new vessels and he reported to Secretary Jones, 'I find the *Saratoga* a fine ship. She sails and works well, she is a ship between the *Pike* and *Madison* on Lake Ontario. The schooner is also a fine vessel and bears her metal full as well as expected. The gallies are also remarkably fine vessels.'[20]

Macdonough soon heard the local scuttlebutt that the British had laid down the keel of a frigate at Isle aux Noix, that two large galleys had been hauled up from the St Lawrence and that one of the vessels sent in frame from England was being transported to the Richelieu dockyard. He wrote to Jones to propose several responses to this news. He preferred to see galleys built, but considered

Commander Pring's squadron consisted of the brig *Linnet*, 16, the *Chub* (ex-*Shannon*, nee *Eagle*), 13, the *Finch* (ex-*Broke*, nee *Growler*), 11, two recently outfitted prizes serving as tenders, the *Canada* and *Icicle*, two other commercial craft and seven gunboats. The squadron had been reinforced by Royal Navy seamen and a Royal Marine detachment, but was still short of hands.

At first light on 14 May the British galleys engaged the guns in Fort Cassin in a long range duel, the first step in the plan for the temporary occupation of the mouth of the river in order to interrupt the American shipbuilding. News of the squadron's slow progress up the lake had been relayed to Macdonough and the local military commanders in the previous days, allowing the

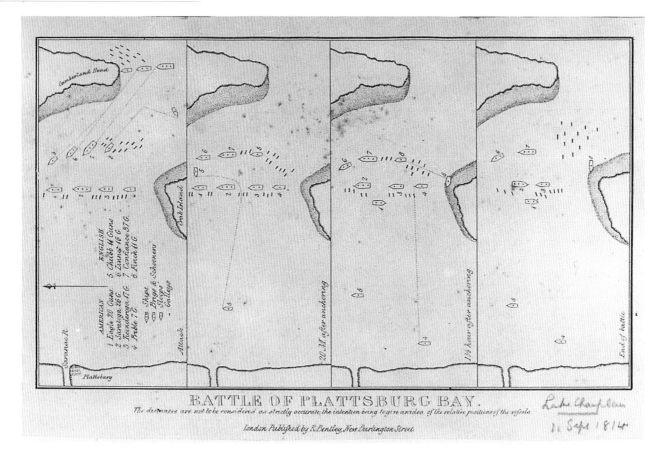

BATTLE OF PLATTSBURG BAY.
The distances are not to be considered as strictly accurate, the intention being to give an idea of the relative positions of the vessels.

London Published by R.Bentley, New Burlington Street

Lake Champlain
11 Sept 1814

This plate originally published in 1837 portrays the sequence of the British advance on the American line in Plattsburgh Bay on 11 September 1814 and the course of the battle as the *Chub*, *Finch* and *Preble* fall out of action. (National Maritime Museum, PAD5853)

them too much of a drain on available manpower, while a brig of 18 or 20 long guns 'would reach [the British] gallies in their skulking places' and be just as economical to build as a handful of galleys and certainly provide better living conditions for the crews.[21] Through June and into July Macdonough wrote repeatedly to Jones for permission to begin building, but the navy secretary was hesitant to grant his approval. Funds still had to be found to cover the invoices from Noah Brown and the steamboat company and Jones was reluctant to allow a shipbuilding contest to develop like the one being conducted on Lake Ontario. When President Madison learned about the situation, however, he instructed Jones to have the work done. As a result, on 18 July Adam Brown delivered Jones's letter of permission to Macdonough on board the *Saratoga* at Pointe au Fer and announced that the department had given him a contract to construct the new brig.

After a quick consultation with the naval commander, Brown went to Vergennes and laid down the keel for a brig on 23 July. Outdoing the speed

with which his brother and Henry Eckford had built warships on the lakes, Brown launched the completed hull on 11 August, nineteen days after its construction started. Its keel was formed from two maple timbers and one of oak, moulded to 18in and sided to 12in. The floors had arms averaging 4ft to 6ft in length and ranged between 11in and 13in moulded and 8in and 10in sided. The first futtocks were bolted to the floors, had similar dimensions to the floors in cross section and their heels met on the centreline of the keel; limber holes were cut in the bottom of the floors and first futtocks. Under the pressure to build quickly, Brown reduced his construction time by omitting the use of knees of any type. Instead, he provided support for the beams and deck by fitting a clamp to the frames that averaged about 12in square, notching it to receive deck beams and giving the waterway similar notches and dimensions of 10in moulded by 12in sided. To stiffen this assembly, Brown riveted the bolts that fastened the clamp to the frames while everywhere else on the hull he appears to have relied on friction alone to keep the bolts in place. Other ways in which Brown expedited the construction of the brig included the use of iron fastenings and a wide range of woods throughout, as well as leaving only a rough finish on some components.

Given its intended effect on the British, the brig was at first appropriately named the *Surprise* by its commander Master Commandant Robert Henley (without seeking Macdonough's permission) but just days before the battle at Plattsburgh Macdonough renamed it the *Eagle*. It measured 117ft 3in between perpendiculars, 106ft 3in by 34ft 9in (moulded beam) by 7ft 3in for a burthen of about 550 tons. Brown built it in a plain style and gave it the shallow midships deadrise of its sister ships (11 degrees) and apparently a plain stem. After fifteen days of fitting out, the new brig sailed to join Macdonough, bringing its much-needed battery of twelve 32pdr carronades and eight long 18pdrs to the squadron. Macdonough had moved to a position off the Chazy River and the brig arrived there on 27 August. There was still many hurried preparations needed on board the vessel, especially in training the short-handed crew in sail and gun drills.

On the British side of the line, affairs were in a much more hectic state. The new frigate *Confiance* was launched on 25 August. It measured 147ft 5in on deck, 37ft 2in abeam by 7ft and was eventually armed with twenty-six 24pdr long guns and four 32pdr carronades on the main deck, one long 24pdr (pivoting) and two 24pdr carronades on the forecastle and four 24pdr carronades on the roundhouse (the poop). So much work had yet to be done on board, however, that even as the ship sailed south for its rendezvous with the Americans, carpenters were building a magazine and fashioning quoins for the ordnance. The long guns were fitted with modified carronade locks and 'in general worked very heavy owing to the decks being rough scraped and a quantity of pitch on them.'[22] Little else is known about the construction of the new British flagship on Lake Champlain other than a later observation that inferior woods had gone into it in abundance. A prominent American marine archaeologist, Kevin Crisman, opined that the dimensions of the vessel 'strongly suggest that her floors had very little deadrise, and she may have had a peculiar raft-like appearance in section.'[23]

Besides the hurried preparations of the *Confiance*, command of the British squadron was thrown into turmoil with the sudden appearance on 1 September of Captain George Downie from the Lake Ontario squadron. In June Commodore Yeo had sent Captain Peter Fisher from Kingston to take over from Pring, who remained in the squadron. Fisher supervised activities at Isle aux Noix all summer, but complaints about his pugnacious manner caused Yeo suddenly to replace him with Downie. That officer raised his pendant in the *Confiance* on 3 September. The ship was not fully manned and over the next few days some Royal Navy officers and men from Lake Ontario and the St Lawrence joined along with a company of Royal Marines, a few members of the Royal Marine Artillery, the Royal Artillery and the 39th Foot. The crew had next to no time to become familiar with its surroundings or the expectations of its officers, let alone develop efficient gunnery skills. Despite the late assistance from the military, the ship remained so short-handed that no men were quartered at its four 32pdr carronades and two of its 24pdr carronades.[24]

The urgency of the *Confiance*'s preparations was heightened by Sir George Prevost's decision to commence a major offensive in September along the Lake Champlain line with Plattsburgh as its main target. Having formed an army numbering more than 10,000, the majority of whom were veterans from Wellington's forces in Europe who had recently arrived at Quebec, Prevost crossed the border on 1 September. Although he knew the *Confiance* needed much work before it was serviceable, Prevost informed Downie that he fully expected the squadron to support his advance. Downie had little time to familiarise himself with his command before ordering Pring on 3 September to sail with the *Linnet* and the rest of the squadron to rendezvous with the army at the Chazy River while he remained at Isle aux Noix to oversee the fitting out of the *Confiance*.

Two-thirds of Prevost's army reached Plattsburgh on 6 September with an intention to attack the next morning, but a lack of information about the terrain and the American positions postponed that plan. Brigadier General Alexander Macomb commanded the American land forces deployed on the south side of the Saranac River; they numbered about 2000 effectives with more than 1000 others infirm or absent and 250 in the squadron. Macdonough had withdrawn his squadron to Plattsburgh Bay on 1 September and anchored it in a northeast-southwest line half way between Cumberland Head and the town, with the *Eagle* at the north and the *Saratoga*, *Ticonderoga* and *Preble* behind. The six galleys and four gunboats were placed in three divisions just west of the warships while the *President* and *Montgomery* were employed as transports.

Prevost decided to delay his attack on Plattsburgh until Downie could arrive to confront Macdonough and wrote daily to Downie to request his prompt support. With his flagship still unprepared, Downie left Isle aux Noix on 8 September and, because of a strong head wind, only managed to reach the Chazy late the next night. Prevost's communications now took on an edge that led to later accusations of his goading the navy into action. Downie replied with assurance that he would do all he could, despite the fact that his flagship was still not completely outfitted, and the next day he proceeded slowly up the lake.

The British appeared off Plattsburgh at dawn on 11 September.[25] Downie reconnoitred the American line and then formed a plan of attack whereby the *Confiance* would anchor between the *Saratoga* and *Eagle*, while the *Linnet* and *Chub* attacked the *Eagle* from ahead, the *Finch* engaged the *Preble* and the gunboats, in three divisions under the command of Lieutenant Mark Raynham, RN, swarmed around the *Ticonderoga*; the scheme apparently did not account for the ten American gunboats and galleys. Macdonough waited for the British to advance, having roused his force with the signal: 'Impressed seamen call on every man to do his duty.'[26] Knowing that a northerly wind was likely to prevail in September, Macdonough had arranged his line so that the British would have to sail up to him and that was the situation that existed as Downie formed his line abreast and steered for the bay. Light airs also retarded the British advance as the opening shots were exchanged shortly after 9:00am. The American broadsides soon poured in such a persistent and raking fire that Downie managed to only get

within 300 yards of the *Saratoga* before he anchored and turned his broadside on Macdonough's flagship. The *Linnet* also failed to reach its intended position and stood off the *Eagle*'s starboard bow while the *Chub* and *Finch* withered under the American fire and accomplished little. The British gunboats proved even less effective when Raynham failed to lead his flotilla into action and later signalled their complete withdrawal from the scene. The *Confiance* and *Linnet* absorbed most of the American broadsides which they returned in kind, but after two hours of fighting (Downie was killed near the outset of the action), the British hauled down their flags. The butcher's bill tallied at about 170 British casualties compared to 110 killed and wounded on the American side.

Prior to the action, Downie and Prevost had agreed that the scaling of the naval guns as the squadron rounded Cumberland Head would be the signal for the army to launch its attack across the Saranac to secure the American batteries and

turn them on Macdonough's vessels. One part of the land force began the drive through the American lines, but Prevost held his main body in place while he watched the naval action and then abruptly called his advanced units back when he saw the squadron surrender. To the amazement of his veteran troops, he cited the loss of the squadron as the reason for giving up his campaign, and withdrew to Canada. Indignation raged through the British camp and when Commander Pring informed Commodore Yeo about Prevost's insinuating statements to Downie, Yeo wrote to the Admiralty with open criticism of the commander-in-chief. Orders were sent from England in December for both men to return home so that the circumstances of the loss at Plattsburgh could be investigated properly.[27]

For winning command of Lake Champlain so decisively, Thomas Macdonough was promoted to captain, effective 11 September, just as Perry had been rewarded one year and a day before. The warships in both squadrons lay shattered by the engagement, especially the *Confiance* which had seventeen of its guns dismounted and between 250 and 300 shot holes in its sides, exclusive of grape shot damage; the *Linnet* had between thirty and fifty holes in its hull. British gunnery had proven less accurate, scoring fifty-five hits on the *Saratoga* and thirty-nine on the *Eagle*. Macdonough's crews patched up the vessels in a couple of weeks and on 29 September the *Saratoga*, *Ticonderoga*, *Confiance* and *Linnet* sailed for Whitehall. Macdonough remained in the *Eagle* with several of the smaller vessels at Plattsburgh, making one short trip north at the end of October to look out for any British activity. Granted permission to give up his command, Macdonough left the *Eagle* in the hands of Lt Charles Budd and headed south to Whitehall. Budd followed shortly after and saw to the laying up of the brig and its cohorts in the narrow confines of the lake just north of the town. Their moment of glory having come and gone, the warships would never sail again.

The US Navy had not begun construction of new vessels on Lake Champlain when the war ended. Macdonough's squadron and the British prizes ended up housed over and moored near Whitehall, New York. (Basin Harbor Maritime Museum)

'Glad to get rid of her'

1815 – 1834

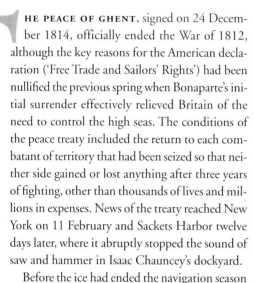

THE PEACE OF GHENT, signed on 24 December 1814, officially ended the War of 1812, although the key reasons for the American declaration ('Free Trade and Sailors' Rights') had been nullified the previous spring when Bonaparte's initial surrender effectively relieved Britain of the need to control the high seas. The conditions of the peace treaty included the return to each combatant of territory that had been seized so that neither side gained or lost anything after three years of fighting, other than thousands of lives and millions in expenses. News of the treaty reached New York on 11 February and Sackets Harbor twelve days later, where it abruptly stopped the sound of saw and hammer in Isaac Chauncey's dockyard.

Before the ice had ended the navigation season in December, the Americans and the British commenced building the ships with which they meant to resume the struggle for control of the lakes in the spring of 1815. At Sackets Henry Eckford started work on a rival for Yeo's *St Lawrence*. Named the *New Orleans*, the ship was so big that Chauncey abandoned his regular building site on the basin and cleared the barracks and batteries off Navy Point so Henry Eckford could launch the First Rate into deep water. Adam and Noah Brown had also arrived at Sackets and opened up a new dockyard nearby at Storrs' Harbor where they pieced together the massive timbers of a near-twin for the *New Orleans*, the *Chippewa*, also meant to carry 100 guns or more. Chauncey had plans on paper to build another strong frigate like the *Superior*, which was intended to be named the *Plattsburgh*, but news of peace kept that project on paper alone and halted all the other work.[1]

Moving quickly to reduce the naval station at Sackets Harbor, the new secretary of the navy Benjamin Crowninshield ordered Chauncey to send the shipwrights back to the seaboard as fast as he could arrange their transport, followed closely by nearly all the naval personnel. Chauncey left the

port in June after handing command of the station to Master Commandant Melancthon Woolsey, who had inaugurated it with the launch of the *Oneida* in 1809. Woolsey retained 134 officers and men under his command and kept the brigs *Jones* and *Oneida* and the schooner *Sylph* in commission. Disposal of the rest of the squadron was debated, with Chauncey suggesting that some be sold off and others sunk for preservation. In May the navy sold the merchantmen which had been converted into gunboats: the *Conquest* earned the most, going at $2540, and the *Asp*, at $155, netted the least. An offer was made to buy the *Oneida*, but it was too low to be accepted and, after some transport work during the summer, the brig went into ordinary with the rest of the vessels under the care of Woolsey's party. Late in 1815

he received permission from the Navy Department to begin roofing over the vessels with surplus wood gathered in store for the First Rates. By the next summer, a lofty building completely enclosed the *New Orleans* (the planking of which had been completed to its upper deck) on Navy Point, and the *Superior*, *Mohawk* and *Chippewa* had been roofed.[2]

The response to peace at Kingston had been nearly identical. Recalled to England to deal with the allegations he had made about Prevost's conduct during the Lake Champlain campaign, Commodore Yeo turned the command over to his replacement, Commodore Edward Campbell Rich Owen, and departed in March 1815. He accepted an invitation from Chauncey to visit Sackets Harbor and with a retinue of officers and

attendants crossed the lake to visit his rival of nearly two years, proceeding from there to New York to obtain the quickest passage to England.

Owen found an ambitious building programme underway at Kingston. Two First Rates to carry 108 guns and measuring 191ft 3in on the gundeck, 157ft 7⅝in by 50ft 8in by 18ft 4in for a burthen of 2152 tons stood framed on the stocks. Thomas Strickland had laid down the first of these (known then as 'New Ship No 1' and later as the *Canada*) in December and John Goudie had taken a contract to build its twin ('New Ship No 2,' later the *Wolfe*) about the same time.[3] Draughts of these vessels show that they were intended to resemble the *St Lawrence* except for having roundhouses upon which six guns could be placed. Strickland had also finished work

The British made careful observations of the American base at Sackets Harbor. This map, done early in the summer of 1816, shows its defences and the squadron hauled into the basin. (National Archives of Canada, NMC7637)

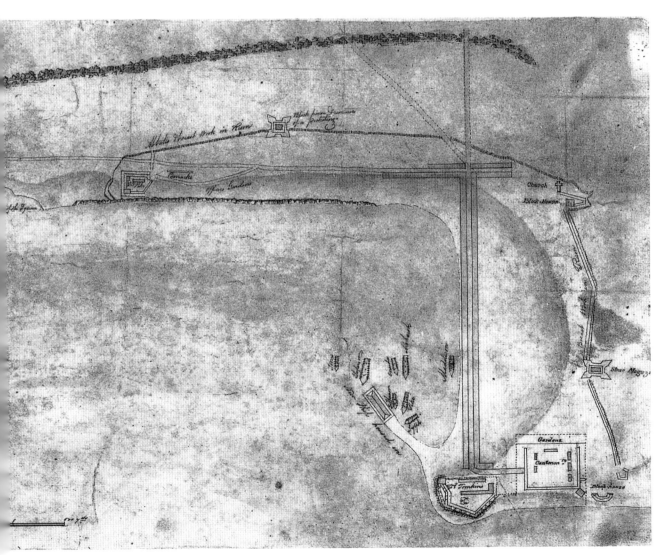

during the winter on three new gunboats, the *Blazer* (43ft on deck by 13ft 3in extreme breadth), *Musquito* and *Boxer* (both 49ft by 13ft 3in), each of them capable of carrying a single 18pdr long gun. In addition Strickland had designed a transport ship at Yeo's request. This vessel was 107ft 5in on the deck, 85ft 8in by 30ft by 12ft 6in for a burthen of 438 tons and featured a flat bottom and rounded bilge to make a hold commodious enough to adequately serve the army's needs. Commodore Owen halted work on the two First Rates and had the tops of their frames and posts covered, leaving the frames open to the elements so that they could season. He allowed work to continue on the transport, which was launched in July 1816 and named, at first, the *Beckwith* and then the *Charwell*. The old *Charwell* (née the *Earl of Moira*) was in ordinary and doing service as a powder hulk by the time the transport swam. The frigate and two brigs sent with the *Psyche* to Canada in frame remained in pieces at Montreal where efforts to sell them failed and they were eventually sent to Halifax.

Thomas Strickland surveyed the warships at Kingston in the spring and summer of 1815 and drew their 'as built' draughts. Owen approved the continued outfitting of the *Psyche* and sent it on two brief cruises up the lake with part of the squadron, informing the Admiralty that the fir frigate 'sails faster than any ship on Lake Ontario.'[4] By summer 1815, however, the *Psyche, Princess Charlotte* (re-named *Burlington* in 1816), *St Lawrence* and *Charwell* were in ordinary, while the *Prince Regent* (re-named *Kingston* in 1816), *Niagara, Montreal* (having been altered to a troopship that spring by the addition of another deck), *Star* and *Netley* were in commission with reduced crews. Officers and seamen began their trek home shortly after the news of peace and by autumn those few who remained worked on roofing over the warships anchored in Navy Bay.

Plans formed by the British late in 1814 had extended well beyond Lake Ontario. Besides the First Rate at Kingston, John Goudie was also contracted to build eleven gunboats, a transport, two large brigs and three 36-gun frigates at Isle aux Noix.[5] Work never began on the brigs and two of the frigates, but Goudie raised the stem and stern and added thirteen floors to the keel of a frigate before the order to stop arrived from Kingston. Enough shipwrights continued under contract, however, to complete a shallow-draught transport named the *Champlain* (68ft 9in on deck by 20ft for a burthen of 111 tons). Goudie also fulfilled his obligation to build gunboats, putting together twelve hulls with large enough scantlings

Thomas Strickland designed the transport *Beckwith/Charwell* but did not live to build it. He died after falling off a horse in September 1815. (Archives of Ontario, f360 OS 13-1)

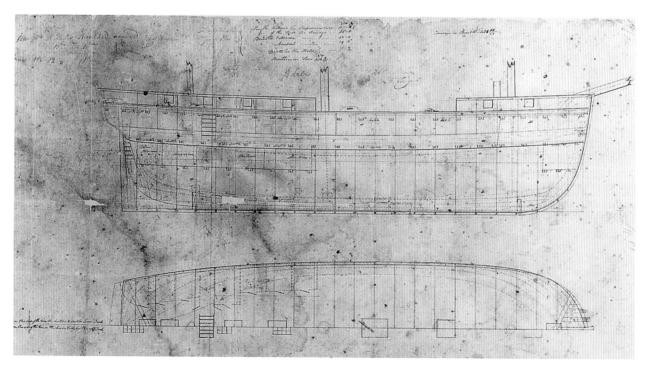

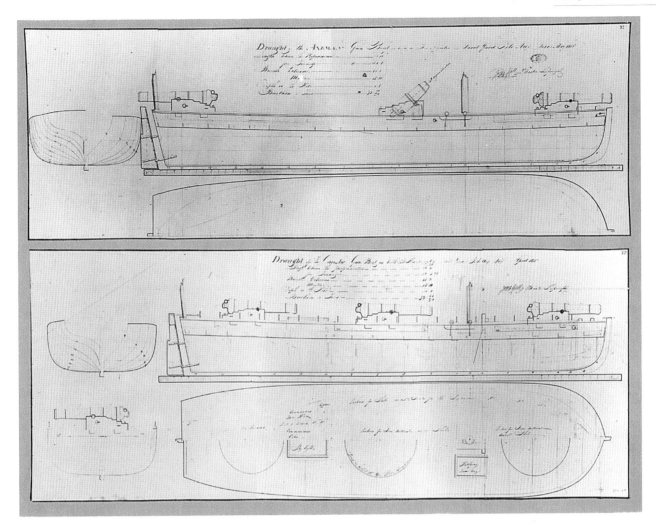

The British had ambitious plans for rebuilding the Lake Champlain squadron in 1815, but only a transport, the *Champlain*, and heavy gunboats like the *Axeman*, top, and *Caustic* were constructed. (National Archives of Canada, MG 11, CO 42/172)

to carry three heavy guns. Constructed in one place at the same time, the new gunboats were more nearly uniform in size than their predecessors: the *Caustic* was the smallest at 59ft 5in (deck) by 16ft 2in by 4ft 1in for a burthen of 73 tons and the *Axeman* was the biggest at 63ft 10in by 16ft 2in by 4ft 4in, 75 tons. Goudie's gunboats brought to a total of twenty-five the number of such vessels at Isle aux Noix. A small naval contingent kept the station open temporarily but it appears that most of the gunboats were drawn up on shore and housed over for preservation, while several of them saw limited service for a brief period.

The Americans did not start any new projects on Lake Champlain. Captain James Leonard, USN, arrived at Whitehall in spring 1815 to take command of the squadron.[6] In July the navy sold the *Chub*, *Finch*, *President*, *Montgomery*, *Preble* and

the four older gunboats for less than $8000 in total, and in August Leonard had the six galleys sunk for preservation. By that summer the *Saratoga*, *Ticonderoga*, *Eagle*, *Confiance* and *Linnet* were roofed over and being pumped dry regularly to keep them afloat at their anchorage in the narrow channel of the lake just north of Whitehall.

A similar approach was taken at Erie. Commodore Arthur Sinclair returned in 1815 to make several brief cruises moving men and munitions and then lay up the squadron.[7] The smaller warships, *Caledonia*, *Porcupine*, *General Hunter* and *Lady Prevost*, were sold while the *Lawrence*, *Detroit* and *Queen Charlotte* were submerged for preservation in Misery Bay off Presque Isle Bay. The *Niagara* remained as a receiving ship and a 60-ton schooner named the *Ghent* was built to function as the navy's sole active element on the upper lakes.

The British increased their presence on the upper lakes after the war as a result of the momentum they initiated while trying to regain what they had lost to Perry in September 1813. In the autumn of 1814 Commodore Yeo, with the full approval of Prevost, ordered Captain Edward Collier to sail to York in the *Niagara,* lay up the ship and head north to Penetanguishene Bay, the site at the southern tip of Georgian Bay that had been chosen for the building of a 44-gun frigate. The *Niagara* had been loaded with the hardware necessary for outfitting the vessel, including twenty of the *Princess Charlotte*'s long 24pdrs, and Collier and his crew were destined to spend the winter hauling the gear along the ninety-mile route to Georgian Bay while axemen felled timber by the inlet at Penetanguishene and shipwrights built the frigate. They had barely begun their task when the news of peace arrived and the project was cancelled.[8]

Nevertheless, the upper lakes became the Royal Navy's most active freshwater station after the War of 1812, in part because the capture of four American schooners in August and September 1814

gave the British an instant flotilla. The *Surprise* (ex-*Scorpion*) and *Confiance* (ex-*Tigress*) spent the winter at the Nottawasaga River, twenty miles southwest of Penetanguishene, while the *Sauk* (ex-*Ohio*) and *Huron* (ex-*Somers*) were taken up the Chippewa Creek and submerged in one of its tributaries, Street's Creek, just in case the Americans tried to recapture them in a raid across the Niagara. The schooners were raised and outfitted in the spring and at the same time Commodore Owen and Commissioner Robert Hall approved the building of two schooners above the falls 'for the Transport of Military Stores upon Lake Erie … [and] to be of sufficient size and strength to be armed as Gun vessels on emergency – to carry two long Twenty-four Pounders abaft the Foremast.'[9] William Bell, who had returned to Canada as the assistant master builder at Kingston, designed the schooners with dimensions measuring 70ft 6in on deck, 52ft 4¾in by 24ft 5in by 9ft for a burthen of 166 tons. They were built at Street's Creek by a gang of 120 artificers who had lately returned from Penetanguishene. Named the *Tecumseth* and

William Bell designed the twin schooners *Tecumseth* and *Newash* that were built in 1815 at Street's Creek for service on the upper lakes. (National Maritime Museum, neg DR4362)

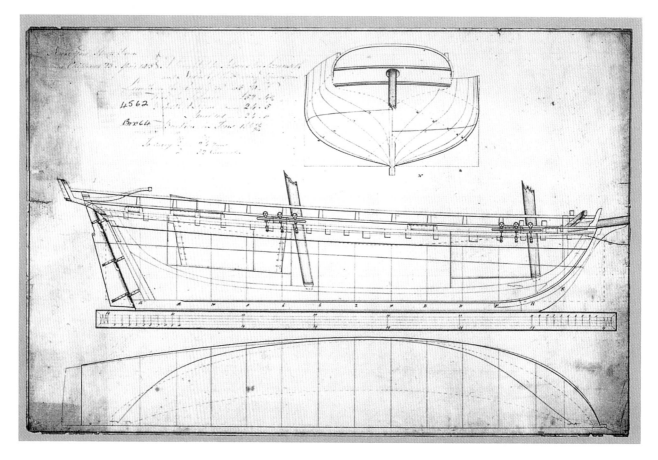

TABLE 45
British vessels launched after 1814

Name	Launch	Place	Rig	Remarks
Lake Ontario				
three gunboats	1815	Kingston	lugger	1820s in ordinary, decayed
Beckwith/Charwell (B)	1816	Kingston	brig	1817 in ordinary; 1830s sold, broken up
Radcliffe	1817	Kingston	gunboat/lugger	1820s in ordinary, decayed
Brock (C)	1817	Kingston	schooner	1820s rebuilt; 1830s sold, broken up
Upper Lakes				
Tecumseth	1815	Street's Creek	schooner	1817 in ordinary, decayed
Newash	1815	Street's Creek	brigantine	1817 in ordinary, decayed
Bee	1817	Penetanguishene	schooner	1820s in ordinary, decayed
Wasp (B)	1817	Penetanguishene	schooner	1820s in ordinary, decayed
Mosquito	1817	Penetanguishene	schooner	1820s in ordinary, decayed
Lake Champlain				
Champlain	1815	Isle aux Noix	schooner	1817 in ordinary, decayed
twelve gunboats	1815	Isle aux Noix	lugger	post 1815 in ordinary, decayed

Source: NAC, MG 12, ADM 106/1997, 1998.

TABLE 46
American vessels launched after 1814

Name	Launch	Place	Rig	Remarks
Ghent	1815	Erie	schooner	1825 sold

Source: Dobbins Papers, p379.

Newash, the vessels were launched on 7 August 1815 and by the end of the month were manned with crews of 50 officers and men and ready for sailing trials. The first excursions on Lake Erie showed a defect in the rig of the *Newash* and it was altered into a brigantine by re-stepping the foremast 10ft aft; the mast of the *Tecumseth* was probably moved as well, although it continued to be labelled a schooner. Rather than having to sail up to Georgian Bay, the vessels wintered at the Royal Navy station that had been opened that year at the mouth of the Grand River to provide a means of maintaining closer contact with posts on Lake Ontario. The *Sauk* and *Huron* were stationed there also while the former dockyard at Amherstburg was reduced to a depot.

The *Tecumseth* and *Newash* were each equipped with long 24s and a pair of 24pdr carronades in the spring of 1816 and put into service transporting troops and provisions between the Grand River and Amherstburg. Although they drew only 7ft 7in of water, the vessels frequently scraped over the bar at the Grand River, so in 1817 officials ordered them to change places with the *Surprise* and *Confiance* which required less water. After a trip to Drummond Island at the very northern tip of Lake Huron where the British had moved their garrison when they returned Mackinac Island to the Americans, the *Tecumseth* and *Newash* arrived at Penetanguishene. The Royal Navy had finally opened its base there after two years at Nottawasaga and the shipwrights had begun work on three schooners that were so small in dimension that they were frequently referred to as Durham boats. These were the *Bee*, *Wasp* and *Mosquito*, measuring about 43ft between perpendiculars, 36ft 6in by 14ft 6in for a burthen of about 40 tons. Although as small as their names suggested, the schooners (rigged without topsails) were to be the way of the future on the upper lakes because of an agreement signed early in 1817 by Britain and the United States.

The British minister in Washington, Sir Charles Bagot, and Acting Secretary of State Richard Rush pursued negotiations for naval disarmament begun by their governments in 1816 and settled the matter in April 1817. Known as the Rush-Bagot Agreement, the arrangement limited the naval strength of each nation to one vessel under 100 tons armed with one 18pdr long gun on each of Lake Ontario and Lake Champlain and two such vessels on the upper lakes. At Kingston the current master builder, Robert Moore, launched two new craft in the spring of 1817. The first was a 2-gun gunboat, the *Radcliffe*, measuring 54ft on deck, 43ft 3in by 15ft 8in by 3ft 3in for a burthen of 56 tons, and the second was the schooner *Brock*, which was 69ft 6in on deck, 55ft 9⅞in by 22ft 3in by 10ft for a burthen of 140 tons. The Rush-Bagot Agreement restricted the service of these vessels, as did the fact that Britain and the United States steadily reduced their stations on the lake as a cost-saving measure.

Command of the British naval forces on the lakes passed to Captain Robert Barrie in 1818, whose official title was that of commissioner; he was granted the title of commodore in the 1820s.

During his long tenure as senior officer on the lakes, Barrie watched the status of his command slowly fade as funding lessened each year and it became more and more difficult to keep the old ships afloat. In spite of the decline in operations he and his officers and men regularly completed lengthy surveys on the condition of the ships and storehouses, sails, ropes and guns and made estimates of the work that needed to be done and the costs it would incur.[10]

One of the more interesting reports filed in the volumes of correspondence exchanged with the Admiralty is Barrie's response to Admiralty queries about the suitability of converting commercial steamboats on the lakes into warships. After explaining that the private steamers were too light in scantling to be of any service, the commodore suggested that the frigate *Psyche* could support an engine and paddle wheels. As his crews had done to some of the other vessels over the years, the *Psyche* had been cut down, hauled up on a slipway, stripped of rotten timbers and rebuilt in frame 'from the best wood that could be procured; her scantling is very large equal to a line of Battle Ship, and she is calculated at present to carry 56 Guns.'[11] Nothing came of Barrie's suggestion and little else was actually accomplished throughout the 1820s, although the British did manage to outlast the Americans in maintaining naval stations on the lakes.

The three US Navy stations on the lakes were closed in 1825. At Erie the brig *Niagara* had been sunk for preservation five years earlier and the schooner *Ghent* had continued under command of Sailing Master Daniel Dobbins, who arranged for its sale in 1825. While the *Niagara* and *Lawrence* remained beneath the waves, the *Detroit* and *Queen Charlotte* were both raised in the 1830s and outfitted as commercial ships. The end of the *Detroit* was dramatic. In September 1841 a group of merchants bought the ship lying derelict at Buffalo, rigged it up and sent it down the Niagara River to crash over the falls; their motivation was to create a spectacle, but the old warship ran aground on a shoal before it could reach the brink and eventually went to pieces.[12]

At Whitehall the galley *Allen* had been raised and outfitted with a long 12pdr so that the

Commodore Barrie submitted this cross section with his proposal to convert the *Psyche* into a paddle-wheeler in 1831. (National Archives of Canada, MG 12, ADM 106/2002)

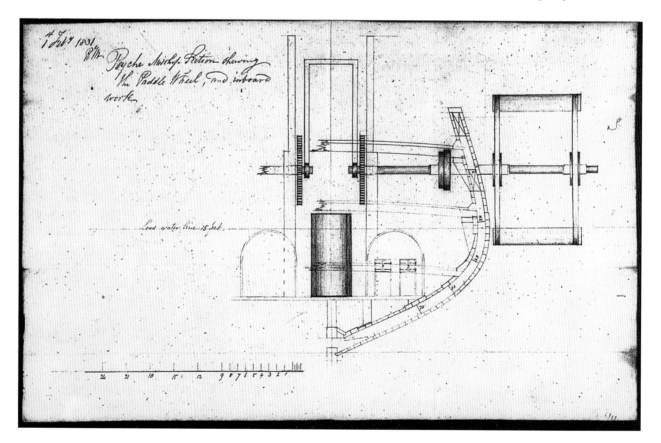

United States could comply with the Rush-Bagot Agreement. Captain Leonard moved the warships from their anchorage to a point a little ways up the Poultney River in 1823 and then oversaw the demolition of the *Confiance* when it washed into the main channel the next year. The remainder of the ships, sunk or heeled over in a line along the shore, were sold at an auction in October 1825 for $6632.83 to salvagers who harvested any iron and serviceable timber they could find.

At Sackets Harbor the *Lady of the Lake* served for a time after 1817 as its nation's only active warship on Lake Ontario, but it was eventually laid up to join the other ships slowly decaying beneath their roofs and sinking at their moorings.[13] Woolsey left the station in January 1825 to take a commission at sea in the USS *Constellation* while his replacement, Lt Samuel Adams, attended to the orders he had received to sell off the ships and their equipment. An Oswego businessman named Robert Hugunin paid $8000 in the spring of 1825 for the right to refloat or dispose of the square-rigged vessels. Hugunin deemed the *Jefferson* worthless and left it at its wharf in the basin, while he appears to have even-

In 1815 the Royal Navy established a new post on the mouth of the Grand River at the eastern end of Lake Erie to reduce the distance between posts on Lake Ontario and Amherstburg. Apart from small boats, no construction was carried on there, although the schooners *Confiance, Surprise, Sauk* and *Huron* were stationed there at the end of their careers. (National Archives of Canada, MG 12, ADM 106/2002)

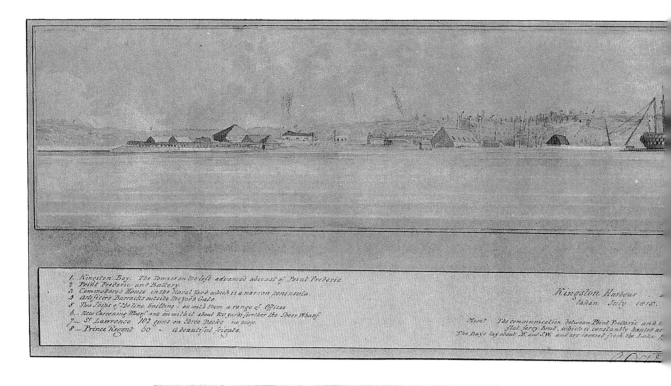

SHIP "ORLEANS" WAR 1812
SACKETTS HARBOR, N.Y.

Right: The last of the 1812ers was the *New Orleans*, shown here in the 1880s after its housing had collapsed and just before it was dismantled. (Courtesy, Jonathon Moore)

Above: This watercolour done in July 1815 shows Point Frederick, Kingston and Point Henry with the British squadron at anchor. The vessels (left to right) are the two First Rates on the stocks, the *St Lawrence*, *Prince Regent*, *Princess Charlotte* and *Psyche*. Deadman Bay, where two of the ships later sank, is to the right of Point Henry. (Royal Military College, Kingston, Ontario)

tually dismantled the *Superior*, *Mohawk*, *Sylph*, *Jones* and *General Pike*; the *New Orleans* and *Chippewa* were retained by the government, the latter ship falling to the wrecking hammers in 1833. Hugunin resurrected and restored the *Oneida* and sold it as a merchantman named the *Adjutant Clitz*; it lasted until beached at Clayton, New York in 1837, perhaps a testament to Woolsey's salting experiment in 1809. The *Madison* became the *General Brady* and survived for a few seasons as a laker before disappearing from the record. The *Lady of the Lake* also went to a private owner and was lost near Oswego in December 1826.

At Penetanguishene, the Grand River, Isle aux Noix and Kingston the ships were fast hogging out of shape or sinking out of sight. Late in 1831 Commodore Barrie received instructions to sell off the ships still afloat in Navy Bay. He advertised in the *Kingston Chronicle* the availability of the *Canada* and *Wolfe* as they stood on the stocks and the *St Lawrence*, *Kingston*, *Burlington* and *Montreal* at their moorings. As Barrie reported to the Admiralty, however,

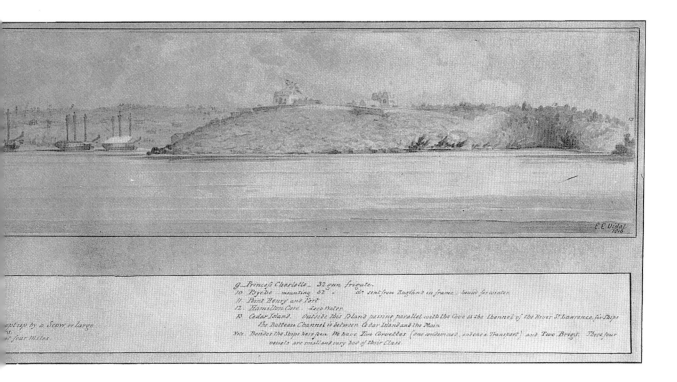

9. *Princess Charlotte* 32 gun frigate.
10. *Psyche* mounting 52 - do. sent from England in frame, housed for winter
11. *Point Henry and Fort*
12. *Hamilton Cove* Deep Water
13. *Cedar Island*. Outside this Island passing parallel with the Cove is the Channel of the River St Lawrence, for Ships The Batteau Channel is between Cedar Island and the Main
Note. Besides the Ships here seen. We have Two Corvettes (one widerrazed, and one a Transport) and Two Brigs. These four vessels are small and very bad of their Class.

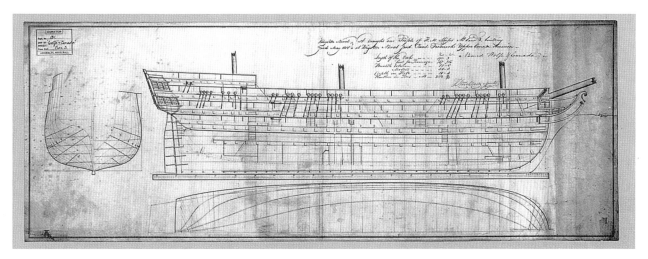

Two First Rates were on the stocks at Point Frederick in January 1815, generally resembling the *St Lawrence*, but with roundhouses to carry more guns and provide additional accommodations on the upper deck. The hull form also showed less deadrise, so would have been more capacious. (National Maritime Museum, neg DR13)

There were no bidders for any of the vessels, except for the *St Lawrence* and she was knocked down for Twenty-five pounds; I should not have allowed her to have gone for that Sum (completely rotten as she is above the water) if the purchaser were not bound to remove her, which will be an expensive job and I was glad to get rid of her on any terms as she is sunk alongside the principal wharf which is in fact useless till she is removed.[14]

The new owner of the largest sailing warship to ever cruise the Great Lakes was Robert Drummond who towed the ship across Kingston Harbour to his property where he stripped it down and used it as a dock. The other vessels were apparently towed away by the navy and sunk. In March 1834 the Admiralty sent Barrie instructions to oversee the closing of all the Royal Navy yards and haul down his pendant. Leaving a watchman in the deserted yard at Kingston, Commodore Barrie departed for England. The final effects at the dockyard were sold off in 1836

and after 1838 no further reference was made in Royal Navy records to the old vessels at Kingston.

Across the water at Sackets Harbor the last of the freshwater warships, the *New Orleans*, remained protected in its boathouse until that sagging structure blew down in a storm in the winter of 1880. Three years later the navy auctioned off the hull for $427.50 to a contractor who managed to accidentally knock it to pieces during demolition in February 1884. Fifty tons of iron, eighteen cords of cedar and vast amounts of oak were picked out of the debris and sold for every purpose from building houses to fashioning decorative knife handles; a cane carved from *New Orleans* oak was presented to President Franklin D Roosevelt in 1929.

By that time the bones of Perry's *Niagara* had been resurrected and were sparking interest in the long forgotten days of warships under sail on the lake. Eight years later divers explored the wrecks in Deadman Bay at Kingston, gathering guns and fittings for display in museums. In the decades that followed, wrecks from the days of early sail were located on each of the lakes while research into archival records revealed their stories. Gradually, the freshwater warships, from the earliest sloops to the mighty *St Lawrence*, have resurfaced to take their places in the historiography of the age of fighting sail.

Above: Underwater archaeologists have done extensive surveys of 1812 wrecks. Here, the scant remains of the once mighty *St Lawrence* are measured and recorded just offshore at Kingston, Ontario. (Photograph by Jonathan Moore)

Right: This view of the Point Frederick dockyard done by John A Roebuck between 1821 and 1824 shows one of the warships drawn up on the slip next to the two unfinished First Rates. Several of the warships were cut down, hauled up and rebuilt during the 1820s. (National Archives of Canada, C121249)

Above: The retrieval of the remains of the *Niagara* at Erie, Pennsylvania in 1913 awoke interest in the days of fighting sail on the Great Lakes. The brig was rebuilt and rigged for centennial celebrations of Perry's victory. The latest reconstruction of the *Niagara*, containing relics of Perry's brig, is now the keystone of the Maritime Museum at Erie. (Pennsylvania Museum and Historical Commission)

Notes

Abbreviations used in Notes
(Full references are given in the Bibliography)
DAB – *Dictionary of American Biography*
DCB – *Dictionary of Canadian Biography*
DHC – E A Cruikshank (ed), *Documentary History of the Campaigns on the Niagara Frontier*
DNB – *Dictionary of National Biography*
NAC – National Archives of Canada
USNA – National Archives of the United States

CHAPTER 1

1. Talon to Louis XIV, 10 October 1670: Preston, *Royal Fort Frontenac*, p102.
2. Admiralty to Keppel, 1754: Pargellis, *Military Affairs in North America*, p51.
3. Grant, 'The Capture of Oswego', pp338-67. MacLeod, *Garrison Drum*, pp6-17. Lyon, *Sailing Navy List*, p299. The only candidate for 'Lt Laforey' is the officer who became Admiral Sir John Laforey, an RN lieutenant in 1748, commander in 1755 and commanding the sloop *Hunter* in Admiral Boscawen's fleet at Louisbourg in 1758 (John Charnock, *Biographia Navalis*, Vol 4, p319); the only other Laforey on the Navy List, Loftus, did not become a lieutenant until 1760.
4. Gardiner, *The Line of Battle*, pp71-80. Gardiner, *The Heyday of Sail*, pp10-17. Chapelle, *American Sailing Navy*, pp27-8.
5. Preston, *Royal Fort Frontenac*, pp254-5.
6. Grant, 'Capture of Oswego'. MacLeod, *Garrison Drum*, pp18-27.
7. A typical ocean-going sloop of 1746 had a hold measuring 9.41ft, while a brig of 1759 had a hold of 10.75 feet: Gardiner, *The Heyday of Sail*, p33.
8. Hamilton (ed), *Adventure in the Wilderness*, pp22-38.
9. *Ibid*, pp278-9. Bradstreet biography, *DCB*, Vol 4, p83. Butler to Johnson, 28 August 1758: Preston, *Royal Fort Frontenac*, p262.
10. Bellico, *Sails and Steam*, pp39-57.
11. Instructions for Loring, 16 March 1758: NAC, MG 13, WO 34, 64, p181. MacLeod, *Garrison Drum*, pp26-37. Loring biography, *DCB*, Vol 4, p486.
12. Dies to Johnson, 19 August 1755: *The Papers of Sir William Johnson*, Vol 3, p862. Bellico, *Sails and Steam*, pp73-86.
13. Webster, *The Journal of Jeffrey Amherst*, pp119-91. Amherst biography, *DCB*, Vol 4, p21.
14. Crisman, 'Struggle for a Continent'.
15. Bellico, *Sails and Steam*, pp86-113. Webster, *The Journal of Jeffrey Amherst*, pp119-91. MacLeod, *Garrison Drum*, pp43-50. Grant biography, *DCB*, Vol 5, p363.
16. Green, 'Corvettes of New France'. Macleod, 'Fight for the West Gate'.

17. Dunnigan, *Pierre Pouchot*, pp188-232.
18. Johnson to Baker, 28 September 1759: *The Papers of Sir William Johnson*, Vol 3, p139; 'Journal of the Niagara Campaign', *ibid*, Vol 13, p129. MacLeod, *Garrison Drum*, pp43-46. Webster, *The Journal of Jeffrey Amherst*, pp127, 205-22. Thornton to Loring, 24 December 1759: NAC, MG 13, WO 34, 65, p2. Here the spelling of *Mississauga* has been standardised since the contemporary spellings varied from *Messasague* to *Messasaga* to *Mississago*.
19. Webster, *The Journal of Jeffrey Amherst*, p223.
20. Sinclair biography, *DCB*, Vol 5, p759.
21. Dunnigan, *Pierre Pouchot*, pp293-320. Doughty, *Knox's Historical Journal*, Vol 2, pp530-56. Webster, *The Journal of Jeffrey Amherst*, pp199-241.
22. Bellico, *Sails and Steam*, pp104-9.
23. Sinclair to Amherst, 22 September 1760: NAC, MG 13, WO 34, 65, p28. Loring to Amherst, 12 January, 13 November 1761: *ibid* pp48, 70. Robertson to Amherst, 20 November 1760: *ibid*, p167. A list of the Vessels on the Various Lakes ... nd (autumn 1762): *ibid*, p109
24. Instructions to Officers of the Different Western Posts, 16 September 1761: *The Papers of Sir William Johnson*, Vol 3, p527.
25. MacLeod, *Garrison Drum*, pp64-72. Nafus, *Navy Island*, pp31-43. A List of Vessels on the Various Lakes ... nd (autumn 1762): NAC, MG 13, WO 34, 65, p109. Dunnigan, 'British Naval Vessels'.
26. Amherst to Loring, 14 June 1762: NAC, MG 13, WO 34, 65, p208.

CHAPTER 2

1. Nafus, *Navy Island*, pp39-53. Dunnigan, 'British Naval Vessels on the Upper Great Lakes'. McConnell, 'Preliminary Survey of the Historical Significance of Navy Island'. Howard Peckham, *Pontiac and the Indian Uprising*.
2. Gage to Halifax, 10 August 1765: Carter, *The Correspondence of Gage*, Vol 1, p62. MacLeod, *Garrison Drum*, pp60-74.
3. Gage's response to a plan by Viscount Barrington, 10 May 1766: Alvord and Carter, *The New Regime, 1765-1767*, p234.
4. Hillsborough to Gage, 15 April 1768: Carter, *Correspondence of Gage*, Vol 2, p61. Gage to Cooper, 22 August 1767: *ibid*, Vol 2, p427. Gage to Cooper, 12 May 1768: *ibid*, p466. Gage to Hillsborough, 5 November 1772: *ibid*, Vol 1, p338. MacLeod, *Garrison Drum*, pp75-94.
5. Return of Shipping on the Lakes, by Grant, 12 June 1775: NAC, Series Q, 11, p226. De Peyster to Powell, 10 October 1781: *Michigan Historical Collections*, 19, p664. MacLeod, *Garrison Drum*, pp92-7.
6. An Inventory of HM Schooner *Dunmore*, 1 May 1778: *Haldimand Papers*, 21804,

p56. Repairs to the *Dunmore*, 15 December 1795: NAC, RG 8, I, 723, p52. A General Return of HM Vessels on Lake Erie: *ibid*, 722 p34. Cornwall to Mathews, 1781: *Michigan Historical Collections*, 19, p674.
7. Andrews to Basset, 17 June 1773: *Michigan Historical Collections*, 19, p304.
8. Morrison to Haldimand, 4 September 1778: *Haldimand Papers*, 21801, p15. Andrews to Haldimand, 3 October 1778: *ibid*, p30
9. Memorandums relative to the Naval Department on the Upper Lakes, by Andrews, Grant *et al*, 13 May 1778: *Haldimand Papers*, 21804, p68. Carleton to Officers at Detroit, Niagara, Oswegatchie and St Johns, 2 July 1777: *ibid*, p20. Remarks on Private Vessels taken into the service, nd: *ibid*, p26. Memorandum by Carleton, 2 July 1777: *ibid*, p20. Colonel Bolton's Opinions in Regard to the Naval Department, 10 May 1778: *ibid*, p59. Regulations, by Bolton, Grant, Andrews, Bouchette, *et al*, 13 May 1778: *ibid*, p66. Grant's position as commissioner on the lakes, dated 23 October 1777 was mentioned in Bolton to Andrews, 25 May 1778: *ibid*, 21801, p3. Memo by Carleton, 21 October 1777: *Michigan Historical Collections*, 19, p333. MacLeod, *Garrison Drum*, pp106-63.
10. Bellico, *Sails and Steam*, pp114-203. Mahan, *Navies in the War of American Independence*, pp6-28. Fowler, *Rebels Under Sail*, pp171-211. Gardiner, *Navies and the American Revolution*, pp28-38, 75-6.
11. Douglas to Starke, 7 July 1776: Morgan, *Naval Documents of the American Revolution*, Vol 5, p1070. Douglas to Stephens, 21 July and 21 October 1776: *ibid*, pp1167, 1340.
12. Lyon, *Sailing Navy List*, p298.
13. Chapelle, *American Sailing Navy*, pp100-114. Lundeberg, *The Gunboat* Philadelphia.
14. Schank biography, *DCB*, Vol 6, p694.
15. General Orders and Regulations for the better Government of His Majesty's Armed Vessels Employed on the Lakes, 1778: *Haldimand Papers*, 21804, p74. Queries and Regulations proposed by Commissioner Schank ..., 30 April 1779: *ibid*, p162. Bolton to Andrews, 25 May 1778: *Michigan Historical Collections*, 16, p346. Regulations for the Naval Armament, 23 July 1781: NAC, RG 8, 722a, p91. Instructions to Captain Grant, 8 September 1781: *ibid*, p94.
16. A General Return of HM Armed Vessels on Lake Ontario, 1 January 1779: NAC, RG 8, 722a, p32. A General Return of HM Armed Vessels on Lakes Erie and Huron, 1 January 1779: *ibid*, p34. Schank to Haldimand, 18 February 1779: *Haldimand Papers*, 21801, p65.
17. Bouchette biography, *DCB*, Vol 5, p100. Pay List for the Snow *Seneca*, 11 November 1777-10 May 1778: *Haldimand Papers*,

21804, p63. La Force biography, *DCB*, Vol 5, p470. Schank to Haldimand, 14 March 1779: *Haldimand Papers*, 21804, p89. Sinclair biography, *DCB*, Vol 5, p759.

18. Bond, 'The British Base at Carleton Island'.

19. Smith, *Legend of the Lake: the 22-Gun Brig-Sloop* Ontario, *1780*.

20. A General Return of the Force on Lake Erie …, 1 August 1782: *Michigan Historical Collections*, 10, p618. Lake Erie Vessels, 1788: *Haldimand Papers*, 21804, p86. Haldimand to Powell, 15 November 1780: *Michigan Historical Collections*, 19, p583. Return of His Majesty's Vessels on the Lakes: *Haldimand Papers*, 21805, p145. Return of Marine Establishments in Lower and Upper Canada, 24 October 1793: NAC, MG 11, CO42, 97, p170. MacLeod, *Garrison Drum*, pp155-165.

21. A Return of the men to be Discharged, 22 May 1783: *Haldimand Papers*, 21805, p90. 18 October 1783: *ibid*, p106. MacLeod, *Garrison Drum*, pp155-165.

CHAPTER 3

1. Carleton biography, *DCB*, Vol 5, pp141.

2. Remarks on the Inland Navigation Ordinance, by James McGill, 19 January 1789: Cruikshank, *Records of Niagara #40*, p74. Report of Committee on Inland Navigation, 9 February 1789: *ibid*, p80. An examination of accounts and outstanding fees is in five volumes of account books and reports covering the period of 1778-93: NAC, RG 14, B 13, 1-5.

3. Mackay to Beckwith, 25 April 1794: Preston, *Kingston Before 1812*, p203.

4. Simcoe to Clarke, 17 June 1793: Preston, *Kingston Before 1812*, p227.

5. Preston, *Kingston Before 1812*, ppxxxvii-lxiv.

6. Bunbury to LeMaistre, 21 August 1789: Preston, *Kingston Before 1812*, p147. Return of his Majesty's Vessels …, November 1793: NAC, RG 8, 723, p26. MacLeod, 'Simcoe's Schooner Onondaga'. MacLeod, *Garrison Drum*, pp69-171.

7. Grant to Simcoe, 2 February 1793: Cruikshank, *Simcoe Correspondence*, Vol 1, p285. Dunnigan, 'British Naval Vessels', pp92-8. 'Stores secured from on board the *Chippewa,* formerly the *Tebicas*', Remains of Ordnance, 1 September 1794 by Byrn: *Michigan Historical Collections*, 12, p124. Abstract of Estimates for Repairs by Reynolds, 15 December 1795: NAC, RG 8, I, 723, p49. MacLeod, *Garrison Drum*, pp169-171.

8. Report of the Committee on Inland Navigation, 9 February 1789: Cruikshank, *Records of Niagara, #40*, p78. MacLeod, *Garrison Drum*, pp170-1.

9. Simcoe biography, *DCB*, Vol 5, p754.

10. Simcoe to Dorchester, 4 November 1792: NAC, MG 11, Q 279, p1.

11. Simcoe to Clarke, 31 May 1793: Cruikshank, *Simcoe Correspondence*, Vol 1, p340.

12. Innis, *Mrs. Simcoe's Diary*, p74.

13. Return of the Marine Establishment, and Return of Additional Armed Vessels, 24 October 1793: NAC, MG 11, CO 42/97, pp170, 172. Simcoe to Clarke, 31 May 1793: Cruikshank, *Simcoe Correspondence*, Vol 1, p340. Schank biography, *DCB*, Vol 6, p694.

14. Dundas to Dorchester, 8 June 1794: NAC, MG 11, CO 42/98, p1.

15. Northumberland to Simcoe, 6 November 1795: Cruikshank, *Simcoe Correspondence*, Vol 4, p128.

16. Return of the Marine Establishment …, 24 October 1793: NAC, MG 11, CO 42/97, p170. Return of Seamen, by Shekleton, 24 June 1802: NAC, RG 8, I, 725, p165. List of Soldiers on Lake Erie between 10 August 1797 and 25 November 1798: *ibid*, 723, p169. List of Soldiers on Lake Ontario, 1798: *ibid*, 724, p22. Selby to Chew, 13 August 1796: *Michigan Historical Collections*, 12, p249. McLean to Green, 18 August 1797: *ibid*, 12, p267. Russell to Prescott, 19 August 1797, Cruikshank and Hunter, *The Correspondence of the Honourable Peter Russell*, p253. MacLeod, *Garrison Drum*, pp197-199.

17. A List of Officers, 6 July 1796: NAC, RG 8, I, 723, p61. Bouchette biography, *DCB*, Vol 5, p101.

18. Enclosures with England to Green, 20 September 1795: NAC, RG 8, I, 723, p40. England to Green, 15 December 1795: *ibid*, p46. Estimates of Expense for building *Maria* and *Francis*, 17 September 1795: *ibid*, pp55,56. England to Simcoe, 31 December 1794: Cruikshank, *Simcoe Correspondence*, Vol 3, p244. Simcoe to Dorchester, 2 June 1794: *ibid*, Vol 2, p256.

19. Mrs Simcoe's Diary, 14 May 1795, cited in: Preston, *Kingston Before 1812*, plxxxiii. Chandler to LeMaistre, 29 October 1794: *ibid*, p238. MacLeod, 'Simcoe's Schooner Onondaga'. Green to Spencer, 12 February 1798: Cruikshank and Hunter, *Russell Correspondence*, Vol 2, p79. Spencer to Green, 6 September 1798: *ibid*, p252. Board of Survey, 5 January 1798: NAC, RG 8, I, 723, p140. MacLeod, *Garrison Drum*, pp200-201. O'Brien, *Speedy Justice*, pp78-81.

20. Grant to Burton, 20 October 1800: NAC, RG 8, I, 725, p39.

21. *Upper Canada Gazette*, 14 September 1799: Firth, *Town of York*, p147. Dennis biography, *DCB*, Vol 6, p187.

22. Spencer to Green, 6 September 1798: NAC, RG 8, I, 723, p152. Ross to Green, 6 June 1800: *ibid*, 724, p133. Board of Survey, 21 February 1803: *ibid*, 726, p11. MacLeod, *Garrison Drum*, pp206-7.

23. MacLeod, *Garrison Drum*, pp205-208.

24. Statement of the Naval Forces on Lake Ontario, 1814, 1815: NAC, MG 12, ADM 106/1997. Craigie to Green, 31 December 1802: *loc cit*, RG 8, I, 725, p212.

25. Proposed Establishment … for 1812, by Pye, 30 August 1811: NAC, RG 8, I, 728, p60. Gray to Prevost, 29 January 1812: *ibid*, p77. Robe to Green, 22 October and 16 December 1804: *ibid*, 726, pp175,184. Robe to Green, 24 October 1803: *ibid*, p87. Earl to Green, 7 February 1804: *ibid*, p124. Estimate for rigging *Moira*, by Dennis, 21 May 1804: *ibid*, p154.

26. Report of a Board of Survey, 16 January 1799: NAC, RG 8, I, 724, p5. Estimate of materials needed by Pearson, 6 November 1800: *ibid*, p171. McClean to Green, 28 April 1801: *ibid*, 725, p16. Campbell to Green, 25 June 1802: *ibid*, 724, p171. England to Green, 27 May 1796: *Michigan Historical Collections*, 12, p209.

27. Craigie to Green, 27 September 1803: NAC, RG 8, I, 726, p75.

28. Robe to Craigie, 27 September 1803: NAC, RG 8, I, 726, p81. Craigie to Reynolds, 27 September 1803: *ibid*, p78

29. Court of Inquiry into the Loss of the *Hope*, 25 November 1805: NAC, RG 8, I, 726, p188. O'Brien, *Speedy Justice*, pp97-110.

30. Grant to Campbell, 3 March 1806: NAC, RG 8, I, 727, p15. Estimates by Dennis, 26 February and 26 December 1806: *ibid*, pp9, 54. A bill of sale the *General Hunter* in 1815 gave its dimensions as 51ft by 17ft by 8ft 0½in for a burthen of 72 tons: bill of sale, 8 July 1815, USNA, US Customs Service (private correspondence from P Rindlisbacher).

31. *York Gazette*, 11 November 1807: Firth, *Town of York*, p132.

32. War Department to Brevoort, 1 September 1806: *Michigan Historical Collections* 40, p84. Dyson to Dearborn, 8 January 1807: *ibid*, p91. 'Dobbins Papers', pp284-6. Gamble to Woolsey, 2 December 1808, enclosed in Woolsey to Smith, 4 December 1808: USNA, RG 45, M148, 9, p185.

CHAPTER 4

1. Casey, 'North Country Nemesis: The Potash Rebellion and the Embargo'.

2. Chapelle, *American Sailing Navy*, p229.

3. Woolsey to Smith, 19 July 1808: USNA, RG 45, M148, 9, p95. Eckford biography, *DAB*, Vol 3, p4. Wheelock, 'Henry Eckford (1775-1832)'. Anon, 'The Old Ship-Builders of New York'.

4. Woolsey to Smith, 8 September 1808: USNA, RG 45, M148, 9, p136. Palmer, 'James Fenimore Cooper and the Navy Brig *Oneida*'.

5. Woolsey to Smith, 4 December 1808: USNA. RG 45, M148, 9, p185.

6. Gamble to Woolsey, 2 December 1808, enclosed in Woolsey to Smith, 4 December 1808: USNA, RG 45, M148, 9, p185. Woolsey to Smith, 22 January 1809: *ibid*, 10, p14.

7. Woolsey to Smith, 2 April 1809: USNA, RG 45, M148, 11, p3. Woolsey to Smith, 29 January 1809: *ibid*, 10, p29.

8. Cartwright to Mackenzie, 2 November 1808: Preston, *Kingston Before 1812*, p261. Tucker and Reuter, *Injured Honor*.

9. Craig to Gore, 24 and 26 January 1809: NAC, RG 5, A1, 9, pp3620, 3634. Gore to Craig, 20 February 1809: *ibid*, p3688.

10. Pye to Gore, 12 March 1809: NAC, RG 5, A1, 9, p3766. Steel to Halton, 21 April 1809: *ibid*, p3897. In this context, the term 'sloop' refers to the class of vessel that would be suitable for command by a Commander rather than a Lieutenant; any vessel below a post ship under commission to a Royal Navy commander was deemed a sloop; the Americans had a similar system. Data for the *Royal George* is based upon several sources, including: the Admiralty draught and various statements (which present conflicting figures) of the naval force on Lake Ontario in NAC, MG 12, ADM 106/1997. Gardiner, *Line of Battle*, pp56-7.

11. Woolsey to Hamilton, 23 August 1809: USNA, RG 45, M148, 12, p141.

12. Kempt to Gore, 2 and 3 April 1809: NAC, RG 5, A1, 9, pp3830, 3835. Grant to Halton, 27 May 1809: *ibid*, p3958. Estimates for workmanship, materials and stores for the vessel at Amherstburg, enclosed in Gore to Kempt, 14 June 1809: *ibid*, p3985.

13. Barclay to Yeo, 2 June 1813: NAC, MG 12, ADM 1/5445, p77.

14. Elliott to Chauncey, 15 January 1814, enclosed in Chauncey to Jones, 23 April 1814: USNA, RG 45, M125, 35, p105. Gardiner, *The Line of Battle*, p62. Enrolment by George Miles, 10 July 1835: USNA, US Customs Service, Certificates of vessels enrolled from various Great Lakes Customs House Districts, Port of Buffalo.

15. Proposed Establishment …, by Kempt, 29 October 1810: NAC, RG 8, I, 1705, p101.

16. Woolsey to Hamilton, 22 August, 22 September, 4 and 11 November 1810: USNA, RG 45, M148,15, pp79, 117, 163, 180.

17. Woolsey to Hamilton, 23 and 30 July, 11 October, 8 November 1811: USNA, RG 45, M148, 17, pp144, 88, 188, 236. Woolsey to Hamilton, 3 January 1812: *ibid*, 18, p5.

18. Hull to Eustis, 6 March 1812: *Michigan Historical Collections*, 40, p362.

19. Armstrong to Eustis, 2 January 1812: *DHC*, Vol 3, p30.

20. Report on the Provincial Marine by Pye, 7 December 1811: NAC, RG 8, I, 373, p29.

21. Brock to Prevost, 2 Decmber 1811, *DHC*, Vol 3, p21. Prevost biography, *DCB*, Vol 5, p693.

22. Brock to Prevost, 2 December 1811, *DHC*, Vol 3, p21. Memo by Brock, January 1812: *ibid*, p28.

23. Gray to Prevost, 29 January 1812: NAC, RG 8, I, 728, p77.

24. Prevost to Liverpool, 14 April 1812: *DHC*, Vol 3, p52.

25. Woolsey to Hamilton, 9, 26 and 28 June, 4 July 1812: USNA, M148, 19, pp19, 63, 72, 82.

CHAPTER 5

1. Barclay to Freer, 9 May 1813: NAC, RG 8, I, 729, p183. Report on the Provincial Marine by Pye, 7 December 1811: NAC, RG 8, I, 373, p29. Data for the schooner *Prince Regent* (renamed the *Lord Beresford* in 1813 and the *Netley* in 1814) is based upon various statements (which present conflicting figures) of the naval force on Lake Ontario in NAC, MG 12, ADM 106/1997.

2. Prevost to Brock, 7 and 10 July 1812: *DHC*, Vol 3, pp113, 120.

3. Woolsey to Hamilton, 21 July 1812: USNA, RG 45, M148, 19, p100. Lossing, *Pictorial Field-book of the War of 1812*, pp367-9.

4. Wells to Woolsey, 4 August 1812, enclosed in Woolsey to Hamilton, 8 August 1812: USNA, RG 45, M148, 19, p142.

5. Phelps to Tompkins, 4 October 1812: *DHC*, Vol 4, p32. Earl to Prevost, 10 October 1813: NAC, RG 8, I, 731, p43. Memo by Tuttle, 29 March 1815: *ibid*, 695, p4

6. Malcomson, *Sailors of 1812*, pp22-3.

7. Strachan to McGill, November 1812: Spragge, *The John Strachan Letter Book*, p28.

8. Prevost to Bathurst, 17 October 1812: NAC, MG 11, CO 42/147, p215.

9. Hamilton to Chauncey, 31 August 1812: Dudley, *The Naval War of 1812*, Vol 1, p297.

10. For Chauncey biography, see *DAB*, Vol 2, p40. Chauncey to Hamilton, 26 September and 8 October 1812: USNA, RG 45, M125, 25, pp79, 106. Malcomson, *Lords of the Lake*, pp38-56.

11. Cooper, *Ned Myers*, p56. Cain, 'Building the *Lord Nelson*'.

12. Chauncey to Hamilton, 5 November 1812: USNA, RG 45, M125, 25, p162. List of Vessels Purchased prior to 3 March 1813 by Chauncey, 15 June 1813: *ibid*, M625, 76. Ordnance in the squadron was frequently altered; this arrangement probably reflects initial armaments.

13. Chauncey to Hamilton, 21 and 27 October 1812: USNA, RG 45, M125, 25, pp137, 148.

14. Chauncey to Hamilton, 8 October 1812: USNA, RG 45 M125, 25, p106.

15. Chauncey to Hamilton, 13 and 17 November 1812: USNA, RG 45, M125, 25, pp176, 183. List of Vessels Purchased prior to 3 March 1813 by Chauncey, 15 June 1813: *ibid*, M625, p76.

16. *Ned Myers*, p57.

17. Chauncey to Hamilton, 21a and 21b November 1812: USNA, RG 45, M125, 25, pp185, 185a.

18. Chauncey to Hamilton, 13 November 1812: USNA, RG 45, M125, 25, p176.

19. Chauncey to Hamilton, 26 November 1812: USNA, RG 45, M125, 25, p192. Voucher signed 10 October 1812: USNA, RG 45, Records of the Treasury Department, 4th Audit of Settle Accounts, Alphabetical Series (this reference provided to the author by Gary Gibson).

20. Sheaffe to Prevost, 23 November 1812: NAC, RG 8, I, 728, p115.

21. Gray to Prevost, 11 and 3 December 1812: NAC, RG 8, I, 728, pp119, 135.

22. Gray to Myers, 9 February 1813: NAC, RG 8, I, 729, p99. Pearson to Freer, 11 March 1813: *ibid*, p111.

23. Surveys of *Simcoe* and *Gore*, 24 February and 6 March 1813: NAC, RG 8, I, 729, pp104,109.

24. Estimate of British and American strength by Gray, 13 March 1813: NAC, RG 8, I, 729, p130. Pearson to Freer, 28 March 1813: *ibid*, p48.

25. Myers to Freer, 9 February 1813: NAC, RG 8, I, 729, p86. Plucknett to Myers, 27 January 1813: *ibid*, p62. Gray to Prevost, 19 January 1813: *ibid*, p34. Gray to Myers, 9 February 1813: *ibid*, p99. Bruyeres to Prevost, 28 January 1813: *ibid*, 387, p15.

26. Gray to Freer, 29 April 1813: NAC, RG 8, I, 729, p173. Clerk to Gray, 25 March 1813: *ibid*, p175.

27. Sinclair to Cocke, 4 July 1813: Malcomson, *Sailors of 1812*, p43. Chauncey to Jones, 6 April 1813: USNA, RG 45, M125, 27, p135. Chapelle, *American Sailing Navy*, p273.

28. Chauncey to Bullus, 16 April 1813: Chauncey Letter Book. Tucker, *Arming the Fleet*, pp88-9. Chapelle, *American Sailing Navy*, pp165-6.

29. Chauncey to Bullus, 16 April 1813: Chauncey Letter Book.

30. Chauncey to Jones, 18 March 1813: USNA, RG 45, M125, 27, p58.

31. Chauncey to Jones, 28 April 1813: USNA, RG 45, M125, 28, p63. Sheaffe to Prevost, 5 May 1813: NAC, MG 11, CO 42/150, p158.

32. Gray to Freer, 29 April 1813: NAC, RG 8, I, 729, p169.

33. Wingfield: NAC, MG 24, F 18, p4.

34. Admiralty to Yeo, 20 March 1813: NAC, RG 8, I, 729, p132. Yeo biography, *DNB*, Vol 21, p1234. Malcomson, *Lords of the Lake*, 112-140.

35. Sinclair to Cocke, 4 July 1813: Malcomson, *Sailors of 1812*, p44. Chapelle, *American Sailing Navy*, pp120-1, 165. Enclosure with Chauncey to Bullus, 16 April 1813: Chauncey Letter Book.

36. Gray to Freer, 29 April 1813: NAC, RG 8, I, 729, p169. Malcomson, *Lords of the Lake*, pp159-62.

37. Harvey to Baynes, 11 June 1813: NAC, RG 8, I, 679, p76.

38. Mcdonogh to sister, 9 August 1813: *DHC*, Vol 6, p325.

39. Sinclair to Cocke, 25 August 1813: Malcomson, *Sailors of 1812*, p48.

40. Yeo to Prevost, 9 August 1813: NAC, RG 8, I, 730, p78.

41. Chauncey to Jones, 13 August 1813: USNA, RG 45, M125, 30, p99.

42. Sinclair to Cocke, 10 October 1813: Malcomson, *Sailors of 1812*, p59.

43. Malcomson, *Lords of the Lake*, pp164-180.

44. Chauncey to Jones, 19 August 1813: USNA, RG 45, M125, 30, p119.

45. Malcomson, *Lords of the Lake*, pp181-211.

CHAPTER 6

1. Elliott to Chauncey, 15 January 1814, enclosed in Chauncey to Jones, 23 April 1814: USNA, RG 45, M125, 35, p105.

2. Barclay to Yeo, 1 June 1813: NAC, MG 12, ADM 1/5445, p71.

3. Dunnigan, *The British Army at Mackinac*, pp10-15. Malcomson, 'War on the Lakes'.

4. Chauncey to Elliott, 7 September 1812: Chauncey Letter Book. Elliott to Chauncey, 9 October 1812, enclosed with Chauncey to Hamilton, 18 October 1812: USNA, RG 45, M125, 25, p127.

5. Hamilton to Dobbins, 11 and 15 September 1812: Dudley, *Naval War of 1812*, Vol 1, pp307, 310.

6. Dobbins to Angus, 2 December 1812: Dudley, *Naval War of 1812*, Vol 1, p360. Dobbins to Hamilton, 12 December 1812: *ibid*, p369. Howell, 'The Arrival of Dobbins at Erie'. Dobbins and Dobbins, 'The Dobbins Papers'.

7. Chauncey to Hamilton, 1 and 8 January 1813: USNA, RG 45, M125, 26, p1, 13. List of vessels purchased prior to March 1813: USNA, RG 45, M625.

8. Jones to Chauncey, 27 January 1813: USNA, RG 45, M149, 10, p231.

9. Chauncey to Brown, 18 February 1813: Chauncey Letter Book.

10. Chauncey to Jones, 21 January 1813: USNA, RG 45, M125, 26, p28. Chauncey to Perry, 20 January and 15 March 1813, Chauncey Letter Book.

11. Rosenburg, *The Building of Perry's Fleet on Lake Erie*. Chapelle, *American Sailing Navy*, pp269-273. 'The Remarkable Statement of Noah Brown'. Atkins, 'Who Designed Perry's Brigs?'.

12. 'The Dobbins Papers', p324.

13. 'Statement of Brown', p106. Inventory and Valuation of the Schooners *Scorpion* and *Tigress*, no date: NAC, MG 24, F 25, p115.

14. Proceedings of a Board of Survey, 16 August 1814: NAC, MG 24, F 25, p118. 'The Dobbins Papers', pp 286-97.

15. Gray to Prevost, 11 and 29 December 1812: NAC, RG 8, I, 728, p119 and 159. Various Estimates and Requisitions, January and February 1813: *ibid*, 729. Myers to Freer, 2 April 1813: *ibid*, p153. Chambers to Freer, 15 April 1813: *ibid*, p159.

16. Barclay to Yeo, 7 June 1813: NAC, MG 12, ADM 1/5445, p77.

17. Barclay to Yeo, 1 June 1813: NAC, MG 12, ADM 1/5445, p71.

18. 'The Dobbins Papers', pp296-7. Elliott to Crane, 15 January 1814, enclosed with Chauncey to Jones, 23 April 1814: USNA, RG 45, M125, 35, p102.

19. Barclay to Yeo, 1 September 1813: NAC, RG 8, I, 730, p126. Enrolment by George Miles, 2 August 1836: USNA, US Customs Service, Certificates of vessels enrolled from various Great Lakes Customs House Districts, Port of Buffalo. Elliott to Crane, 15 January 1814, enclosed with Chauncey to Jones, 23 April 1814: USNA, RG 45, M125, 35, p102.

20. Humphrey McGrath, cited in Malcomson, 'HMS *Detroit* 1813'.

21. Malcomson, 'The Crews of the British Squadron at Put-in-Bay'. Malcomson and Malcomson, *HMS* Detroit. Skaggs and Altoff, *A Signal Victory*.

22. Cruikshank, *Drummond's Winter Campaign*, pp25-9.

23. Malcomson, *Lords of the Lake*, pp284-5.

24. Dunnigan, *The British Army at Mackinac*, pp19-31. Malcomson, 'The US Brig *Niagara*: A History'. Malcomson, 'War on the Lakes'.

25. Sinclair to Jones, 23 September 1814: USNA, RG 45, M 125, 39, p92.

CHAPTER 7

1. Barclay to Freer, 9 May 1813: NAC, RG 8, I, 729, p183. Yeo to Prevost, 31 May 1813: *ibid*, p201. Yeo to Prevost, 22 July 1813: *ibid*, 730, p55.

2. Memorial of John Goudie, 24 June 1818: NAC, RG 8, I, 739, p116.

3. O'Conor to Freer, 16 December 1814: NAC RG 8, I, 731, p179. O'Conor to Freer, 8, 22, 27 and 30 October, 3, 5, 19 and 24 November 1813: *ibid*, pp8, 60, 79, 96, 86, 100, 131, 133. Record to Freer, 24 November 1813: *ibid*, p140.

4. NAC, MG 12, ADM 106/1997. Statement of Naval Force on Lake Ontario by Yeo, 14 April 1814: NAC, MG 12, ADM 1/2737, p78. Gardiner, *The Naval War of 1812*.

5. NAC, MG 12, ADM 106/1997. Statement of Naval Force on Lake Ontario by Yeo, 14 April 1814: NAC, MG 12, ADM 1/2737, p78. Gardiner, *The Heavy Frigate*.

6. Moore, 'Frontier Frigates and a Three-Decker'.

7. Sykes to Prevost, 10 March 1814: NAC, RG 8, I, 732, p61. Creighton to Prevost, 7 February, 1814: *ibid*, p23. O'Conor to Freer, 8 February 1814, : *ibid*, p25. Yeo to Beckwith, 10 February 1814: *ibid*, p32. Racin to Yeo, 12 February 1814: *ibid*, p57. Malcomson, *Lords of the Lake*, pp230-240.

8. A list of His Majesty's Gunboats, by O'Conor, 26 January 1814: NAC, MG 11, CO 42, 160, p320. Beattie, *Gunboats on the St Lawrence River*. Malcomson, 'Gunboats on Lake Ontario'.

9. Jones to Chauncey, 19 September 1814: Dudley, *Naval War of 1812*, Vol 2, p581. Chauncey to Jones, 8 October 1813: USNA, RG 45, M125, 31, p146.

10. Crisman, *The Jefferson*. Chapelle, *American Sailing Navy*, pp255-63. Ridgely to Chauncey, 18 September 1814, enclosed with Chauncey to Jones, 20 September 1814: USNA, RG 45, M125, 39, p71.

11. Jones to Bullus, 30 November 1813: Bauer, *The New American State Papers*, Vol 4, p328.

12. Chauncey to Jones, 11 June 1814: USNA, RG 45, M 125, 37, p54. Chapelle, *American Sailing Navy*, pp164, 168-9.

13. Malcomson, *Lords of the Lake*, pp284-5. Chapelle, *American Sailing Navy*, p274.

14. Croker to Yeo, 29 January 1814: NAC, MG 12, ADM 2/1379, pp93, 131.

15. Drummond to Prevost, 27 and 28 April 1814: NAC, RG 8, I, 683, pp57 and 61. Prevost to Drummond, 30 April 1814: *ibid*, 1222, p107. Drummond to Prevost, 7 May 1814: *ibid*, 683, p105. Yeo to Croker, 9 May 1814: NAC, MG 12, ADM 1/2737, p43. Malcomson, *Lords of the Lake* pp263-77.

16. Chauncey to Walton and Co, 9 April 1814: Chauncey Letter Book. Chauncey to Jones, 2 June 1814: *ibid*. Popham to Yeo, 1 June 1814: NAC, MG 11, CO 42/156, p327. Malcomson, *Lords of the Lake*, pp276-83.

17. Chauncey to Jones, 8 June 1814, USNA, RG 45, M125, 37, p31. Chauncey to Jones, 19 August 1814: *ibid*, 38, p113. Brown to Chauncey, 13 July 1814: *DHC*, Vol 1, p64. Brown to Chauncey, 4 September 1814: *ibid*, Vol 2, p444. Malcomson, *Lords of the Lake*, pp284-98. Malcomson, 'Dobbs and the Royal Navy at Niagara'.

18. Yeo to Prevost, 13 April 1814: NAC, RG 8, I, 683, p19. O'Conor to Prevost, 3 February 1814: *ibid*, 732, p20. Yeo to Prevost, 10 March 1814: *ibid*, p59. O'Conor to Freer, 12 April 1814: *ibid*, p123. Dimensions of a ship ... by O'Conor, 13 April 1814, enclosed with O'Conor to Freer, 13 April 1814: *ibid*, p129. Malcomson, 'HMS

St. Lawrence: The Freshwater First-Rate'.

19. Chauncey to Jones, 10 August 1814: USNA, RG 45, M 125, 38, p85. Moore, 'Frontier Frigates'.

20. *Kingston Gazette*, June, July and August 1814.

21. Yeo to Croker, 24 October 1814: NAC, MG 12, ADM 1/2737, p214. Malcomson, *Lords of the Lake*, pp294-310.

22. Yeo to Croker, 14 October 1814: NAC, MG 12, ADM 1/2737, p219.

23. Prevost to Bathurst, 19 November 1814: NAC, MG 11, CO 42/157, p260.

24. Douglas to Bathurst, 20 December 1814: NAC, MG 11, CO 42/149, p175. Prevost to Bathurst, 21 April 1813: *ibid*, 150, p143.

25. Warren to Croker, 1 December 1813: NAC, 'Report 9: Copies of all Correspondence and Orders …', *Papers Relating to the War with America*, Extracts of House of Lords, Accounts and Papers, Vol 75, 1815, p11. Kerr to Melville, 23 November 1813: The Melville Papers, William L Clements Library. A 'Loyalist' to Croker, 23 November 1813, enclosed in Barrow to Bunbury, 25 November 1813: NAC, MG 11, CO 42/155, p198. Enclosures with Hull to Jones, 26 September 1814: USNA, RG 45, M 125, 39, p102. Malcomson, *Lords of the Lake*, pp240-1, 262-3, 314. T Malcomson, 'HMS *Psyche*'.

CHAPTER 8

1. Smith to Hamilton, 16 June 1812: Dudley, *Naval War of 1812*, Vol 1, p275. Hamilton to Macdonough, 28 September 1812: *ibid*, p319. Everest, *The War of 1812 in the Champlain Valley*. Names for the 1808 gunboats are mentioned in Chapelle, *American Sailing Navy*, p298 and Crisman, *The Eagle*, pp99-100.

2. Macdonough to Hamilton, 14 October and 20 December 1812: Dudley, *Naval War of 1812*, Vol 1, pp325, 370.

3. Everest, *1812 in the Champlain Valley*, p64. A Statement of HM Naval Force on Lake Champlain, by O'Conor, 26 January 1814: NAC, MG 11, CO 42/160, p320. Taylor to Stovin, 3 June 1813: NAC, RG 8, I, 679, p10.

4. Tucker, *Arming the Fleet*, pp182-3.

5. Macdonough to Jones, 23 November 1813: USNA, RG 45, M 147, 5, part 1, p169. Proposed Establishment of the Provincial Marine, by Pye, 30 August 1811: NAC, RG 8, I, 728, p60. General Order by Baynes, 6 September 1812: *ibid*,1168, p249. A Statement of the Naval Force on Lake Champlain, by Moore, 6 June 1817: NAC, MG 12, ADM 106/1998. Lewis, *British Naval Activity on Lake Champlain*. Charbonneau, *The Fortifications of Île Aux Noix*.

6. Macdonough to Jones, 1 May 1813: USNA,

RG 45, M 148, 11, pp2, 5. Everest, *1812 in the Champlain Valley*, pp92-3.

7. Macdonough to Jones, 14 August 1813: USNA, RG 45, M 147, 5:1, p106. Plan for a Marine Corps in Gunboats, by Eliot: NAC, RG 8, I, 729, p180. General Order by Baynes, 11 September 1812: *ibid*, 1168, p253. A Statement of the Naval Force on Lake Champlain, by Moore, 6 June 1817: NAC, MG 12, ADM 106/1998.

8. Taylor to Stovin, 3 June 1813: NAC, RG 8, I, 679, p10. Macdonough to Jones, 22 July 1813: USNA, RG 45, M 148, 12, p42.

9. Prevost to Bathurst, 18 July 1813: NAC, MG 11, CO 42/151, p69. General Order by Baynes, 19 July 1813: NAC, RG 8, I, 1170, p314.

10. Sheaffe to Prevost, 25 July 1813: NAC, RG 8, I, 730, p67. Everard to Prevost, 3 August 1813: *ibid*, 679, p340. Macdonough to Jones, 3 August 1813: USNA, RG 45, M 148, 12, p66.

11. Macdonough to Jones, 14 August and 28 December1813: USNA, RG 45, M 147, 5:1, p106, 197. Names for the 1813 gunboats are mentioned in Chapelle, *American Sailing Navy*, p298 and Crisman, *The Eagle*, pp99-100.

12. Pring to Prevost, 5 August 1813: NAC, RG 8, I, 677, p362. Pring to Prevost, 18 October and 8 November1813: *ibid*, 731, pp52, 109.

13. Macdonough to Jones, 14 May 1814: USNA, RG 45, M 147, 5:2, p128. Crisman, *The* Eagle, pp215-7. Chapelle, *American Sailing Navy*, pp272, 299. Washburn, '*Linnet*: A Brig from the War of 1812'.

14. Edgecombe to Freer, 7 March 1814: NAC, RG 8, I, 732, p65. A Statement of the Naval Force on Lake Champlain, by Moore, 6 June 1817: NAC, MG 12, ADM 106/1998.

15. Jones to Macdonough, 7 December 1813: Dudley, *Naval War of 1812*, Vol 2, p605.

16. Emery, 'Whitehall Project 1995'.

17. Crisman, *The Eagle*, pp21, 211. Chapelle, *American Sailing Navy*, pp297-9.

18. Crisman, *The History and Construction of the United States Schooner* Ticonderoga.

19. Simons to Freer, 23 May 1814: NAC, RG 8, I, 732, p174. Pring to Freer, 27 April 1814: *ibid*, p156. Yeo to Prevost, 13 April 1814: *ibid*, p133. Edgecombe to Freer, 20 May 1814: *ibid*, p169.

20. Macdonough to Jones, 29 May 1814: USNA, RG 45, M 147, 5:2, p134. Macdonough to Jones, 9 and 23 July 1814: *ibid*, p4 and 8.

21. Macdonough to Jones, 11 June 1814: USNA, RG 45, M 147, 5:2, p145. Crisman, *The* Eagle, pp136-89.

22. Lake Champlain Court Martial: NAC, MG 12, ADM 1/5450, p20.

23. Crisman, *The Eagle*, p216.

24. Lake Champlain Court Martial: NAC, MG

12, ADM 1/5450, p106, 113.

25. Crisman, *The Eagle*, pp63-96. Everest, *1812 in the Champlain Valley*, pp161-192. Hitsman, *The Incredible War of 1812*, pp248-67.

26. Cited in Crisman, *The Eagle*, p70.

27. Malcomson, *Lords of the Lake*, pp301-303. Hitsman, *The Incredible War of 1812*, pp274-7.

CHAPTER 9

1. Chauncey to Crowninshield, 23 February 1815: USNA, RG 45, M 125, 42, p164.

2. Chauncey to Crowninshield, 10 March 1815: USNA, RG 45, M 125, 43, p34. Crisman, *The Jefferson*, pp160-9. Palmer, 'Sackets Harbor and the *New Orleans*'.

3. Strickland to Navy Board, 29 October 1814: NAC, MG 12, ADM 106/1997. Laws, Pratt and Strickland, 6 January 1815: *ibid*. Statement of the Naval Force on Lake Ontario, by Moore, 6 January 1817: NAC, MG 12, ADM 106/1998. Preston, 'Broad Pennants on Point Frederick'.

4. Hall to Admiralty, 24 June 1815: NAC, MG 12, ADM 106/1997. T Malcomson, 'HMS *Psyche*'.

5. Contracts with Goudie, 14 February 1815: NAC, MG 12, ADM 106/1997. Survey of His Majesty's Frigate at Isle aux Noix, 23 August 1820: *ibid*, 1998. Statement of the Naval Force on Lake Champlain, by Moore, 6 January 1817: NAC, MG 12, ADM 106/1998.

6. Crisman, *The Eagle*, pp97-99.

7. Severance, 'What Became of Perry's Fleet?'. Carone, 'Preserving the US Brig *Niagara*'.

8. Malcomson, *Lords of the Lake*, p313.

9. Hall to Navy Board, 18 May 1815: NAC, MG 12, ADM 106/1997. Malcomson, 'Tallships at Discovery Harbour'. Killing, 'The Designing of HMS *Bee*'.

10. Statement of the Naval Force on Lake Ontario, by Moore, 6 January 1817: NAC, MG12, ADM 106/1998. Preston, 'Broad Pennants on Point Frederick'.

11. Barrie to Admiralty, 5 March 1831: NAC, MG 12, ADM 106/2002.

12. Malcomson, *HMS Detroit*, pp128-9.

13. Crisman, *The Jefferson*, pp169-76. Palmer, 'Sackets Harbor and the *New Orleans*'. Huginin to Bainbridge, 23 March 1825: USNA, RG 45, Navy Commissioners, Letters Received, Sackets Harbor. Stewart to Mallaby, 4 June 1833: *ibid* T829, Roll 287, p614 (these latter references were supplied to the author by Gary Gibson).

14. Barrie to Admiralty, 25 January 1832: NAC, MG 12, ADM 106/2002. Preston, 'The Fate of Kingston's Warships'. Stacey, 'The Ships of the British Squadron on Lake Ontario'.

Bibliography

PRIMARY SOURCES – UNPUBLISHED

National Archives of Canada

MG 11, CO 42, Original Correspondence, Secretary of State, Lower Canada

MG 12, ADM 1, Secretary's Department: In Letters From Captains; Reports of Courts Martial

MG 12, ADM 106, Navy Board In Letters From Yards, Canada, 1814-1832

MG 13, WO 34, Amherst Papers

MG 24, F 18, 'Four Years on the Lakes of Canada', David Wingfield

MG 24, 25, Great Britain, Admiralty Lake Service

RG 5, A 1, Upper Canada Sundries

RG 8, I, 'C Series', British Military and Naval Records

RG 14, B 13, Vols 1-5, Accounts Books, Freight

National Archives of the United States

RG 45, Naval Records Collections
M125, Letters from Captains
M147, Letters from Commanders
M148, Letters from Officers below Commander
M149, Letters by Secretary of the Navy
M625, Area Seven File

British Library: Frederick Haldimand Papers (microfilm copies at Brock University, St Catharines, Ontario)

New York Historical Society, New York: Chauncey Letter Books, April 1809-September 1812; August 1813-July 1814

William L Clements Library, University of Michigan: Chauncey Letter Books, September 1812-August 1813; July 1814-1817

William L Clements Library, University of Michigan: The Melville Papers

PRIMARY SOURCES – PUBLISHED

Anon (ed), *The Papers of Sir William Johnson* (Albany, NY 1921-1961)

Bauer, K Jack (ed), *The New American State Papers* (Wilmington, Delaware 1981)

Carter, Clarence Edwin (ed), *The Correspondence of General Thomas Gage … 1763-1775*, 2 vols (London 1933)

Collections and Researches made by the Pioneer and Historical Society of the State of Michigan, Vols 10, 12, 19, 40, (Lansing 1888, 1888, 1892, 1929)

Cooper, James Fenimore (ed), *Ned Myers; or, A Life Before the Mast* (reprint: Annapolis 1989)

Cruikshank E A (ed), *Records of Niagara, 1784-9* #40 (Niagara nd)

———— (ed), *The Correspondence of Lieut Governor John Graves Simcoe* (Toronto 1923)

———— and A F Hunter (eds), *The Correspondence of the Honourable Peter Russell* (Toronto 1936)

———— (ed), *Documentary History of the Campaigns on the Niagara Frontier in 1812-1814*, 9 vols (Welland, Ontario 1896-1908)

Doughty, Arthur G (ed), *Captain John Knox: An Historical Journal of the Campaigns in North America for the Years 1757, 1758, 1759 and 1760* (Toronto 1914)

Dudley, William (ed), *The Naval War of 1812: A Documentary History*, 2 vols (Washington 1985, 1992)

Dunnigan, Brian (ed), *Pierre Pouchot: Memoirs on the Late War in North America Between France and England* (Youngstown, NY 1994)

Hamilton, Edward P (ed), *Adventure in the Wilderness: The American Journals of Louis Antoine de Bougainville, 1756-1760* (Oklahoma 1964)

Innis, Mary Quayle (ed), *Mrs. Simcoe's Diary* (Toronto 1965)

Malcomson, Robert (ed), *Sailors of 1812: Memoirs and Letters of Naval Officers on Lake Ontario* (Youngstown, NY 1997)

Morgan, William J (ed), *Naval Documents of the American Revolution*, Vols 5 and 6 (Washington, DC 1970, 1972)

Preston, Richard A (ed), *Royal Fort Frontenac* (Toronto 1958)

———— (ed), *Kingston Before 1812: A Collection of Documents* (Toronto 1959)

Spragge, George (ed), *The John Strachan Letter Book: 1812-1834* (Toronto 1946)

Webster, J Clarence (ed), *The Journal of Jeffrey Amherst* (Toronto 1931)

SECONDARY SOURCES – BOOKS

Alvord, Clarence W and Clarence E Carter (eds), *The New Regime, 1765-1767* (Springfield, Illinois 1916)

Antal, Sandy, *A Wampum Denied: Procter's War of 1812* (Ottawa 1997)

Beattie, Judith, *Gunboats on the St Lawrence River (1763-1839)* (Ottawa 1967)

Bellico, Russell P, *Sails and Steam in the Mountains: A Maritime and Military History of Lake George and Lake Champlain* (Fleishmann, NY 1992)

Chapelle, Howard, *The History of the American Sailing Navy: The Ships and Their Development* (New York 1949)

Charbonneau, André, *The Fortifications of Île Aux Noix* (Ottawa 1994)

Charnock, John, *Biographia Navalis …* (London 1798)

Crisman, Kevin J, *The History and Construction of the United States Schooner* Ticonderoga, (Alexandria, VA 1982)

————, *The Eagle: An American Brig on Lake Champlain during the War of 1812* (Shelburne, VT 1987)

————, *The* Jefferson*: The History and Archeology of an American Brig from the War of 1812* (Ann Arbor, Michigan 1989)

Cruikshank, E A, *Drummond's Winter Campaign* (Niagara Falls c1900)

Dictionary of American Biography, 22 vols (New York 1958-64)

Dictionary of Canadian Biography, 16 vols (Toronto 1976-88)

Dictionary of National Biography, 65 vols (London 1885)

Dunnigan, Brian Leigh, *The British Army at Mackinac* (Mackinac 1980)

Everest, Allan S, *The War of 1812 in the Champlain Valley* (Syracuse 1981)

Firth, E G (ed), *The Town of York, 1793-1815* (Toronto 1962)

Fowler, William M, *Rebels Under Sail,* (New York 1976)

Gardiner, Robert (ed), *Navies and the American Revolution: 1775-1783* (London 1996)

————(ed), *The Line of Battle: The Sailing Warship, 1650-1840* (London 1992)

————, *The Heavy Frigate, Eighteen-Pounder Frigates: Vol 1, 1778-1800* (London 1994)

———— (ed), *The Heyday of Sail: The Merchant Sailing Ship, 1650-1830* (London 1995)

———— (ed), *The Naval War of 1812* (London 1998)

Hitsman, Mackay, *The Incredible War of 1812* (reprint, Toronto 1999)

Lewis, David M, *British Naval Activity on Lake Champlain During the War of 1812* (Plattsburgh 1994)

Lossing, Benson, *The Pictorial Field-book of the War of 1812* (New York 1868), pp367-9.

Lundeberg, Philip K, *The Gunboat Philadelphia and the Defense of Lake Champlain in 1776* (Basin Harbor, VT 1995)

Lyon, David, *Sailing Navy List: All the Ships of the Royal Navy – Built, Purchased and Captured, 1688-1855* (London 1993)

Mahan, A T, *The Major Operations of the Navies in the War of American Independence,* (New York 1913)

Malcomson, Robert, *Lords of the Lake: The Naval War on Lake Ontario, 1812-1814* (London 1999)

———— and Thomas Malcomson, *HMS* Detroit*: The Battle for Lake Erie* (Annapolis 1991)

Nafus, Roland L, *Navy Island: Historic Treasure of the Niagara, Heritage, Archaeology, Folklore* (Youngstown, NY 1998)

O'Brien, Brendan, *Speedy Justice: the Tragic Last Voyage of His Majesty's Vessel* Speedy (Toronto 1992)

Pargellis, Stanley (ed), *Military Affairs in North America, 1748-1765* (Boston 1969)

Peckham, Howard, *Pontiac and the Indian Uprising* (New York 1947)

Rosenburg, Max, *The Building of Perry's Fleet on Lake Erie, 1812-1813* (Harrisburg 1987)

Skaggs, David Curtis and Gerard T Altoff, *A Signal Victory: The Lake Erie Campaign, 1812-1813* (Annapolis 1997)

Smith, Arthur Britton, *Legend of the Lake*: the *22-Gun Brig-Sloop* Ontario, *1780* (Kingston 1997)

Tucker, Spencer, *Arming the Fleet: US Naval Ordnance in the Muzzle-loading Era* (Annapolis 1989)

———— and Frank T Reuter, *Injured Honor: The* Chesapeake-Leopard *Affair, June 22, 1807* (Annapolis 1996)

SECONDARY SOURCES – ARTICLES

Anon, 'The Old Ship-Builders of New York', *Harper's Monthly Magazine* 65 (1882), pp223-41

Atkins, Kenneth S, 'Who Designed Perry's Brigs?', *Inland Seas* 47 (1991), pp245-50

Bond, C C J, 'The British Base at Carleton Island', *Ontario History* 52 (1960), pp1-16

Cain, Emily, 'Building the *Lord Nelson*', *Inland Seas* 41 (1985), pp121-29

Crisman, Kevin J, 'Struggle for a Continent: Naval Battles of the French and Indian Wars', in George F Bass (ed), *Ships and Shipwrecks of the Americas: A History Based on Underwater Archeology* (New York 1988)

Casey, Richard P, 'North Country Nemesis: The Potash Rebellion and the Embargo of 1807-1809', *New York Historical Society Quarterly* 64 (1980), pp31-49

Carone, Anthony C, 'Preserving the US Brig *Niagara*, 1813-1988', *The Journal of Erie Studies* 17 (1988), pp103-12

Dobbins, Daniel and William Dobbins, 'The Dobbins Papers', *Buffalo Historical Society Publications* 8 (1905), pp283-379

Douglas, W A B, 'The Anatomy of Naval Incompetence: The Provincial Marine in Defence of Upper Canada Before 1813', *Ontario History* 71 (1979), pp3-25

Dunnigan, Brian L, 'British Naval Vessels on the Upper Great Lakes, 1761-1796', *Telescope* 31 (1982)

Emery, Eric, 'Whitehall Project 1995: A Preliminary Report on the Excavation and Study of the USN Row Galley *Allen*', *The INA Quarterly* 22 (1995), pp9-14

Grant, W L, 'The Capture of Oswego in 1756', *Proceedings of the New York State Historical Association* 13 (1914)

Green, Ernest, 'Corvettes of New France', *Ontario History* 35 (1943), pp29-38

Howell, William M, 'The Arrival of Dobbins at Erie', *Inland Seas* 51 (1995), pp32-4

Killing, Steve, 'The Designing of HMS *Bee*', *Freshwater* 1 (1986), pp21-4

MacLeod, Carol, 'The Tap of the Garrison Drum: The Marine Service in British North America, 1755-1813', unpublished manuscript, Parks Canada, Historical Research and Records Unit, (Ottawa 1983)

Macleod, Malcolm, 'Fight for the West Gate', *Ontario History* 58 (1966)

———— 'Simcoe's Schooner *Onondaga*', *Ontario History* 59 (1967)

Malcomson, Robert, 'War on the Lakes', *The Beaver* 70 (1990), pp44-52

————, 'HMS *Detroit* 1813: The British Flagship at Put-in-Bay', *Seaways' Ships in Scale* 2 (1991), pp26-32

————, 'The US Brig *Niagara*: A History', *Seaways' Ships in Scale* 3 (1992), pp30-4.

————, 'Gunboats on Lake Ontario in the 1812 War', *Seaways' Ships In Scale* 7 (1996), pp31-9;27-32; 40-4

————, 'The Crews of the British Squadron at Put-in-Bay', *Inland Seas* 51 (1996), pp16-29, 43-56

————, 'Tallships at Discovery Harbour', *Model Ship Builder* 112 (1998), pp33-43

————, 'Dobbs and the Royal Navy at Niagara', *Fortress Niagara* 1 (2000), pp1, 7-10, 11-13

Malcomson, Thomas, 'HMS *Psyche*: A Frigate in Frame', *Seaways' Ship in Scale* 4 (1993), pp16-21

McConnell, David, 'Preliminary Survey of the Historical Significance of Navy Island', *Research Bulletin of the National Historic Parks and Sites Branch* 43 (Ottawa 1977)

Moore, Jonathan, 'Frontier Frigates and a Three-Decker: Wrecks of the Royal Navy's Lake Ontario Squadron', in Kevin Crisman, *Shipwrecks of the War of 1812* (in print, 1999)

Palmer, Richard, 'James Fenimore Cooper and the Navy Brig *Oneida*', *Inland Seas* 40 (1984), pp90-9

————, 'Sackets Harbor and the *New Orleans*', *Bulletin of the Jefferson County Historical Society* 8 (1984), pp3-16

Preston, Richard A, 'The Fate of Kingston's Warships', *Ontario History* 44 (1952), pp85-100

————, 'Broad Pennants on Point Frederick', *Ontario History* 50 (1958), pp81-92

'The Remarkable Statement of Noah Brown', *Journal of American History* 8 (1914), pp103-8.

Severance, Frank H, 'What Became of Perry's Fleet?', *Buffalo Historical Society Publications* 8 (1905), pp401-4

Stacey, C P, 'The Ships of the British Squadron on Lake Ontario', *Canadian Historical Review* 34 (1953), pp311-23

Washburn, Erika, '*Linnet*: A Brig from the War of 1812', *INA Quarterly* 23 (1996), pp14-19

Wheelock, Phyllis DeKay, 'Henry Eckford (1775-1832), an American Shipbuilder', *The American Neptune* 8 (1947), pp177-95

Glossary

abaft Towards the stern, behind or astern.

abeam When calculating a ship's dimensions the measurement 'abeam' is the width or breadth of the hull at its widest point. A wind blowing toward a ship's side is 'abeam,' as is any vessel located to the side of the ship as opposed to ahead or behind (abaft).

bar An obstruction in the mouth of a stream or river consisting of sand and/or gravel.

bar shot A projectile consisting of an 8ft to 14ft bar connecting two solid hemispheres; also known as dismantling shot as it was used to damage rigging.

batteau An open, flat-bottomed boat powered by oars and/or a simple rig, commonly used for transportation of troops, arms and provisions.

beam A heavy squared timber supporting the deck, located athwart a vessel and attached to the frames.

bear up To turn into the wind.

Bermudoes A sloop rig popular with small merchant vessels in the Atlantic and West Indies during the 1700s; thought to originate from Bermuda, the rig was also termed Bermudian or Bermudan.

berthing deck The deck where the majority of the crew members slept.

between perpendiculars The measurement between the stem and sternposts, roughly equivalent to the length of the gundeck.

block A 'pulley' through which lines are run in order to gain a mechanical advantage.

boom A spar to which is fastened the lower edge of a fore-and-aft sail or studding sail.

bowsprit The spar extending forward from the forecastle over the bow.

brig A two-masted, square-rigged vessel.

brigantine A two-masted vessel with square sails on the foremast and fore-and-aft sails on the mainmast.

brig-sloop A naval brig commanded by a commander (RN) or master commandant (USN).

broadside The flanks of a ship, and by extension all of a vessel's ordnance on that side; also the simultaneous discharge of all those weapons.

bulwark The planking or woodwork along the side of a vessel above the upper deck.

burthen The capacity of a vessel calculated by a conventional formula from the dimensions, the resulting figure being rendered in tons. It was a primitive forerunner of gross tonnage and did not measure displacement.

cable Heavy rope used for fastening an anchor to a vessel, its size usually based on the ratio of one inch in circumference to every two feet in the vessel's beam.

canister A projectile fired by ordnance, consisting of a tin can filled with small lead bullets, referred to by the Royal Artillery as 'case shot'.

capstan A large, cylindrical crank fitted with bars against which seamen apply pressure to turn the capstan as cables wrapped around it raise heavy objects like anchors, spars or boats.

careen To haul a vessel as far over on one side as possible, without upsetting it, so that its hull can be repaired or scraped clean.

carlines Short fore-and-aft timbers connecting the deck beams of a vessel.

carriage The wooden framework upon which a piece of ordnance is mounted so that it may be fired and moved.

carronade A piece of ordnance with a short barrel and a wide, smooth bore, developed in the 1770s and employed on warships because it was lighter in construction than a long gun, required a smaller gun crew and smaller charges than a long gun and could fire large calibre projectiles, though its effective range was limited to about 500 yards.

caulk To seal the joints between planks by driving oakum or rope junk into them using a hammer and caulking iron.

ceiling The interior planking fastened to the lower portion of a vessel's frame.

chain shot A projectile consisting of a piece of chain 8ft to 12ft long connecting two round shot; a form of dismantling shot used to damage rigging.

circle A pivot mount for ordnance, consisting of a gun carriage fastened to a skid with rollers on its underside that ran on a circular track (or racer) in the deck, allowing the gun to be rotated to fire in virtually any direction.

cleat A two-armed block of wood around which a rope may be temporarily fastened by taking several overlapping turns around the arms of the cleat.

cockpit The accommodation for midshipmen and master's mates; low in the ship, in action it was often used as the surgery.

columbiad A smooth-bore weapon similar to a carronade developed by the American George Bomford.

commander In the RN, a commissioned officer ranked between lieutenant and post captain. Any vessel that he moved into was formally rated as a sloop during his commission.

commission The document issued to officers of lieutenant rank and above in the RN, and including surgeons, surgeon's mates and pursers in the USN after 1812, certifying them to serve in specific positions until replaced and/or transferred to other positions.

commission pendant A long, slender flag flown at the masthead of a vessel commanded by a commissioned officer, white with the red St George's cross in the RN. Pronounced and therefore sometimes spelt 'pennant'.

commodore A temporary position of responsibility awarded to a naval captain, involving the overall command of more than one warship for a specific assignment.

corvette-style Built with a flush upper deck, *ie* without a raised quarterdeck or forecastle.

cradle The structure constructed around the lower section of the hull to keep it upright during its launch.

cross chock A piece of timber laid across the keel joining the lower frame timbers.

cutter A decked vessel with one mast having a fore-and-aft rig, plus (usually) a square topsail.

cutwater The leading edge of the bow; usually a separate timber ahead of the stem proper.

deadrise In cross section, the angle at which the frames of a vessel rise above the lateral plane of the keel.

deadwood The blocks of timber affixed to the upper surface of a keel fore and aft, but narrower than the keel, to receive the heels of half frame timbers.

deck clamp A thick plank running fore and aft under the ends of deck beams.

drag The amount by which a vessel draws more water aft than it does forward.

draught A plan for a vessel. Also, the depth of water taken up by a vessel.

driver A long narrow square sail raised on a gaff to the outer peak of the spanker gaff and set to draw just aft of the spanker; often confused with and therefore used synonymously with spanker.

Durham boat A large, open craft, similar to a batteau but closer in proportion to a gondola.

edge away To gradually move away from a specific point or specific course.

extreme breadth The overall width of a vessel including the thickness of the planking.

fashion pieces The aftermost timbers in the run of a vessel's hull which form the shape of the stern.

fathom A length of six feet.

Fifth Rate In the RN, a warship rated 30 to 44 guns carried on one or two gundecks.

First Rate In the RN, a warship with 100 guns or more on three gundecks.

fittings All the individual pieces of equipment used to operate a vessel.

flag officer Admiral (an officer flying his own distinguishing flag).

floor The large timber fastened across the keel to which the futtocks are fastened.

flotilla A group of small boats, such as batteaux or gunboats.

forecastle A deck over the forward part of the weather deck, or, in a flush-decked vessel, the portion of the upper deck between the foremast and the bow.

foremast The mast closest to the bow of the vessel.

fore-and-aft rig A vessel has a fore-and-aft rig when most of its propulsion is achieved through the use of sails set along the centreline of the vessel rather than athwart the vessel, like square sails.

foresail The lower sail or course (whether square or fore-and-aft) on the foremast.

Fourth Rate In the RN, a warship with between 50 and 60 guns, originally on two gundecks but after 1815 the largest frigates were so rated.

frames The rib-like components of a vessel's hull, consisting of overlapping timbers known as futtocks (up to four on each side of the hull), fastened to the keel and secured by the keelson longitudinally and beams athwart the hull.

frigate A ship (RN Fifth and Sixth Rates) originally developed to carry around 28 guns on one main gundeck but later improved to carry more than 40 guns. Too small to fight in the traditional line of battle, it was used as an extension of a fleet or on independent missions. A frigate was an appropriate command for a full (or 'post') captain and in the RN an officer's initial commission in a frigate or other 'post' ship meant automatic appointment to the Admiralty's seniority list.

futtock A component of a frame, overlapped with other futtocks (up to four on each side of the hull) to form the frame.

gaff A spar to which is fastened the upper edge of a fore-and-aft sail.

galley *See* row galley.

gondola A barge-like open river craft popular in Colonial America for the transportation of goods; also gundalo or gundalow.

grapeshot A projectile fired from ordnance consisting of a canvas shroud quilted over nine small round shot (resembling grapes, of notably large proportion) positioned around a iron spindle fitted into a circular iron plate.

gunboat A small armed vessel, varying considerably in size, rig and strength from a batteau fitted with a carronade or small-calibre long gun, to a purpose-built craft with rowing benches and two or three guns on slides or circles, to converted merchantmen outfitted with one or more pieces of heavy ordnance.

gunbrig A brig commanded by a lieutenant (RN or USN).

gundeck A deck with guns located along its entire length.

gunport The opening through which guns are fired, usually closed with a hinged cover on vessels with more than one deck of guns.

gunwale In a vessel, the wide cap fastened to the top of the bulwark. In a boat the cap fastened to the topmost planks in the sides.

gusset A bracket used to strengthen the fastening between two components.

half floor Half a floor timber that is fastened to the opposite half floor at a scarf on the keel.

halliard A line for raising or lowering yards except for the courses, which, being heavy, are raised by a stronger tackle known as jeers.

hanging knee A knee installed vertically to fasten and brace the frame of a vessel to a

deck beam.

hawser A heavy cable.

headsails The fore-and-aft sails set between the foremast and the bowsprit and its booms.

impressment The practice of forcibly enlisting seamen for service in a warship.

jib The triangular fore-and-aft sail usually set from the foremast to the jibboom, which is attached to the bowsprit. A flying jib could be set ahead of the jib.

kedge To move a vessel by laying out the anchor and hauling the vessel up to it by use of the capstan.

keel The backbone of a vessel, made from up to seven pieces of large dimension timber joined (scarphed) together to which are attached the stem- and sternposts and the frames.

keelson An assembly of several large dimension timbers joined together and laid over the floors of the frames to secure them to the keel.

knee A right-angled brace usually fashioned from the natural curve of a single crook of timber.

larboard The left, or port, side of a vessel facing forward.

lateen A large triangular shaped sail fastened to a long angled yard that is set with the forward end of the yard secured low to the deck and the after end aloft; common on small craft in the Mediterranean, and employed on the mizzen masts of square-riggers until replaced by the spanker sail in the middle of the eighteenth century.

leeward The downwind side of a vessel. A lee shore was a shore towards which the wind was propelling a vessel.

lieutenant The lowest rank of commissioned officer; could command small craft in his own right but usually a subordinate officer of a larger ship.

limber hole A slot cut in the lower extreme of a floor or first futtock adjacent to the keel to allow waste water to run down to the pump well.

lodging knee A knee installed horizontally to fasten and brace a deck beam of a vessel to the frames.

long gun Commonly known improperly as a 'cannon', a piece of ordnance with a smooth-bore barrel, the calibre of which was determined by the weight of shot it fired. Called a long gun to distinguish it from a carronade.

lower mast The bottom, and thickest, section of the mast assembly.

lugger A small fore-and-aft rigged vessel, usually having two or three masts carrying trapezoidal-shaped sails set on spars that are hoisted from a point about a third of their length from the forward end. The spar is thus to one side of the mast, and depending on whether or not the sail is lowered when the ship goes about, it is defined as a 'dipping' or 'standing' lug rig.

magazine A compartment in which barrels of gunpowder and 'fixed' cartridges, which have been prepared for use, are stored.

main boom The spar extending the lower edge of the largest fore-and-aft sail on a cutter, sloop or schooner.

mainmast The tallest mast on a vessel, located abaft the foremast.

mainsail The lower sail or course (whether square or fore-and-aft) on the mainmast.

mast A vertical spar to which are attached smaller spars (the yards) and their sails. The term refers to the entire structure from the step to the truck and may also refer to each of the component parts of the mast since most masts consist of a lower section to which are attached one or more upper sections (topmasts and topgallants and even royal masts).

master The senior warrant officer in the RN in charge of navigation and pilotage, among other tasks, equal in status to the lieutenants and accommodated with them, but rarely promoted from his position.

master and commander A rank used only in the Provincial Marine during this period (the RN had used this term until 1794 when it was simplified to commander).

master commandant A rank used only in the USN during this period, equivalent to a RN commander. The vessel under his command was classed as a 'sloop' regardless of its rig.

master's mate A superior midshipman being groomed for advancement to lieutenant in both services, but more often mentioned in RN records. Also, in both services, a highly skilled seaman or mate from a merchantman with potential to become a master or, rarely, to gain a commission.

midships deadrise In cross section, the angle at which the midships frames of a vessel rise above the lateral plane of the keel.

midshipman A 'young gentleman' who had three year's experience at sea could be rated a midshipman and thereby be in line to attain a commission in the RN. In the USN this was an entry level appointment, certified with a warrant, which provided training necessary to earn a commission.

mizzen The aftermost mast of a three-masted vessel. Also mizen.

moor To anchor using two anchors, one to either side of the bow with their cables fastened to a swivel so that the vessel may swing with the wind and current, or with one anchor ahead and one behind, or, in modern usage, secured afore and abaft to a quay.

mooring A permanent location in a harbour where vessels can be secured without having to use their own anchors.

mortar A short, squat piece of ordnance designed to fire explosive projectiles (*see* shells) in a high, curving trajectory, its calibre determined by the diameter of its bore.

mortise Part of a wood joint – a hole into which a tenon is meant to be inserted.

moulds The patterns, usually drawn on thin, flexible pieces of board, used for shaping individual components of frames.

moulded The dimension of a timber in its shaped direction (*ie* the one offered up to the moulds); the opposite of sided, which was a constant dimension.

moudled breadth The overall width of a vessel at the frames, minus the thickness of the planking.

musketoon A short musket with a large bore.

oakum Tarred fibres picked from condemned ropes.

ordnance All 'artillery' used aboard vessels or on land, including long guns, carronades, swivel guns, howitzers and mortars.

orlop deck A deck below the waterline used for accommodations and storage.

petty officers In both services, generally, assistants to warrant officers, such as quartermaster's, master's mates, gunner's mates, master-at-arms.

pilot An individual hired to share his knowledge of local waters

pilot boat A speedy sloop or schooner employed to transport pilots to vessels entering a port on the seaboard.

plank sheers The covering of the timber heads; also the gunwale.

poop deck A deck built above the aft portion of the quarterdeck to create additional accommodation and as a platform for ordnance. Also termed the 'roundhouse'.

port The left, or larboard, side of a vessel, facing forwards.

post captain In the RN, the rank above commander whereby the officer was granted a commission for a Sixth Rate warship, or larger, and was posted to the seniority list, which meant that he could attain the rank of admiral if he lived long enough to rise to the upper echelons of the list. The seniority of captains in the USN was noted, but since that service had no flag officers advancement to the rank of captain did not hold the additional perk of being 'posted'.

post ship In the RN, generally a Sixth Rate warship of 20-24 guns (smaller than a frigate but large enough for a post captain's command), although a smaller vessel entered that class, temporarily, if its commander was advanced to 'post' rank.

profile The appearance of a vessel from end to end as seen from the side.

quarterdeck A deck over the after part of the weather deck, or, in a flush-decked vessel, the portion of the upper deck between the mainmast and the stern.

quarter gallery The curving projection on either side of the stern quarter of a vessel, forming part of the accommodations of the cabins and usually used as lavatories.

quarters The places to which members of a crew are assigned during an engagement; also the after part of the broadside of a vessel.

quickwork The interior planking between gunports.

rabbet The slot ('rebate') cut into a keel, stem and sternpost to receive the strakes of planking.

radeau A flat-bottomed, floating battery powered by sweeps and a simple rig.

rake The angle, either aft or forward, at which a mast, stempost, sternpost or any other upright element is stepped in relation to the perpendicular.

receiving ship An old warship moored in a harbour to provide temporary accommodation for seamen awaiting re-assignment.

ribs The frames of a vessel.

rider Timbers laid, often diagonally, across the frames between the keelson and beams to add stiffness to a hull.

Rig The configuration of the masts and sail-plan.

rigging The lines attached to spars and sails; traditionally divided into standing rigging which is more or less permanent and braces the masts, and running rigging which is used in handling the sails.

round shot A solid, spherical, iron projectile, its calibre determined by its weight. A typical 9pdr shot measured 4 inches in diameter, whereas a typical 24pdr shot measured 5.33 inches in diameter.

row galley A long and narrow craft powered chiefly by oars and a simple rig and sometimes decked rather than being open like a gunboat.

royal The sail fastened to the royal yard, the fourth yard above the deck.

running rigging *See* rigging.

sailing master In the USN, equivalent to the RN master, which see.

scale the guns To fire a charge of powder from a piece of ordnance in order to remove any rust that might have formed in its bore.

scarph A joint at which cut away portions of timbers overlap each other and are fastened.

schooner At this period a two-masted vessel, rigged primarily with fore-and-aft sails. It was considered a topsail schooner when square topsails and topgallants were added to its foremast.

scroll head A curved piece of timber fastened at the head of a vessel in place of a figure.

Second Rate In the RN, a warship with 90 to 98 guns on three decks.

sheer In profile, the upwards curve toward the bow and stern of decks, wales, strakes, etc with the lowest point being amidships.

shell A hollow, iron projectile filled with powder and ignited by a fuse so that it will explode near the enemy.

shipwrights Labourers skilled in the multi-faceted craft of building vessels.

shoe A filler piece fastened to the bottom side of

a timber in the keel to makes its dimensions equal to the next run of keel timber.

shot A round projectile fired by a piece of ordnance.

shrouds The heavy lines in the standing rigging that brace the lower masts to the sides of the hull and brace the topmast and topgallants masts to their tops.

sided The constant dimension (thickness) of a beam or strake.

Sixth Rate In the RN, a warship with 20 to 30 guns; the larger of them were regarded as frigates, but those with fewer guns were referred to as 'post ships'.

skylight A windowed framework that allows light vertically to the deck below.

slide Part of the mounting for a carronade or gunboat gun – a flat platform with a centre-slot in which the ordnance, fastened to a conventional carriage or a flat 'bed,' slid when it recoiled. It was often attached to a pivot in the gunport and had a pair of small wheels for traversing the mounting.

sliding keel A centreboard-like feature concealed within a well in a vessel's hull adjacent to the keel which can be lowered beneath the hull to reduce leeway.

slipway The platform upon which a vessel is built, commencing with its keel, and down which the vessel slides during its launch

sloop As a rig, a single-masted vessel with fore-and-aft rig; as a warship description ('sloop of war'), a small vessel of about 10-18 guns, usually ship- or brig-rigged, in the charge of a commander or master commandant. In fact, any naval vessel so commanded was formally rated a sloop.

snow A two-masted vessel with square sails on both masts (much like a brig) but with an auxiliary mast (the trysail mast) located right behind the mainmast from which a trysail (similar to a spanker) was set.

sound To measure the depth of water.

spanker The fore-and-aft sail set behind the mizzen and used in place of a mizzen sail, or mizzen course.

spar deck The uppermost deck of a vessel in which the waist is planked over, in effect connecting the forecastle and quarterdeck to create a continuous deck from bow to stern.

spars All the 'poles' (masts, yards, booms, gaffs) employed in the rig of a vessel.

square rig A vessel has a square rig when most of its propulsion is achieved by sails set athwart the vessel rather than along its centreline (as in fore-and-aft rigs).

standing rigging All the lines used to brace and support the masts and yards.

starboard The right hand side of a vessel, facing forward.

stations The places to which crew members are assigned to conduct manoeuvres in sailing or fighting a vessel.

stays The heavy lines in the standing rigging

which brace the masts to the deck behind (backstays) and ahead to the deck and to the other masts and bowsprit.

staysails Fore-and-aft sails suspended from the stays when in use or furled to the mast ahead when not in use.

stem The curved, upright bow timber of a vessel to which planking is fastened.

step The wooden structure built on and around the keelson to receive the foot of the lower mast.

step the mast To set a mast in its step.

stern lights The windows along the stern allowing light into the cabins.

sternpost The straight, upright stern timber of a vessel to which planking is fastened and to which the rudder is attached.

strake A single run of planking.

studding sails Supplementary sails used when wind conditions were extremely light and blowing from the stern. They were laced to spars extended past the yardarm of the topsail and topgallant sail yards (usually) and fastened to similar booms on the yard below.

sweeps Long oars used to power a large gunboat, galley or small warship.

swivel gun A short, small calibre long gun-like weapon mounted on a pivot located in the bow of a small boat or on the gunwale of a vessel.

tack To change a vessel's course so that the bow of the vessel passes through the eye of the wind – when the ship is on 'the starboard tack' the wind blows from over the starboard bow, but tacking brings it on to the larboard bow (larboard tack), or vica versa.

tackle When pronounced *taykle*, the ropes and pulleys (blocks) used to move heavy objects like guns or to trims sails and yards; when pronounced *tackle*, the rigging and general equipment of a ship, including cables and anchors.

tenon In a wooden joint, the protruding part of one piece cut to fit a corresponding mortice (or slot) in the other.

Third Rate In the RN, a warship with 64 to 80 guns on two decks.

top The platform built around the head of the lower mast and the topmast. It provided a structure to which the upper shrouds could be fastened and it was also the quarters of sharpshooters during an engagement.

topgallant breeze A wind of up to 5-6 knots that allows the topgallant sails to be set safely

topgallant forecastle A light deck built to cover the fore part of a flush upper deck.

topgallant mast The mast section fastened to and standing above the topmast.

topgallant sail The sail fastened to the topgallant yard, the third yard above the deck.

topmast The mast section fastened to and standing above the lower mast.

topsail The sail fastened to the topsail yard, the second yard above the deck.

toptimber The uppermost component in a single frame of a vessel.

troopship A vessel delegated for transporting troops, often a warship that had most of its guns removed to accommodate large numbers of passengers.

truck The cap of a mast, fitted with sheaves through which halliards run to raise flags and pendants.

trucks The heavy, small-diameter 'wheels' on a naval, or garrison, gun carriage.

trunnions The two cylindrical 'axles' mounted opposite each other near the middle point of a gun's length, which support the gun on its carriage and allow it to be elevated.

waist The part of the upper deck between the forecastle and the quarterdeck, often open, apart from gangways along the sides, to the gundeck below.

wales The thickest exterior strakes on a hull, positioned about the waterline of single-decked vessels and below the gundecks of larger vessels.

wardroom The officers' 'mess' aboard a large warship, located between the rows of officers' cabins (situated against the hull in the stern).

warrant officer Officers warranted by the Navy Board (RN) with specialised skills, including masters, surgeons, pursers, chaplains, boatswains, carpenters, gunners and schoolmasters. In the USN, boatswains, carpenters, sailmakers and gunners.

watch bill The roster allocating tasks and timetables to the members of a crew.

waterways The heavy planks adjacent to the frames by which the deck is attached to the timbers of the frame and along which waste water is conducted to the scuppers.

wear To change a vessel's course so that the stern of the vessel passes through the eye of the wind – when the ship is on 'the starboard tack' the wind blows from over the starboard side, but wearing brings it on to the larboard side (larboard tack), or vice versa.

whaleboat A very seaworthy double-ended open boat with sharp lines and steep sheer, originally employed to harpoon whales.

xebec frigate A Mediterranean ship type ultimately derived from the galley and originally lateen-rigged on two or three masts, at one time much favoured by the Barbary States (currently Morocco, Algiers, Tunisia and Libya), with two masts featuring a lateen rig and armed with about twenty guns. It was powerful and fast, and could be rowed in a lull.

yard A spar attached to a mast, usually athwart the vessel in a horizontal position, to which a sail is fastened.

yardarm The outside end of a yard.

Index

Unless otherwise specified, ships are British or British-Canadian.

Page references in *italic* refer to illustrations, in **bold** to tables.

Abbreviations

Cdr = Commander
Cdre = Commodore
Fr = France
Lt = Lieutenant
US = United States of America